THE ADEQUACY OF FOSTER CARE ALLOWANCES

Studies in Cash and Care

Editors: Sally Baldwin and Jonathan Bradshaw

Cash benefits and care services together make a fundamental contribution to human welfare. After income derived from work, they are arguably the most important determinants of living standards. Indeed, many households are almost entirely dependent on benefits and services which are socially provided. Moreover, welfare benefits and services consume the lion's share of public expenditure. The operation, impact and interaction of benefits and services is thus an important focus of research on social policy.

Policy related work in this field tends to be disseminated to small specialist audiences in the form of mimeographed research reports or working papers and perhaps later published, more briefly, in journal articles. In consequence public debate about vital social issues is sadly ill-informed. This series is designed to fill this gap by making the details of important empirically-based research more widely available.

The Adequacy of Foster Care Allowances

NINA OLDFIELD

Routledge
Taylor & Francis Group

LONDON AND NEW YORK

First published 1997 by Ashgate Publishing

Reissued 2018 by Routledge
2 Park Square, Milton Park, Abingdon, Oxon, OX14 4RN
711 Third Avenue, New York, NY 10017, USA

Routledge is an imprint of the Taylor & Francis Group, an informa business

Publisher's Note
The publisher has gone to great lengths to ensure the quality of this reprint but
points out that some imperfections in the original copies may be apparent.

Disclaimer
The publisher has made every effort to trace copyright holders and welcomes
correspondence from those they have been unable to contact.

A Library of Congress record exists under LC control number: 97071458

ISBN 13: 978-1-138-34203-3 (hbk)
ISBN 13: 978-0-429-43986-5 (ebk)

Contents

List of tables

Preface

This research was initiated by foster parents in the late 1980s and is dedicated to the promotion of fostering activities. Paul Kind, a fellow researcher and foster parent, identified the problem of altruism versus affordability and I am grateful for his support in the early days. I express my sincere thanks to the thirty-two foster families who gave their time and effort to talk about a subject of some sensitivity. My thanks also to the seven foster families who took part in the pilot study. There was honesty, humour, pain, caring and above all sincerity in their accounts.

My gratitude to the academic national informants of Belgium, Netherlands, Luxembourg, Denmark, France, Germany, Greece, Italy, Norway, Portugal, Spain, USA, Ireland and Australia. In addition Larry Bond of Combat Poverty Ireland and Trish O'Neil of Foster Care Association of Western Australia Inc for their help.

I am grateful to have been given the opportunity to contribute to the work of the Family Budget Unit and indebted to Professor Jonathan Bradshaw for his caring supervision, his advice, lucid criticism and encouragement during the four years of study.

I acknowledge the financial support given by the Economic and Social Research Council without which the research would not have taken place.

I am also indebted to Marilyn Thirlway for her proof reading skills, editorial comments, patience and understanding. Also thanks to the editorial staff at Ashgate for publishing the book.

Not least, I thank my colleagues and family for their support.

Definition of terms

Foster parent and foster carer

The terms 'foster parent' and 'foster carer' are used interchangeably in this book. Traditionally, the term 'foster parents' was understood to mean a two parent household which had experienced parenting and would take the role of local authority foster mother and father for another child temporarily in their care. During the 1980s, the term 'foster carer' was used in recognition that single people, non parents were eligible to become carers of foster children, and that non parenting tasks could be performed by foster parents.

Non-foster child

Different terms have been used to describe the child/ren born to or adopted by the foster parents, these are 'other child/ren', 'normal children', 'non-foster child/ren', 'natural child/ren'. No moral judgement is intended in the use of these terms.

Introduction

This study explores the financial consequences for foster parents of fostering a child. It develops a method for estimating the direct and indirect costs to foster families of a foster child, and draws conclusions about whether the foster care allowance is adequate to cover these costs.

The level of social security benefits in the UK is determined by the Government. In making their judgement:

> the government gives due regard to the relationship between benefits levels and the rewards available to those in work, and to the total resources available for public spending. (DSS 1988 Paragraph 5.3)

In the case of foster care allowances, the local authorities similarly have regard to the resources that are available and take into account local supply and demand factors. In addition, the judgement about the level of foster care allowances is formally required to meet the costs of a foster child. The principal aim of this study is to inform those judgements by undertaking empirical research on the costs of a foster child. It is also through the development of method a general contribution to research on adequacy and living standards.

The importance of fostering

Currently foster care is the most common form of care and accommodation for children 'looked after' by the state in most regions of Britain. On the last day of March 1991 (DOH 1992), there were approximately 34,000 children in foster placements in England. However, the trend towards short term placements and the high incidence of placement breakdowns during the last decade mean that the actual number of children

1

in foster care during one year is very much understated in cross sectional statistics (Rowe, Hundleby, Garnett 1989). Furthermore, the average child placed in foster families today is much more difficult to look after than previously (Knapp and Fenyo 1988). Foster care represents the cornerstone of the modern child welfare system in Britain, consequently maintaining a healthy supply of volunteer carers is very important for some of the country's most vulnerable children.

The role of foster care allowances

In most circumstances, foster parents give their services to children for no pecuniary reward. The foster care allowance is paid merely to reimburse the carer for the financial cost of the foster child's upkeep:

> foster parents are paid an allowance which is expected to cover the additional costs of maintaining their foster child. (The Family Welfare Association, 1990:26)

The level of allowance is determined by each local authority on a sliding age-band scale which reflects an assumption that older children cost more to feed and clothe than younger children.

However, the foster care allowance takes into account factors other than the assumed costs of a foster child. First, in the absence of a national standard allowance, and with the possibility and practice of cross boundary placements, the allowance has to be sensitive to the local problems of supply and demand (Bebbington and Miles 1989, Berridge 1987 et al). A consequence of this is that there are considerable differences in the allowances paid by different authorities. These differences raise questions about equity in the treatment of foster parents between local authority areas. Second, within a given area, differences also arise due to the practice of paying discretionary enhancements to the basic rate to some foster parents but not to others for the care of children with different (but also sometimes similar) degrees of caring difficulty.

The nature of foster care is changing primarily for two reasons: more children are being maintained successfully in their own homes and children who would ordinarily be accommodated in residential care are found in foster placements. This means that the cost to foster families is likely to be increasing.

In the face of this, if the foster care allowance is inadequate, a problem in the supply of foster parents may well emerge. In most placements, although all household members contribute, it is the foster mother who has the dominant role in the physical and psychological care of the foster child. The labour market now offers more opportunities to women for flexible, unskilled and often service sector remunerative work. Furthermore, with a growing community based elderly population, women may have to take a greater caring role in this area. Therefore, potential foster parents, facing increasingly difficult foster children, may find themselves less able to combine fostering and employment with a growing pressure to occupy themselves in other community activities.

The perceived adequacy of the foster care allowance

There has been little research on the perceptions of a foster parent's fostering costs. Culley (1975) in a US study, suggests foster parents frequently meet costs that are over and above that of natural children. Various articles in fostering journals suggest high costs in general (Kavanagh, 1988a, 1988b) but are not specific about them. Rhodes (1989) suggests high transport costs, and the National Foster Care Association (NFCA) (1988 to 1993) believes the direct costs of a foster child could be 50% more than a natural child in the same family.

There is evidence of foster parents' dissatisfaction with the level of the foster care allowance. A NFCA campaign for better allowances in 1987 reached confrontational levels but had little impact on the situation:

> In the present times of recession it is even more important that foster parents are paid realistic allowances or local authorities will find that foster parents will be unwilling to continue fostering when children already placed have left their care. (NCFA 1988:3)

Social workers appear to endorse the foster parent claims of inadequacy:

> We ask much of these people. It is high time that they were treated properly and accorded the wages, training and status they deserve. ....
> After all, if foster parents decided to withdraw their services tomorrow, the entire care system would collapse. (Cousins, 1988:25)

Initiated by foster parents, innovative and market orientated schemes are beginning to emerge. One group of local authority approved foster parents have privatised their child care service and charge the local authority a weekly fee of £254.00 per child (NFCA 1993:64). It is in this context that this study of the adequacy of the foster care allowance has been mounted.

What is adequacy?

A dictionary states adequacy as 'sufficiency', 'proportionate to need' and that which is 'satisfactory', but these definitions are not helpful in themselves as Cooke and Baldwin (1984) found when exploring the notion of the adequacy of the supplementary benefit scales:

> Adequacy is a subjective notion - a matter in the end, of judgement.
> (Cooke and Baldwin 1984:4)

3

Similarly the Government review of social security in 1985 cast doubts that adequacy could ever be defined:

> There have been many attempts to establish what would be a fair
> rate of benefit for claimants. But, it is doubtful whether an attempt
> to establish an objective standard of adequacy would be fruitful.
> (DHSS, 1985:21)

There is no real answer, but Veit-Wilson (1994) suggests adequacy can be understood if it is explicitly stated (or implicitly assumed) what objective the benefit is designed to meet. The achievement of an adequate standard of living (socially recognised and approved as decent) is the target of much income maintenance policy. For example, an adequate standard of living is one of children's 'rights' accorded by the 1993 'UN Convention on the Rights of Children' which is ratified by 126 countries including the UK[1] (*Guardian*, 1993):

> State Parties recognise the right of every child to a standard of living
> adequate for the child's physical, mental, spiritual, moral and social
> development. Article 27. (Newell 1991:105)

The Boarding Out Regulations (1988) state the authority is obliged to:

> care for the child placed with the foster parent as if he were a
> member of the foster parent's family. (Boarding Out Regulation Cm
> 2184:15)

Any definition of adequacy in terms of foster care allowance must therefore be related to the standard of living of the placement family, and not to the foster child's natural home which is likely to be lower (Schorr 1992, Bebbington and Miles 1988). Research has shown that foster families in the 1980s are characterised generally as having median lifestyles (Bebbington and Miles 1988).

How can adequacy be evaluated?

One way of considering the notion of adequacy in the short term is to allow it to be determined naturally by the market. The market uses the price mechanism to adjust for the quantity and quality of supply, for example, when demand outstrips supply the price rises. There are problems with relying entirely on market mechanisms to ensure adequacy. Foster parents are not motivated entirely by financial incentives. There is

---

[1] The UK government became a signatory to the UN Convention on the Rights of a Child in December 1991. (Lansdown 1992)

clearly a considerable degree of altruism in supplying their service as foster parents. If there was no altruism involved the market price for fostering would certainly be considerably higher than it is. The foster care allowance is supposed to cover the costs of a child. If a pricing policy over-exploits altruism by paying allowances below real costs, local authorities may well have to lower their expectations about the quality of care parents can afford to give and or jeopardise supply (and altruistic supply) in the long term. In addition the resources of the local authority are limited. A fostering service inevitably competes for funding with other local authority services, such as services for the elderly or child protection services. If problems of supply and demand lead to fostering becoming too expensive to sustain then the local authority will look for less costly alternatives to provide the same service.

There is also considerable evidence that the motivation to foster is not affected by increased payments to carers and therefore cannot be left to the market to regulate (Rowe 1973, Smith 1988, Shaw and Lebens 1977). The House of Commons Social Services Committee in 1984 reported that in view of this it was even more important that allowances should be equitably and reasonably fixed (NFCA 1988). Smith (1988) also argues that in a materialistic society foster parents should have their 'fair share'. This necessitates developing a method of measuring the adequacy of foster care allowances independently of the market.

There may be no objective or independent test of adequacy but nevertheless there are a variety of criteria that can be employed to evaluate the adequacy of a standard of living. These have been developed in previous studies.

Previous studies

A number of studies have used different criteria to assess the adequacy of state benefits. Cooke and Baldwin (1984) suggested adequacy of the supplementary benefit (SB) scales could be judged by the following criteria:

- The way in which the level of the scale rates was originally set, and whether this level has maintained its value in real terms over time.
- Equity in the scales paid to different types of claimant.
- The extent to which the scale rates meet basic needs.
- Differences in the living standards of SB recipients and those of households not on SB.
- Normative standards - that is, views about the standard of living the SB scheme ought to provide. (Cooke and Baldwin 1984:5)

Bradshaw and Holmes (1989) explored the living standards of families living on income support in Tyne and Wear using a broad range of standard of living indicators. Bradshaw and Morgan (1987) analysed the living standards of families on supplementary benefit in the Family Finances Survey by representing their commodity expenditures in terms of a basket of goods. Murphy-Lawless (1992) in a similar methodological study used Irish expenditure data to explore two standards of living of low income and average income in relation to a family with two children. In these cases the conceptual framework of adequacy was a range of household consumption.

In this study the following five criteria form a framework to assess the adequacy of the foster care allowance:

- The extent that foster care allowances have maintained their value over time.
- The extent that allowances meet the normal costs of child rearing.
- The extent that allowances meet the extra costs of fostering.
- The extent that the indirect costs to the foster parents of fostering are compensated.
- The extent that UK foster care allowances are comparable with those paid elsewhere.

Structure

The evaluation of the adequacy of the foster care allowance using these five criteria is presented in the following five chapters.

The first chapter explores the origins of the foster care allowances. Foster care was first covered by legislation in 1870 although the history of public payment for foster care goes back more than a hundred years. The history of foster care is well documented by Beatrice and Sidney Webb (1910, 1929), Heywood (1978), Packman (1975) and George (1970), albeit from an ideological rather than financial stance. During the late 1970s and 1980s attitudes towards payment to foster parents appeared to change largely because of the changing nature of children in the care of the local authority. This affected the supply and demand for carers, perceptions about adequacy of payment to cover costs and aspirations for professional recognition. Using information collected on the foster care allowance over the last 50 years, an assessment is made of whether the allowance has maintained its value in relation to prices, wages and benefit levels.

The second test of adequacy explores the notion that the foster care allowance should cover all the 'normal' direct costs of child rearing. Budget standard methods are used in this study to explore the household consumption of children at a 'modest-but-adequate' standard of living. The budgets for children of different ages, sex and in different sized families are derived from family budgets created by the Family Budget Unit (1992). The cost of children's housing, fuel, clothing, food, household goods and services, transport, child care, leisure goods and services, pocket money and personal care are all explored and compared with the standard foster care allowances.

Chapter 3 is based on a sample survey of foster families in North Yorkshire designed to identify and estimate the extra costs to foster parents of fostering a child. Budget standard methods were used to create additional budgets for foster households and the extra costs were expressed in terms of the average fostering household.

Associated with the direct costs are the indirect cost of foster care and this is the subject of Chapter 4. Previous research has focused mainly on the direct costs of a child (Piachaud, 1979, 1981; Lovering 1984) or the extra costs of fostering (Culley 1975). There has been little research on the indirect costs of foster children, although the indirect costs of 'normal' child rearing has been assessed by Joshi (1987, 1992). This book deals with the indirect costs of a foster child by estimating the extra time spent in caring for the foster child.

Finally, other countries make different arrangements to pay foster parents a fostering allowance, including benefits in kind, and sometimes fostering wages. A comparative analysis of the foster child support package was made to explore differences and similarities and to reflect on the appropriateness of the UK payment system. Fifteen countries were compared with the UK: Belgium, Denmark, France, Germany, Greece, Ireland, Italy, Luxembourg, Netherlands, Portugal, Spain, Australia, Norway and the United States. The foster care allowances and additions were converted to a common currency using purchasing power parities to allow cross country comparison.

The conclusion summarises the evidence and its implication for policy and research.

1 The dynamics of foster care allowances

Introduction

This chapter explores the adequacy of foster care allowances from an historical perspective. First, there is a brief exploration of the interplay of policy, payment and foster care practice during the last two centuries to gain an insight into the nature and objectives of the foster care allowance. How was the allowance originally determined and by whom and what purpose was it intended to serve? Second, an attempt is made to explain why payment for foster care has become an important issue during the last decade, what changes have taken place and the impact these changes had on the payment levels and objectives of fostering. Four issues are examined: the changing balance of care and the effects on the demand for and supply of foster parents and the role of fostering allowances on the supply side; the perceived adequacy of the maintenance allowance; the changing perceptions of foster parents on their role as foster mothers and expectations for payment; and the changing role of mothers in a competitive market place. Finally, as far as possible, given the paucity of information on actual foster care rates through the ages, the issue of whether the allowance has maintained its value in real terms is explored.

There is no national fostering allowance in Britain, the amount varies widely between and sometimes within the same authority. The law, through its statutory instrument (Foster Placement [Children] Regulations 1991), allows local authorities to define the appropriate level of maintenance to reimburse the foster parent for the upkeep of the child. The local authorities as a collective body, however, have not chosen to adopt a national scale of boarding out allowance, each authority or voluntary scheme pays according to its own policy. The allowances are funded from the County Council Block Grant provided by central Government. Consequently, any increase in fostering allowance is allocated locally 'in preference to other pressing priorities' (North Yorkshire County Council Memo of March 1990).

Each April the NFCA Fostering Allowances Working Party carries out a survey of allowances paid by local authorities and voluntary organisations in Britain. The variations in basic allowance between and within major regions are shown in Table 1.1. The lack of standardisation is greatest in England where the variation is wide. The highest paying authorities are in the London region.

Table 1.1
Allowances April 1992: The highest and lowest paying authority in each area in relation to oldest and youngest age group. £ per week.

Region	Lowest paying 0-18	Highest paying 0-18
London	61.10 - 110.00	148.72 - 239.44
England	33.32 - 63.91	103.11 - 166.25
Wales	28.07 - 58.24	43.33 - 86.73
Scotland	38.76 - 71.45	58.97 - 119.12

Source: NFCA (1992) *Foster Care Finance*: p.54.

The basic fostering allowances and repaid expenses are not counted as earnings and therefore are not eligible for tax or national insurance purposes. Similarly, fostering allowances are not counted as income in the foster family assessment of means tested benefits (income support or family credit etc), although any reward element would be. Child benefit is not payable in respect of a foster child provided a foster care allowance is paid by the local authority or voluntary organisation. Foster parents can, however, claim a series of benefits in respect of a foster child with a disability, such as the Disability Living Allowance, Invalid Care Allowance and others - although any reward or fee part of the fostering allowances is counted as income in general in the benefit system.

The origins of foster care allowances

During the period 1782 to 1834 the boarding out of 'poor law' children was public policy in some parishes. Parishes were responsible for the relief of their own pauper population and the Gilberts Act 1782 decreed that the children of paupers receiving work relief under the Old Poor Law system could be boarded out with local rate payers. The contract to care for the pauper child was 'let' by means of competitive tendering to the lowest bidder despite the risk of low standard care, overcrowding (baby farming) and profiteering. At best the Gilberts Act encouraged responsible people to come forward to care for pauper children, on the other hand, boarding out was a means of saving public expenditure and an opportunity to profit on the part of the foster parent. This type of fostering, where allowances were paid according to the market, lasted until 1834.

The Poor Law Amendment Act of 1834 introduced the concept of uniformity in the treatment of paupers, 'less eligibility' and the workhouse test which was designed to stop the payment of 'out relief' as a deterrent to the state of pauperism. Strictly speaking, boarding out was contrary to the principles of the 1834 legislation because it

9

was considered by the Boards as a form of 'outdoor relief'. The notion of 'less eligibility' was that no person should receive in 'poor law relief' more than the lowest earnings of a labourer. The principle of 1834 was non interventionist beyond keeping the destitute alive (Webb 1910:270). As far as children in the workhouse were concerned, however, the 'less eligibility' was no deterrent to pauperism which was in the hands of their parents. For the first time children were beginning to be seen as a special group, blameless for their pauper state which was brought about by their 'inadequate' parents. They were the deserving poor who, along with future generations, could be saved by rehabilitation (Horsburgh 1983). It was taken for granted that workhouse children should be educated (trained for adulthood), even though universal education had not been introduced, at the risk that this may encourage parents to become paupers (Crowther 1981). Barrack schools and later district boarding schools separated the poor law children from their parents. In general, this type of institutional care remained the norm for the majority of pauper children. Some exceptions were made by the Poor Law Commission for the boarding out of orphaned and abandoned children preferably outside their areas of origin in farming or rural locations.[1]

The issue of boarding out was finally brought to a head by two Poor Law Board reports: The Boarding Out of Pauper Children in Scotland, and in Certain Unions in England, Parliamentary Papers number 176, dated 1870. In England, boarding out was first regulated by statute in 1870 and 1877. Subsequent legislation in 1889 and 1905 had regard to the distinction between fostering children within and outside their present area of residence. This distinction disappeared when the statutes governing fostering were clarified and codified under the same order of 1911. The weekly boarding out sum in 1870 was not more than 4 shillings (increasing to 5 shillings) for the child's maintenance, although payment for clothing, school money and medical attention were at the discretion of the individual boards of guardians (Heywood 1978:82). The allowance, however, was especially low for relatives acting in the capacity of foster parents, Webb 1929:745 suggests sometimes as low as two shillings and sixpence a week with 10 shillings a quarter for clothing - an ambiguity still seen in some local authorities today (Jervis 1990, Rickford 1992). During the last quarter of the 19th century the amount of allowance received by foster parents was three and sometimes four times that of the cost of a child on outdoor relief which Webb (1929) suggested was far in excess of what the ordinary labourer could spend on his children. During this period, the Central Authority controlled local authority spending on foster care by capping foster care allowances. This hold on foster care rates was not to be relinquished until the regulation was rescinded on May the 3rd 1920.

Government regulations authorised the setting up of voluntary committees to supervise and regulate the contractual arrangements between parents and Union. The duties of foster parents were stated in 1889 as:

---

[1] Boarding-out took two forms: selected foster home of known respectability, usually outside the union in rural areas; or relative of the child's dead parent. The latter was considered to provide a lower standard of home (Webb 1929:743).

He will bring up the child as one of his own children, and provide the child with proper food, lodging and washing, and endeavour to train the child in truthfulness, obedience, personal cleanliness and industry, as well as in suitable domestic and outdoor work[2] so far as may be consistent with the law; that he will take care that the child shall attend duly at church or chapel according to the religious creed to which the child belongs, and shall attend school .... provide for the proper repair and renewal of the child's clothing .... report such illness to the guardians and to the boarding out committee; ... permit the child to be visited and the house inspected ... and upon the demand of a person duly authorised ..... give up possession of the child. (Boarding out without the Union Order, 1889 cited in Webb 1910:196)

The selection of foster parents excluded any person in receipt of poor relief, or whose sole income would be the foster care allowance. Only in special circumstance were children boarded with relatives. The foster father could not be employed in night work and manual outdoor workers were preferred to indoor sedentary workers. Attention was paid to accommodation offered in the home including separate sleeping rooms for different sexes and the number of children placed was limited to two. The clothing provided was to be good and of ordinary character with no resemblance to a workhouse uniform. Furthermore, the foster child could only be employed in work with the permission of the guardians. The view that foster parents were only interested in the money was gradually rejected as confidence grew in the selection process which served to eliminate 'hard up' volunteers.

The Central Authority, however, did little to encourage the expansion of boarding out, it was described as just one method for removing children from the workhouse (Webb 1910:195). The Poor Law Institutions Order 1913 prohibited (other than very short term) the maintenance of children aged between three and 16 in the workhouse. Children, however, were more often placed in local authority and voluntary residential children's homes or sent on emigration ships to Canada than found foster homes. During the post war period (1914-18) there was a decline in boarding out for poor law children which Webb (1929:743) suggests was partially attributed to the level of payment to foster parents[3]. Some guardians responded by increasing the payment per week to 7s and 10s.

---

[2] The term 'domestic and outdoor work' was omitted by 1905 because taken literally, it was understood as licence to overtax the working capacity of children.

[3] Other reasons for the decline in fostering included the introduction of a pension for children orphaned by the war which lifted them out of the poor law system of relief and placed them under the protection of the Ministry of Pensions. Voluntary boarding out committees were accused of failure in their attempt to find sufficient new foster homes to meet the demand. (George 1970: 31, 32)

Once removed from the natural family the child tended to stay in the care of the local authority until adulthood. There was no vision of prevention work or rehabilitation of the child and family. The Children and Young Persons Act 1933 extended the grounds for bringing the neglected child into 'the care' of the local authority, establishing a principle of placing the child's welfare first. Confusion and defects in the administrative system, however, were manifested in the death of a foster child, Dennis O'Neill in 1945, and a subsequent public enquiry. The Monckton Enquiry highlighted the urgent need to overhaul the system of caring for deprived children and this led to a Royal Commission on the Care of Children - Cmd 6922 (1946) referred to as the 'Curtis Report'.

The Curtis Report identified an assortment of government departments and regulations managing foster care: the Ministry of Health (through local authority departments) was responsible for the destitute, homeless evacuees, children fostered for reward under the age of nine years and those pending adoption; the Home Office was responsible for those children removed for care and protection by order of the courts; the Board of Control was responsible for mentally disordered children; the Ministry of Education responsible for children with physical or mental handicap; and the Ministry of Pensions had responsibility for war orphans (Cmd 6922 s99). The supervision of children, the selection of foster homes and the calculation of fostering rates in each area was the responsibility of three main committees: Public Health, Public Assistance and Education. Curtis (1946 s130) finds little evidence of common policies between committees with the exception of some instances of sharing visitors. Other instances revealed conflict between the departments (s131 ibid) leading to inequality in the treatment of similar children. The rates of payment to foster parents for the boarding out of children were usually derived separately by the various authorities though sometimes the result was similar. Moreover, the allowance for a child placed outside the authority would frequently reflect the authority of origin and not that in which the child was placed. Curtis (Cmd 6922 s362) suggests that the repercussions of paying sometimes three different levels in a locality and three different levels from outside the area in the same locality, for a similar child, caused resentment in the lower paid group of foster parents and could not be justified on any economic basis.

Curtis examined 41 counties in England and Wales and found the lowest and highest payments a week for the maintenance of a child under 14 years was 10 shillings and twenty shillings and sixpence respectively with no allowance for school dinners. There were instances of special rates for children with special difficulties. It was usual to increase the payment with age in three age bands with some exceptions, for example, some committees added a supplement for a child below the age of 7 years. The total sum in this case was:

- twenty shillings and sixpence for a child under 3 years
- fifteen shillings and sixpence for a child 3-7 years
- thirteen shillings for a child over 7 years.

In another area a uniform rate was paid at 16 shillings per week regardless of the child's age. In addition to the maintenance allowance, all authorities paid something towards clothing, from 30 shillings to 52 shillings and sixpence each quarter and in some areas one or two pairs of boots were also provided. Through inspection of the wardrobes of foster children, Curtis concluded the allowance was inadequate to provide for the child in this respect.

There was no fixed allowance for maintenance or clothing in the case of the private fostering of illegitimate or unwanted children. The allowance in voluntary organisations tended to be lower than that paid by the local authority for often more difficult children.

The boarding out of children by the Ministry of Pensions who had its own board of visitors had a tendency also to pay lower allowances than local authorities.

The Children Act 1948 laid upon the local authority a duty to find every child in care a foster home. At the same time the Act was revolutionary in expecting the local authority to restore children to their own families when (or if) the particular crisis was resolved (Children Act 1948, S.1, Part 3). The two way flow of children gave local authorities some control over the number of children expected in a rapidly expanding service. The work of child care experts such as Bowlby (1951) served to legitimise the political decisions of the day. Bowlby provided evidence to a receptive audience about the effects of maternal deprivation in childhood and claimed foster care as the best solution for those children deprived of their parent and home. Bowlby, however, was a proponent of the development of a quasi-professional foster care service in marked contrast to the traditional British view of the volunteer mother.

The new local authority children's departments were given the responsibility to supply, supervise and determine the payments in regard to foster parents. The duties of foster parents laid down by statute in 1946 and 1955 were little changed from those of 1889. The foster parents had to agree to 'look after him as they would a child of their own'. The 1946 memorandum (Cmd 6922 s355) however, included the recognition of the child as an individual with personal ownership of clothing and personal possessions, and a need for recreation appropriate to his age. The most desirable foster families continued to be those where the mother did not work and the father was in regular employment. The nature of household budgeting in terms of economies of scale however, would in a practical sense allow the fostering allowance to be counted in terms of total family income without compromising the fostering altruistic ideology.

The cost of maintaining fostered children was borne by the county and county borough rates with no direct grant from the Exchequer. Fostering allowance expenditure in common with other expenditure of local authorities, however, is taken into account in the calculation of the Exchequer block grant (Cmd 6692 s30) just as it is today. Between 1948 and 1955, the number of children in foster care greatly increased.

The 1951/52 Select Committee on Estimates, 6th Report (para 6), cited in Packman (1968:17), was considerably alarmed by the rise in public expenditure costs in line with the increasing numbers of children in the care of local authorities. The weekly fostering allowances in 1956 for the maintenance of children boarded out in the Coventry area (Barnes 1979:51,89) ranged from 22s.for a child of 0-5 years to 40s. for a child of 17 years. Eight years later in 1964 this had increased by approximately 30% and the majority of children in care, with the exception of some inner city areas, were in foster homes (Stroud 1975:71). The Select Committee recommended more attention should be paid to preventing the break up of families as the least expensive option. This notion was crystallized in the Children and Young Persons Act 1963. The motto of the Coventry children's department was 'the nation that destroys the family destroys itself' (Barnes 1979:109).

The adequacy of payments made for the upkeep of the child has rarely been on any agenda but payments as a means of an incentive to encourage a positive supply of foster placements have. There was some discussion in the Association of Children's Officers in 1967 about higher payments but these were discouraged on the grounds of morality. Instead of higher payment, emphasis was given to raising the status and awareness of fostering. In Coventry, for example, the Lord Mayor gave civic recognition to the foster parents with a reception in their honour expressing the hope that other people would respond to this need.

The period between the late 1960s and early 1970s showed a decline in long term fostering and residential care but an increase in the use of short term places and prevention work with families in the home. This was a radical period. The social service departments were restructured, as envisaged by Seebohm, in an attempt to secure an effective family service through generic social work practices (Barnes 1979). The Children and Young Person Act 1969, Section 13, released local authorities from their statutory duty to find every child 'in care', a foster home leaving the way open for specialist work with some children. The National Foster Care Association was set up in 1974 against a backdrop of a high number of: fostering placement breakdowns, 'tug of love' media focus as a number of natural mothers 'brutally' removed foster children from long term foster care, an estimate by Rowe and Lambert (1973) of 7,000 children said to be spending their childhood unplanned 'in care', and the incorporation of a large number of disturbed and delinquent children into the child care system as a result of the closure of Approved Schools.

In the 1970s some authorities belatedly took up the recommendation of Curtis (1946 s.471) and Bowlby (1952) to introduce 'Professional Foster Parent' schemes. The pilot schemes were not widespread and the principles on which they were based differed between authorities. In Reading Social Services, the appointments were 'regarded as staff', members of an area team and accountable to a staff member. The salary was approved by the National Joint Council Scheme with increments and nationally negotiated increases although classified as 'Miscellaneous' in the local authority accounts. The actual level was reached by making the annual cost rather less than that of residential care (Hartnell 1974). The children included in the scheme were previously in long term residential care and the majority of professional foster parents were from a child care work environment. Hartnell, overwhelmed by applicants, believed they had plugged

14

into a new market for potential carers who had experience, commitment and a less ambiguous working relationship with the department.

The debate on a fostering wage, which started quietly in the public domain with Curtis, gained professional backing in the 1970s. A DHSS Working Party on fostering practice in 1976, for example, recommended that foster care be recognised as a child care service in financial terms with compensation for the child's upkeep as the bottom line. The argument for remuneration of foster care put forward by Curtis (1946) was that the mother is working for a public authority in caring for the child and should be paid for her labour. In paying for her labour the authority would then be entitled to put pressure on the parent to maintain a defined standard of care. Arguments against paying a reward included the notion that the acceptance of payment for work cuts at the root of the foster mother-child relationship. Curtis believed there to be conflicting evidence as to whether the prospect of financial gain was an important incentive to foster parents and concluded that it should not be seen as a serious motive to foster care.

George (1970) and Adamson (1968) suggested that commentators were coming round to the view that foster parents should be paid more than the maintenance and other expenses of the foster child. There was, however, no real evidence of a foster parent desire for change in the occupational status of foster care at this time. Policy seemed to be directing the way, nevertheless, many authorities no longer included a serious assessment of foster parent financial circumstances and the potential to foster was seen in diverse family types.

The changing climate of foster care in the 1980s and early 1990s

The supply and demand of foster carers

A popular misconception of the 1980s was the expansion of fostering. There were less than 35,000 foster children and 20,000 foster families in England (Bebbington 1989). The myth of expansion arises because of the growth in the proportion of foster children compared to a declining number of children 'in care' in England. Table 1.2 shows in 1980 that 37% of children 'in care' were placed with foster parents. By 1991 this proportion had risen to 57% and the trend looked set to continue. The numbers of children in foster care has remained fairly static but with a slight downward trend towards the end of the decade, whereas the aggregate number of children 'in care' has fallen dramatically.

Table 1.2
Children 'in care' by mode of accommodation as at the 31st March,
1980-1992.

Totals rounded in 000s

	1980	*81*	*85*	*86*	*87*	*88*	*89*	*90*	*92*
In care	95	92	70	67	66	64	62	60	55
In foster care	35	35	35	35	35	35	34	34	32
% foster care	37	38	50	52	53	54	55	57	58

Source: Derived from the Department of Health, Personal Social Services Table 7.7. 1992 and 1993.

In a major study of 10,000 placements, Rowe et al (1989) found official figures based on a once a year count held few clues to the actual situation in terms of turnover, that is, the number of children actually going through the system for short periods of care, the number of times a child has experienced a disruption in the placement or the numbers of foster families waiting for a child to be placed. Rowe et al (1989) concluded that the 'foster care rate' was in fact much closer to the 'residential care rate' than government statistics suggested and therefore both of equal importance as a resource.

The present instability of foster placements leading to high breakdown rates is also more assumption than fact as there is little systematic recording of fostering outcomes by local authorities. Furthermore, a breakdown of a placement does not necessarily mean loss of a foster parent although there is generally an investigation of cause which gives a 'cooling off' period before (or if) other children are placed.

The definition of a breakdown is complicated as disruptions may be initiated by the foster carer, the foster child or the fostering agency. Strathclyde in 1982 found 13% of the children in its residential homes had experienced fostering breakdowns, whereas Berridge et al (1987) claimed 30% in 1984. For long term fostering it was common to find studies such as Napier (1972) and Triseliotis (1989) reporting 50% of placements breaking down within three to five years. Short term placement breakdown rates were lower. Rowe (1987) found 13% within an 8 week period but the rate was much higher for adolescents than other children (Triseliotis 1989). The impact of fostering breakdown on the supply of foster parents is exacerbated by the emphasis placed on 'matching'[4] which can generate a pool of foster parents and a waiting list for places at the same time.

Foster families are a scarce commodity, consequently, generalities are expressed about their 'specialness'. Bebbington and Miles (1988b) found this to be true when the characteristics of foster families and a sample of average families from

---

[4] 'Matching' is used here in the general sense, but also with specific reference to the 1989 Children Act ,which for the first time places a duty on local authorities to have regard to racial origin and culture and linguistic background when providing day care or recruiting foster carers. Tunnard (1991: 74)

the General Household Survey (GHS) were compared. The description of a typical foster family given below applied to 75% of a sample of almost 3,000 foster families, but to only 31% of the 8,500 families in the GHS:

> Includes a woman in the 31-55 years age group, living in a home with three or more bedrooms, is a two parent family, one parent working and the other not, and they have older children only. (Bebbington et al 1988b:1)

An exploration of the existence of this family type has helped to explain geographical variations in the demand and supply of foster families. The estimator for potential fostering families is the incidence of the Bebbington archetypal family in an area in relation to the number of children in care in the same area. Ironically, Bebbington found the potential supply of foster homes was best in areas which had less need for foster families. The reason for this was that the level of deprivation in an area bore some relation to the numbers of children in care and the affluence of families of the given type. Deprived areas of Newcastle upon Tyne had a predicted supply per 10,000 families of 9.8 with a ratio of children in care to predicted supply of 6.8. North Yorkshire had a higher potential pool of fostering families and a lower need for the service - 11.9 per 10,000 families and a ratio of children in care to predicted supply of 2.4. The London Boroughs were shown to have a lower potential than Newcastle upon Tyne for foster families and a similar need for care. In the London Boroughs practically all the potential families would need to be turned into actual foster families to meet the demand for carers. This has left some authorities with little option but to seek cross border placement families.

Exploring the role of allowances in the supply of foster carers, Bebbington et al (1989) provided evidence that local authorities were sensitive to their supply position. Bebbington found a significant negative correlation between the allowances paid and the supply indicator. The greater the number of suitable families locally, the lower the boarding out allowance. In areas of low numbers of suitable families with a high need for foster families, the local authorities were found to encourage fostering supply with above average amounts paid relative to the basic rate and use of enhancements as further incentive. The difficulty in recruitment was particularly acute in the metropolitan authorities' areas which had increasingly placed children outside their areas, despite the regulations to the contrary. The London Boroughs paid substantially higher rates and met all the costs of travel between the two areas (Knapp 1982).

The cost of foster placements

One reason for the robustness of the modern foster care system has been the public and professional understanding of the comparative cost of the alternatives. In 1972 the average cost of a residential placement was £21 per week, the cost of a foster placement £4 - a huge saving of public expenditure with a value for money differential of 81%. In the period 1984 to 1985 cost statistics produced by the DHSS (an annual requirement of the Child Care Act 1980) showed the differential between foster placement and residential placement had widened to 86% cost saving (£42 per child per week in foster care and £304 per average child per week in residential care, Knapp and Fenyo 1988:176).

The cost savings to local authorities through pursuing a policy of boarding out, however, is claimed to be greatly exaggerated when a comprehensive cost analysis of residential and foster care is attempted. Knapp and Fenyo (1988) claimed that when hidden costs such as administrative and senior management overheads, health and education inputs are included, the fostering estimate just based on boarding out allowances, was 50% more. Costs are further increased in short term foster care because of the higher rate of recruitment, selection, training, and the 'matching' of foster families and foster children. Much of the variation in cost per child in different settings, however, is suggested to be related to the degree of difficulty in caring for the child.

Changes in the nature of foster care

Changes in child care practice during the 1980s profoundly affected the nature of foster care and subsequently perceptions about the role of foster care allowances. The average degree of difficulty in caring for children increased in both residential and boarding out settings. These changes were brought about by restructuring and establishing new child care practice. 'Easy to care for cases' (children on the border line of coming into care) were either prevented from coming into care by social workers working with families at home, stayed in care for only short periods or found permanent rather than temporary solutions to their situations. A large number of disturbed and delinquent children had been incorporated into the care system with the closure of Approved Schools during the 1970s. Awareness of hidden forms of abuse, the 1980s saw a catalogue of revelations about incest, sexual abuse, satanic rituals, bullying, AIDS/HIV, home alone children and children as child murderers, bringing a plethora of damaged children with new problems into the care system. In addition, many children's homes had closed due to falling numbers and a preference for foster care because of assumed cost savings and assumed best practice. Consequently, the population of fostered children or those waiting for a foster placement included more children with behavioural problems, fewer infants, many more older children, a disproportionately high number of black children, sibling groups[5], ill and distressed children, children with disabilities, and children in foster homes who were 'on remand'.

The Boarding-Out of Children (Foster Placement) Regulations 1988, Regulation six, asked for a new undertaking from foster parents

---

[5] Sixty per cent of young children enter care with siblings. (Bullock 1990: 43)

> To care for the child placed with the foster parent *as if he were a member of the foster parent's family...* (Cm:2184 P 1, Para 1)

Previous emphasis in foster parents' directives had dwelt on caring for foster children 'as if' they were the foster parents' own. The difference is subtle, treating the child as a family member gives emphasis to individualism, special need and treatment instead of the more intuitive child rearing of the natural child. This may still not be a good enough directive as some specialist adolescent placement aims are not to integrate the child into the carer's own family. Nevertheless, foster parents are obligated to make a written agreement to complete certain tasks for the child which it is suggested, are more demanding of foster parents than social workers.

In general, a foster parent is expected to develop a personal, caring and trusting relationship with the foster child to develop the child's self esteem, overcome previous rejections and moves, increase the child's range of positive life experiences and encourage new ways of behaviour by exercising authority appropriately. The placement family as a whole is expected to provide a good role model for the child in its relationships and behaviour with others. The foster parent has the task of teaching the foster child social and practical skills to stimulate the child through encouragement of recreational activities and community links. Moreover, the foster parent should be able to liaise and share information with the social worker to give a more complete picture of the child's home background, liaise with the child's school, maintain contact with relevant agencies, such as 'educational child guidance', hospitals or the probation office. At a professional level the foster parent is expected to attend case conferences and reviews, to maintain diary notes regarding development and incidents, and be able to summarise these at meetings, to assist in preparing court reports and at times attend court at the request of the local authority to give evidence on behalf of the child. Placements are frequently open ended, that is, foster parents are expected to take part in pre-placement work, post-placement work and support, assessment work and the matching of the child to a foster family. More recently, foster parents have been involved in their own selection processes, the approval of new carers and adoption panel members.

The task of foster parents includes working with the natural parent often in support of the partnership between authority and natural parent - a concept of total 'inclusive' fostering (Holman 1975, Goldstein et al 1973). Bullock (1990) suggested a wider view of the 'natural parent' which includes kinship networks, friendship networks and community links. It is now well documented that parental access to the child enhances the prospects of the child's return to its own environment. The principle has been enshrined in the 1989 Children Act which provides a framework for partnership orientated services to children (Marsh 1990). Foster parents are often given the task of teaching the natural parent parenting skills and supervising their access visits when appropriate.

19

Changes in the nature of foster parent type. The 1980s saw not only a change in the level of difficulty in caring for a foster child but also a change in the type of family willing to foster. Families with special qualities and skills were recruited to take difficult to care for children supported within fee paying schemes. Kavanagh (1988) argued, however, that if the basic maintenance levels were inadequate to pay for the upkeep of their foster children, then any reward or 'wage' paid for skills, within a fee paying scheme, was in reality used to make up the day by day expense deficiency.

Legislation obligates authorities to take note of cultural, locational, linguistic and religious aspects when matching foster children to foster families and implicit in this statement is that extreme difference in living standards is not in the child's best interest. It may be considered therefore to be in the best interest of the child to match foster children from low income families with foster parents from a similar background. Similarly, the controversy about matching by race, as Rhodes (1991) explained, moved local authorities from a policy of 'colour blindness' to one of racially matched placements which stimulated the recruitment of black foster families with a sensitivity to culture rather than the image of 'middle classness'. As a consequence, the sum paid to maintain the child's upkeep takes on a new importance and dimension.

It could be concluded that fostering allowances have a role to play in adjusting the balance between the foster parents' expectations and aspirations of fostering and the stress and strain of fostering tasks. The NFCA believes that payment of a more generous allowance does have an impact on recruitment. The success of the fee-paid fostering schemes seem to support this view. Verity (1988), President of the NFCA suggested that policy makers who fix allowances too low contributed to the breakdown rates of placements as families who continually have to dip into their own pocket to meet the daily costs of upkeep feel resentful. Moreover, Leat (1990) found the offer of payment was not just an incentive in the recruitment of foster parents but a financial necessity. The effect of increasing fostering payments was explored in a US study. Simon (1975), concluded that the regression results of annual fostering data across a large number of states over a three year period showed a substantial and positive relationship between the level of foster care payments and the number of foster homes offered. The elasticity of the supply of foster homes in relation to the level of allowances is between 0.5 to 1.00, that is, doubling the fostering payment produced an increase in the supply of foster homes of 50 to 100 per cent. The authorities, however, remain unconvinced, the House of Commons Social Services Committee Report in April 1984 stated that:

> There is no evidence that the exact level of allowance has any great impact on potential foster parents; nor would we expect it to do so. (Cited in NFCA 1987:2)

Are foster children more expensive to raise than other children?

The typical foster family's living standard could be described as average on a living standards' scale and the typical foster child as from a deprived background both economically and psychologically. The NFCA claim that foster carers who have monitored their own expenditure find foster children cost at least 50% more than other children. Foster children are more expensive than non foster children as a result of deprivation which manifests in greater demands on all physical aspects of care: food, clothing, household expenses, health care expense, education and transportation.

Culley (1977, 1975) and Oldfield (1990) found evidence that foster children were more destructive or harder on clothes than other children, and foster parents chose to buy brand named clothes for their foster children to improve the child's self image. Foster parents claimed they bought more toys for foster children than for their natural children, especially if the turnover of children in a placement was high. Destructiveness and a desire by foster parents to compensate for earlier deprivations by gifts were common reasons given.

There is strong evidence that children's health is compromised by poverty. Bebbington (1989) examined the background of 2,500 children admitted to care in England, finding material and social deprivation and entry into care closely associated. Schorr (1992) also highlighted poverty as a factor in the natural families of children 'in care' of the local authority:

> The chance of a child between five and nine in families receiving
> Income Support being admitted into care is one in ten; for
> families not on Income Support the chance is 1:7000. (Schorr in
> Dean 1992)

Blackburn (1991) states that in 'poor' families children usually fare better than their parents in terms of meals but are deprived of healthy food through lack of income at a time when their need for nutrients is at its greatest. Poor diets in childhood are associated with poor physical and intellectual growth and development, obesity, dental cavities and diseases associated with vitamin and mineral deficiencies such as anaemia and rickets. Blackburn suggest there is a body of evidence which indicates that the major public health problems of the decade, in particular, coronary heart disease, have their origins in childhood. In addition, abused and 'or' neglected children frequently display a variety of eating behaviours which reflect their situation. Demb (1991) suggested:

> Disturbed eating and disturbed growth... neglected children who
> were apathetic, did not gain weight normally, and whose
> developmental milestones were delayed.... Psychosocial
> dwarfism in which height growth and weight growth were

dramatically slowed as a result of emotional factors. (Demb 1991:77)

Demb (1991) also described a disproportionate number of foster children, who were not observed to be obese, or to be suffering from any childhood diseases, but who had severe over eating problems. Culley (1975) also found foster children ate more. Kavanagh (1988) suggests that there is wastage of food because of faddiness, over-eating and as a result of the foster parent not knowing the child's likes and dislikes. Foster parents believe food plays a major part in the health improvement of foster children. Meal-times offer the opportunity to promote good eating habits, prevent and correct former dietary deficiencies and create an environment of stability and security. Foster parents suggest that children grow faster in the initial stages of foster care as a consequence of improved appetites.

Aldgate (1990) suggested that studies in the UK and US showed that children 'in care' do not perform as well educationally as other children. Overall there is some uncertainty about the causes, but several studies conclude that, 'a poor start' is one factor and 'increased mobility due to placement breakdown', 'poor nurturing', 'poor self image', 'poor social adjustment' have all been linked to low levels of educational attainment. Additional schooling costs for foster children were noted by Culley et al (1975), Oldfield (1990), and Kavanagh (1988), these include extra tutoring and heavy wear and tear on school equipment and clothes.

Rhodes (1989) pointed to the extra transportation cost of foster children as a result of changing fostering practices. First because of the development of group methods of recruitment, assessment, training, post-placement support etc. It is economically efficient for the foster parents to be counselled in a group instead of individual home visits. Second, there are new and increased travel needs in fostering because of the high proportion of children fostered who have special needs, such as extra visits to GPs, assessment centres, hospitals and special schools. Rhodes suggested that more and more foster parents were expected to take an active role in the total care of their foster children involving courts, schools, police, adoption procedures, transport between natural parents and extended family and their own home.

Perceptions of adequacy

Traditionally the fostering allowance was regarded by foster parents and agencies as a token towards the daily expense of foster care. Regarded in this way, the adequacy of the maintenance allowance was not an issue. Recruitment of foster families was from largely median living standard families with the implicit aim of raising foster children out of poverty to a better life. The median living standard image was encouraged through allowances which were substantially more than that paid in poor relief to the natural family and the recruitment process excluded low income families from fostering by means testing. In pragmatic terms, the cost of the child's upkeep was largely dependent on the lifestyle of the family and therefore adequacy of the allowance was probably less of an issue the higher up the living standards' scale a foster family was placed. In the late 1980s, however, Leat (1990) found the principle of adequacy of payment important even for placement families with sufficient private income to carry the true cost of an extra child:

> It's not a matter of whether you can afford it, it's a question of whether you should have to. They tell you to treat the child as your own and then won't give you the money to do it..... (After all) you couldn't possibly leave him at home, he's part of the family so you end up paying yourself. (Leat 1990:32)

Foster parents' aspirations for payment

Traditionally foster parents have not perceived fostering as work outside the domestic sphere but as an extension of natural parenting. This image has left foster mothering as low status because virtually the only skills and attributes needed to perform a mothering role were those believed by some to be biologically bequeathed to females as mothers. The 1980s discourse has raised the perceptions and aspirations of foster parents, first because this myth of motherhood has been exposed through feminist writers, second because the role of the foster mother has moved away from that of the natural mother and third because one of the precursors of change have been the tasks of fostering which are increasingly recognised as skilful.

Changing perceptions of motherhood

Traditional values about foster mothering have followed the same route as ideologies about motherhood Feminist writers have contributed to the liberation of the foster mother by raising awareness of women's issues (Smith and Smith 1990, Cousins 1988, Meyer 1985, Rhodes 1991, et al). Meyer suggested that the status of foster mothers is lower than that of natural mothers. Southern (1986), found evidence through an international comparative study of payment to adoptive and foster families that a decline in the recruitment of foster carers was linked to a rise in the women's movement towards emancipation. The drop in volunteer mothers means that fostering must compete for workers with other paid caring occupations.

Foster parent perceptions about payment may be related to how they perceive their own fostering role at any particular point in time[6]. From a role perspective, if a foster mother sees her role as or very close to the natural mother she will perceive taking payment for caring for the child in the same light. The definition of role used in this instance is a set of rights and obligations to which people will strive to conform in varying degrees. This refers to how parents feel they are expected to behave and not necessarily to actual behaviour. The foster parent, for example, may feel expected to work with the natural parent but in reality not able to do so. The de-construction of the role of foster parent and natural parent gives a framework for identifying the similarities and differences between the roles. George (1970:52), based on the work of McCoy in 1968, suggested there were three levels of characteristics which make up the whole: pivotal, relevant, and peripheral. The foster parent's role traditionally included few of the 'pivotal' attributes such as blood ties and possession which enabled the parent to make choices concerning residency, religion, education and life plans for the child. 'Relevant' attributes were common to foster and natural parents' roles, for example, caring for the day to day emotional and physical needs of the child. 'Peripheral' roles did not effect role behaviour but the way in which tasks were performed by natural or foster parents which could differ within and between the groups and be a source of stress. There were also reciprocal aspects to roles. A natural mother may expect love in return for caring whereas foster children may find it hard to reciprocate in this way.

In the late 1960s, George (1970) provided evidence that 92% of long term foster mothers perceived themselves as if they were natural or adoptive parents. There was, however, marked differences if a foster parent cared for the child for short periods. In this case only 25% perceived themselves as the child's mother. The majority thought their role was as a relative. Other studies such as Adamson (1968), provided evidence of high proportions of foster mothers who perceived themselves in the role of natural or adoptive mother, the former 68%, the latter 77%. George (1970:56) found a negative correlation between the perceptions of the long term foster mother as mother of the foster child and the desire to be paid a reward for caring: 15% of the sample believed payment should cover maintenance plus a reward for the trouble of caring, and 11% maintenance plus a payment for professional skill. The majority of foster parents (George 68%, Adamson 77%) believed they should only receive a maintenance allowances plus other expenses. From a traditional British standpoint, this evidence seems to suggest that the

---

[6] Role theory has adequately been used in the past as a framework to explain foster parent perceptions (George 1972, Fanshel 1961, Glickman 1980). Role ambiguity in foster care can include lack of clarity about the scope and responsibilties of fostering and has been highlighted as a source of stress (Glickman 1980: 28).

24

closer the perception of foster mothers to natural mothers the greater the reluctance to making profit out of children:

> A large number of foster mothers have difficulty in carrying out their role: they are carrying out the role of substitute adoptive parent. This is reflected in their views about payment. Mothers are not paid, therefore substitute mothers should not be paid. (Adamson 1968:269)

The last decade has seen a growth in the use of short term placements for many reasons[7]. Consequently, many more fostering mothers today see their fostering role as carer rather than substitute mothers to their foster children and are not averse to the idea of taking payment for care.

The role framework also sheds light on the way professionals working in the field of boarding out hold different perceptions about payment for foster caring. George (1970) examined the opinions of Child Care Officers on the relationship between foster parents and foster children. A much lower percentage, 36%, looked upon long term foster parents as natural or adoptive parents and none believed short term foster parents held this role. The majority of Child Care Officers believed the role of foster parent should be that of 'relative' and in the case of short term foster parents, 10% of Child Care Officers believed foster parents should be paid employees.

A later study in the US by Glickman (1980) identified a similar trend towards a desire for extra payment for fostering in line with a moving away from the image of foster parent as 'natural parent' to that of 'worker'. A number of foster parents saw themselves as being members of a team or in para-professional roles. At the same time, foster parents expressed a sense of powerlessness, their skills and knowledge unrecognised by agency workers. Bullock (1990) argued that the roles of foster carers have had to change with more complicated cases. This meant that foster parents could no longer retain a passive role, but were compelled to be actively engaged in partnership with social workers.

George (1970) suggested 'role-training' could re-model foster parents perceptions of themselves in view of conflicting roles and in the light of the changing expectations of fostering. The result of paying foster parents would be higher quality care which would benefit the agency, foster children, natural families and foster parents. Glickman (1980:281) also advocated a reformation of the foster parent role towards para-professionalism, payment, work status and certification based on special training.

---

[7] There was greater commitment towards planning and permanence in long term fostering. Abortion law and greater acceptability of lone parenting contributed towards fewer children spending their childhood in foster placements.

In the 1980s and beyond, mothers faced more opportunities and greater pressure to work outside the home or in the mixed economy and this created competition for activities such as fostering.

Fee-paid foster care schemes began in the mid 1970s, these were described as 'specialist' schemes as opposed to the usual non paid 'traditional' fostering. Sometimes these schemes were sponsored by a voluntary organisation such as Barnardos. They went under many names: Professional, Specialist, Contract Fostering, Teenage Fostering, Family Placement, Family Support, Family Relief, Family Plus, Family Links, Teencare, Youthcare, InPlace, Links, Children First, and Mainstay (Shaw & Hipgrave 1989). They have in common 'time-limited' placements and 'contract-based' conditions. The fee is paid in recognition of the agency's high expectations of professional foster parents. As well as offering a secure, loving home, the foster parent is expected to implement an agreed development plan, keep a diary of the child's progress, contribute to six monthly reviews and liaise with other professionals. The foster parent is seen by the agency as 'self employed' under the terms of a contract between agency and carer in which compulsory training is written into some agreements. Shaw and Hipgrave (1989), however, suggest there is a lack of standardisation of definition which is leading to claims of rewarding some carers and not others.

Shaw and Hipgrave (1989) noted the bewildering complexity and variety of fee payments and methods of calculation. They found a few schemes with individual rates negotiated with management, some linked to residential child care officer or social worker scale, and one paid the equivalent of a married woman's personal tax allowance. The low fee and high expectations of the quality of care is an indication that fee paid fostering has not moved into the private market but that the degree of altruism present is extremely high.

Leat (1988) asked if such low levels of payment would deter women from the labour market. In respect of adult family placement carers evidence shows that money plays an ambiguous role, it is both crucial and irrelevant presenting a mix of caring values, labour market values and social justice. Leat claimed that carers were not selfless altruists because in today's society market values predominate: the point of reference is the paid labour market rather than unpaid family caring. Favourable or unfavourable comparison is made with previous employment or alternative jobs open to carers. (Adult carers are paid through the Department of Social Security about £100 a week [ibid:140].) Leat concluded that foster carers were the least money orientated of the groups of carers[8] interviewed.

In an enterprise culture supply and demand is the mechanism by which the market determines price. Knapp (1982) suggested the effect of increasing demand for foster parents in a supply led situation was the 'reservation wage' of fostering.

---

[8] Four groups of carers interviewed: foster parents, adult family placement carers, childminders and agency carers.

The concept of a reservation wage is described as the lowest level of compensation, payment and support that the parent will except for the task of foster caring. The most highly motivated foster parents will already be fostering, therefore, to reach the marginal potential foster families, the conditions of recruitment will need to be clearly defined.

Indication of foster parent dissatisfaction is seen in the setting up of independent services by groups of foster carers and the continued high drop out rate of newly recruited foster families (Department of Health 1991). In England fostering agencies run by foster parents which sell placements to the local authorities have emerged. In the 'seamless personal service' described by ministers, foster carers may well be there as private or voluntary agents bidding for contracts, ready to emerge as an independent profession.

Foster care in competition with other activities

NFCA (1992) claim fostering is a full time job which can rarely be combined with other work and yet more than before mothers have aspirations and 'needs' to take up employment. Fostering represents for many carers no employment or employment with lost earnings through reduced hours. Abrams (1986) suggested that reliance on the non-paid help of volunteers in general to care for non kin in the community in some parts of the country conflicted with labour market forces. In the US it was suggested by Wulczyn (1993) that one reason for a dramatic rise in foster care between 1986 to 1992 was the introduction of a policy in 1987 to pay relative or kin foster carers. In the UK, Rhodes (1989) pointed to communities, such as the Afro Caribbean, where combining paid employment and bringing up a family is vital both culturally and as a way of maintaining an acceptable standard of living. In other words, to consider fostering as an alternative to other forms of employment would not be unusual. As previously explained, in some areas there has been a relaxing of the exclusion of low income families from fostering by financial incentives such as enhancements attached to basic rates and only partially (or not at all) counted as income in an entitlement to benefits calculation.

Demands that fostering be incorporated in the formal economy as a fee paid or salaried service have increased in line with the growing prominence of fostering as a major child care resource. Maclean (1989) suggested that the advantages of fee paying far outweighed its drawbacks. In brief, fee paying:
- enhances the status of foster carers
- allows the authority to make explicit the roles and expectations of carers
- reduces unplanned moves and breakdown of placement
- aids recruitment
- offers equal opportunities policies for carers.

In addition, a salaried situation offers in-work protection for carers, National Insurance payments, tax benefits, holiday entitlement, sick pay, pension provision,

27

insurance, union protection, maternity and paternity leave, career breaks and other benefits received by other professionals working as civil servants. The main argument against is the cost of running such a service.

An attempt to adopt a professional approach to payment for foster care has been made by the NFCA by devising a 'payment for skills' system. Previously, a common system of enhancements was used by local authorities to reward carers whose children had special time consuming, or expensive needs. The problem was as the child's needs stabilised or reflected normalisation because of the good work of the foster parent, the enhancement disappeared. The enhancement scheme had the added disadvantage of labelling the child as a 'problem'. Whereas the new system (if adopted) labels the foster parent as skilled and pays for skill and experience at three levels, even if these skills are not utilized for every placement.

The appropriate level of payment is suggest to be the Residential Child Care Officer grade 4 at one third, two thirds and mid point on the scale, and is paid regardless of a current placement (NFCA 1993, Curry 1993).

The next part of this chapter examines whether the foster care allowance has maintained its value over time, or increased its value to reflect the changing climate of foster care.

The value of foster care allowances over time

The question of whether the foster care allowance has maintained its value over time is measured by three indicators:
- Prices
- Wages
- Benefits.

The comparative foster care allowance rates for particular years are chosen for specific reasons and, in view of the lack of accurate historical accounts, the 1945 rates are from the Curtis Report (1946) and are typical of a number of local authorities. The 1956 and 1964 rates are recalled by Barnes (1979) from a yearly diary of child care in Coventry. The years 1977, 1986 and 1992 are from the historical accounts of the NFCA. The rates are frequently paid by local authorities in England. 1977, was the first year local rates were collected by the NFCA, and 1986 was chosen because it was just prior to the social security reforms. Implicit in the post 1945 foster care rates is that the cost of a foster child increases with age. Before this period the younger child had higher foster care rates.

Prices

The comparative value of foster care allowances over time is measured in relation to the Retail Price Index (RPI). The RPI has been used for about 50 years to measure the monthly changes in prices of a comparative basket of goods and services. The basket of goods is set each year from the FES and the price changes monitored throughout the year. The prices are weighted to represent regional variations and variations in types of items. The index is not weighted for spending by different income/expenditure levels, household types etc, and therefore represents average spending in all households. The index reflects median spending styles but does not differentiate between the spending of families with children and those without. Changes in technology and techniques of weighting in the early days of its use were less complex than in recent times and, therefore, comparison of price over a long period of time is not as accurate as over the short term.

Table 1.3. shows the foster care allowances at 1992 prices. In just under 50 years of payment the foster care allowances have increased much faster than prices. The 1992 fostering rates have therefore significantly improved in real value compared to the original allowance and the increase in value is evident at each point on the scale.

Table 1.3
Foster Care Allowances 1945 to 1992 at constant 1992 prices, uprated by the RPI.

Age	1945	1956	1964	1977	1986	1992
0-4	14.84	15.86	17.74	26.89	38.15	51.11
5-10	11.27	18.42	19.82	33.26	46.67	62.54
11-15	9.43	22.92	24.07	40.03	55.14	74.48

Sources of foster care allowances: Curtis Report 1946, Barnes 1979, NFCA Fostercare Finance 1977-1992.

Table 1.4 shows the percentage yearly increase over time according to the age of the child. Overall, in just short of 50 years, older children have done better than younger children. The annual average real percentage increase measured by prices is 5.2% for children 0-4 years, 9.7% for children aged 5-10 years and 14.7% for children 11-12 years. During the last decade, however, the real per cent increase was approximately 6% per year for all age groups.

Table 1.4
The percentage real increase in foster care allowances by age of foster child, 1992
constant prices.

Period by age of child	Real increase in foster care rate £s	Real % increase	Annual real % increase
Age zero to four years			
1945-56	1.02	6.9	0.6
1956-64	1.88	11.9	1.5
1964-77	9.15	51.6	4.0
1977-86	11.26	41.9	4.7
1986-92	12.96	34.0	5.7
1945-92	36.27	244.4	5.2
Age five to 10 years			
1945-56	7.15	63.4	5.8
1956-64	1.88	11.9	1.5
1964-77	13.44	75.7	5.8
1977-86	13.41	40.3	4.5
1986-92	15.87	34.0	5.7
1945-92	51.27	454.9	9.7
Age 11 to 15 years			
1945-56	13.49	143.1	13.0
1956-64	1.15	5.0	0.6
1964-77	15.96	66.3	5.1
1977-86	15.11	37.7	4.2
1986-92	19.34	35.1	5.8
1945-92	65.05	689.8	14.7

Source of foster care rates as previous table.

Average wages

The foster care allowance is compared with the average wages of male manual workers in all industries at each period in time. This comparison gives some notion of how 'well off' a foster family would feel in relation to their overall income. Records of wage levels are collected annually by the Department of Employment and the historical annual statistical records are from 1945.

Table 1.5 shows that as a proportion of average wage, the allowances have maintained their relative value over time, with the exception of 1964. 1964 was during a period when foster care was a more popular activity compared with other periods in time. By 1977, the popularity of fostering had waned and the proportion of allowance to average wages had increased. In 1945, the allowance represented about an eighth of the average wage, by 1992 this proportion had increased to just less than a quarter of the average wage.

30

Table 1.5
Average male manual worker weekly wage (all industries) in relation to Foster Care Allowances (average 0-15yrs), 1945 to 1992.

Year	Foster care rate	Average wage	FCA as a % of AW
1945	192d	1521d	12.6
1956	404d	2947d	13.7
1964	528d	4479d	11.8
1977	£11.73	69.50	16.9
1986	£34.74	170.90	20.3
1992	£63.47	268.3	23.7

Source: Wages - Historical Labour Statistical Records, *Labour Market Statistics* 1964-1992, Foster care rates - Curtis 1946, Barnes 1979, NFCA *Foster Care Finance* 1977-1992.

Supplementary Benefits

Supplementary Benefit child scale rates have been the subject of much investigation over the years (Cooke and Baldwin 1984, Field 1985, Piachaud 1979 et al). The child scale rates originated as part of the National Assistance scales in 1948 but at a lower rate than had been recommended by Beveridge in 1942 (based on empirical research related to actual needs). Moreover, the focus on the inequality of benefit for older children resulted in adjustment out of line with inflation in the early 1980s. It is therefore the least reliable of the indicators used to test the adequacy of foster care allowances.

The significance, however, of using supplementary benefit child rates as an indicator of the movement of foster care allowances originated in the historical trend for measuring foster care allowances against the current payment of poor relief. At the turn of the century foster care allowances were three times that of outdoor relief. In 1948 foster care allowance was seven times the National Assistance for young children. For older children the foster care allowances remained equivalent to the turn of the century value.

Table 1.6 shows supplementary benefit as a proportion of foster care allowances. In 1964, for all ages of foster child, the Supplementary Benefit child rates were approximately 50% of the foster care allowance. The trend from the 1970s to the 1990s in relation to benefit levels, was for the foster care allowance to move further away from the amount judged adequate to meet the needs of children of the 'poor'. During this period, the youngest and oldest age groups of foster child allowance appear to have done slightly better than the 5-10 foster child age group. From 1986 this appears to be the effect of changes in the age-banding of Income Support rather than relative changes in the foster care allowances.

Two of the three indicators, prices and average manual wage, show that the foster care allowance has in real terms not only maintained but increased its original value since 1945. The supplementary benefit child scale rates as a proportion of foster care allowances show an increase in relative value to foster care allowances since the 1960s. Benefit rates, however, are the least reliable of the indicators because of the re-structuring of benefit rates and contraction of the age-bandings.

Table 1.6

Supplementary Child Scale Rate in relation to Foster Care Allowances 1945 to 1992.

Year	Foster care (d./£s)	S.B Rate (d./£s)	SB as a % of FCA (rounded)
Age 0-5 years			
1945*	246	37.5	15
1956	333	65	20
1964**	453	252.5	56
1977	9.32	4.10	44
1986	28.07	10.20	36
1992	51.11	14.55	29
Age 5-10 years			
1945*	186	45	24
1956	387	77.5	20
1964**	506	275.0	54
1977	11.54	4.95	43
1986	34.34	10.20	30
1992	40.57	14.55	36
Age 11-15 years			
1945*	156	52.5	34
1956	482	90	19
1964**	614	307.5	50
1977	13.89	6.75	49
1986	40.57	15.30	38
1992	74.48	21.40	29

Source: Foster care rates - Curtis 1946, Barnes 1979, NFCA *Foster Care Finance* 1977-1992. SB rates - DSS Annual Statistics.

* Supplementary Benefit rate 1948
** Supplementary Benefit rate 1965

Conclusion

This chapter has explored the dynamics of the foster care allowances both from a historical and contemporary perspective. From its origin the allowance functioned to pay for the child's maintenance, that is 'proper food, lodgings and washing, and the repair and renewal of clothing,' as it purports to do today with additional emphasis on the child's social development. The allowance was determined locally and funded from local taxes as is now the case. There are still significant differences between the lowest and highest paying authorities, especially in England.

Foster care was recognised in the early 19th century as a passport to more effective training for adulthood, an alternative to the workhouse and later as residential care for 'poor law' children. The actions of philanthropists, the church and voluntary organisations promoted foster care as an altruistic activity of moral, employed, working class, religious families who would raise the child as if it were their own. To this end 'hard up' potential carers were eliminated in the selection process. Nevertheless, by the end of the 19th century, authorities were paying carers three and four times the amount the same child would receive in out-door relief (the forerunner of National Assistance).

The heyday of fostering was probably the 20 year period after World War Two, when a certain dignity and respectability was attached to the then large army of volunteer mothers, and legislation placed a duty on local authorities to accommodate children 'in care' in foster families. It was ironic that allowances at this period of time were comparatively low, just keeping pace with prices and only twice the National Assistance child scale rates.

The 1970s proved to be a radical period for foster care. Issues such as children's and foster parent's rights came to the fore, as did the high breakdown rate of placements and the number of children in long term care without permanence or planning in their lives. A large number of disturbed and delinquent children were in the child care system and the climate of foster care was changing. Debate had been renewed on the payment of fees or wages to certain foster carers who would look after difficult to care for children. By 1977, the gap between benefits and allowance had widened, and in relation to wages and prices the allowance had gained some ground.

The last decade has seen an advancement in the understanding of the cost of foster care compared with the alternatives, and a growing awareness of the problems of meeting the demand for foster parents. The supply of foster parents has remained constant for more than a decade. Foster care allowances in the 1990s, in terms of prices, have increased in real value by 6% per annum for all ages of children. As a proportion of average wages, the foster care allowance has risen from 20% in 1986 to 24% in 1992. The Income Support child rate (the traditional barometer of foster care rates) as a proportion of the foster care allowance stands at approximately 31% in 1992.

The comparative value of foster care allowances has been important in government policy decisions in directing authorities to contract or expand the fostering service and the extent that alternative services are used. This type of evaluation of foster care allowances, however, tells us little about how adequate the amount is to meet the costs of caring.

Foster children are now on average more difficult to care for than previously. The task of caring demands higher levels of skill. Placements are more often time limited and task centred, and there are some indications that the aspirations of foster carers for payment to care have changed. The contemporary (and increasingly the traditional) foster mother looks less upon herself as a substitute 'mother' to foster children and more as a child care 'worker'. Analysis of policy shows legislation and regulations are also moving in this direction.

To conclude, foster care allowances not only have a role to play in adjusting the balance between foster parent expectations and the stress of fostering tasks but also in competing for new foster parents in an expanding labour market for women with 'caring' skills. As these jobs are low paid it is an indication that this field of work has not moved into the free market but that the degree of altruism as a motivation to foster care remains high. It could be that modern foster care also calls for a redefinition of altruism with a need for an extra element of explanation for commercialism in the motivation to foster. Commercialisation is said by Titmuss (1970) to repress expressions of altruism and sense of community. Culyer (1973) however suggests that altruism is only a state of mind held by many more than those who actually give. Whether a person presents others with a gift depends on their circumstances, that is, the intensity of the desire to give (altruism) and the cost to the person of giving (generosity). Compensation is one influence in Culyer's argument that frees a person to increase generosity without compromising the intensity of altruism. Payment for all foster care however, may result in some limitations such as the loss of freedom to exercise choice about which children to care for, and it infers contractual accountability and labour market commitment and rules. On the other hand, it enables the agencies to complete for quality care in a mixed economy without fears of a diminution of the gift of caring.

2 The direct costs of a child

Introduction

The direct costs of a child are explored in order to measure the adequacy of the foster care allowance in meeting a foster child's basic needs: that is, the costs of feeding, clothing, housing, health care, leisure, education and so forth, at median living standards.

Methods of estimating child costs

Behavioural, consensual and budget standard methods have been used to estimate the direct costs of a child. In practice, however, research often combines a number of different approaches.

The behavioural approach is based on surveys of what households actually spend, often in relation to their income. Public officials collect social statistics so that policy makers can be informed about the need for public services. The household is the typical unit of analysis with few child-related costs separately identified. Attempts at analysing the actual expenditure of a child from household data has been more successful in America than in Britain. One method compares the expenditure of families with children to similar families without children to determine the child's share of family expenditure (Olson 1982, Epenshade 1977); another way identifies 'child only' costs, leaving the collective consumption of families to be shared by some other method. Edwards (1981) from the United States Department of Agriculture (USDA), used the latter method and a per capita approach to sharing collective expenditure. In the United Kingdom (UK), Baldwin (1985) sought to identify the extra financial costs for families with a disabled child. Baldwin compared the income and expenditure of a control group of families from the Family Expenditure Survey and a group of families drawn from the Family Fund register. One way to identify child costs is to collect the information when the household expenditure survey is carried out.

Bradshaw and Holmes' (1989) relatively small scale study in Tyne and Wear involved children filling in expenditure diaries to complement family data.

Economists use large surveys of expenditure to construct equivalence scales to infer the comparative cost of a child. An equivalence scale attempts to capture the extent to which large families need more resources than small families at the same standard of living. The scales represent the cost of a child as a ratio of the cost of an adult(s). The reference household is usually taken to be a married couple without children or a single childless adult.

There are many different equivalence scale estimates and there is some controversy about which scale is best (McClements 1978, Whiteford 1985, Banks and Johnson 1993). The traditional approach to calculating equivalence scales is based on Engels' work which presupposes that there is some measurable part of a household characteristic that relates to the household's well being. Engels used food to measure well-being and others have used iso-prop techniques grouping together spending on a number of necessities. The 'Rothbarth' technique, for example, selects an 'adult' set of goods consumed in exactly the same way in households with and without children living at the same standard (such as alcohol, tobacco or adult clothing). Recent developments in computation and econometric theory, however, have produced a number of equivalence scales which attempt to measure welfare explicitly. Banks, Blundell and Preston (1991), and Pashardes (1991), for example, attempted to estimate scales which reflected spending over a period of time. These recognised that the spending decisions of households are made with more than one period in mind and for some households this can result in 'intertemporal transfers'. Pashardes (1991) suggests:

> that parents may provide for their children by drawing on savings or borrowings as well as by reducing current consumption. This means that child costs may be partly paid from reducing consumption in periods when the children themselves are not in the family. (Pashardes (1991:191)

Some limitations of equivalence scales are that they measure differences between different household types and they cannot test the adequacy of standards of living. An equivalent standard of living is reached by grouping households together by levels of income or expenditure whilst ignoring issues of debt or savings, gifts from others and quality of life indicators. Equivalence scales do not necessarily remain constant over time. Changes in relative prices and average income will affect spending in families differently. Equivalence scales are notorious for being unspecific about their make up. Some scales utilise components in expenditure surveys which contain anomalies such as low clothing expenditure and under reporting of alcohol expenditure. Other scales exclude major items such as housing and expenditure on durable goods.

The consensual approach has rarely been used to estimate the costs of children. It involves asking individuals what they think they need to spend on selected budget items or services. Van Praag (1982) pioneered this method in major research covering eight countries. Respondents were asked the minimum income required by someone in their circumstances. Piachaud (1987) points to inescapable conceptual problems in asking people for a prescription of how others may live given the conclusions the respondent may draw from the purpose of the question or research. In relation to estimating child costs, however, the approach is useful when combined with other methods to reveal the common values held by society at a particular point in time. Piachaud suggests:

> perhaps the most attractive feature of the social consensus approach is that it seeks to cast aside self-appointed, self-opinionated experts and let the people decide. (Piachaud 1987:149)

Piachaud's (1981) survey of 91 teenagers employed this method as a basis for estimates of older child costs. The teenagers were asked how much they or their parents spent in 14 categories and to give an estimate of the minimum expenditure needed. The teenagers' broad range of socio-economic characteristics made generalisation difficult. Current work by Walker (1992 on-going) aims to broaden the subjective concept of child costs by exploring the aspirations of children and parents through a large national survey.

The budget standards approach attempts to measure what people ought to spend rather than what they actually do (or think they need to). A characteristic of budget standard methodology is that *normative (expert) judgement* is used to create a 'basket of goods' which represents the type of commodities, quantities and quality of family consumption. Budget standards is an exact technique involving the counting of items, the calculation of periods of time before replacement of the item and the establishing of pricing mechanisms. Each item in the budget represents a function of the lifestyle it represents. Preference is exercised by consumers choosing an alternative item to perform the same function for a similar price.

Budget standards are among the oldest methodological tools in the social sciences for estimating living costs. The method was pioneered by Rowntree at the beginning of this century (1898, 1905, 1936) and informed Beveridge's recommendations for the setting of the National Assistance scales in 1946. There were three components in Rowntree's 'minimum necessary expenditure', food, household sundries and rent, of which Rowntree considered food was the most important. The cost of a basket of food according to age and sex was calculated by:

- looking at the function of food in the body
- the quantity necessary to fulfil the function
- the kind of food
- and the cost of food.

Differentials in children's food consumption at three, eight and 16 years were unfortunately lost due to averaging the final calculation (Field 1985).

Since the Second World War the budget standard method has been little used in the UK with the exception of Piachaud (1979). Piachaud estimated the cost of a child as a 'modern minimum set of requirements', which was, 'intended to reflect prevailing social attitudes'. The costs were not the total costs of a child aged two, five, eight and 11 years to its parents, as collectively consumed articles such as furniture, appliances and rent were excluded from the budgets. Piachaud's budgets have been described by Lynes (1979) and others as 'meagre', nevertheless, they illustrated the inadequacy of the child rate for families claiming supplementary benefit.

An international comparative study of the costs of children (Wynn 1972) provided budget estimates from the United States and Europe to demonstrate that the method had not been neglected outside Britain. A typical aim of 'budgetary studies' was to construct unit consumer scales so as to measure the cost of household members according to age and sex and compare these costs to a standard adult. In Australia, Lovering (1984) collected national and international normatively derived inventories for children and priced them at two standards of living. Housing was excluded on the basis of its variation in type and cost. Today, in Canada, Sweden, Norway and Denmark, and in some states of America, household budgets are still constructed and updated regularly, usually with the individual as the unit of analysis and subjective notions of economies of scale.

One of the most important outcomes of budget standard work is that it offers an alternative way of constructing equivalence scales based on other than expenditure surveys which are constrained by income and taste. The effort required to produce budgets for each family type, however, means few studies have been comprehensive enough to provide a range of scales which are age and family size related.

The Family Budget Unit

In Britain in 1985, a group of social scientists and researchers interested in the domestic economy in the UK set up the Family Budget Unit (FBU). The aim of the FBU was to construct a UK budget standard based on the budgets of a number of model family types at a modest-but-adequate standard of living. The FBU budgets improve on many of the former methods by taking model family types as the unit of analysis in place of the individual. Furthermore, 'normative estimates' are informed by behavioural evidence of median consumption from other sources.

The task of the FBU in drawing up each budget was to decide which items to include, their quantities, qualities, prices and, where the items are purchased intermittently or occasionally, how long they should last. The budgets were unconstrained by taste or household income. The approach to carrying out these tasks varies between commodities in the budget but in general the following procedures were used:

- Those responsible for preparing the budget for each commodity were supported by a team of experts. For example, the food group comprised of nutritionists and experts on food consumption.
- This expert advice was supplemented by seeking behavioural information about what people actually do. The transport budget, for example, was informed by The National Travel Survey.

- The budgets also took into account recommended standards laid down by official bodies. The housing budget, for example, was drawn up with regard to the housing fitness standard set in the Local Government and Housing Act 1989 and the General Household Survey common bedroom standards.
- Previous budgets, particularly the Swedish, Canadian, and Norwegian budgets, were also drawn on when no other authoritative information could be found.
- The judgement of the FBU researchers over-rode that of the 'experts' or behavioural evidence when questions about what was 'right' was in doubt.
- A second stage validated the budgets by comparing them with actual expenditure patterns based on the annual Family Expenditure Survey.
- Democratisation of the budgets was achieved by returning to the groups of experts and consumers for confirmation or adjustment.

The modest-but-adequate standard of living

The FBU *modest-but-adequate* standard of living is based on a median lifestyle. The Watts Committee (1980) describes a similar lifestyle as the *Prevailing Family Budget:*

> This standard affords full opportunity to participate in contemporary society and the basic options it offers. It is moderate in the sense of lying both well above the requirements of survival and decency and well below the levels of luxury as generally understood. (Watts 1980, p.vii)

The median income of a family with two adults and two children was used by Watts to represent this standard of living.

Lifestyle assumptions of the model families

A number of crucial assumptions have to be made about the lifestyles of the model families, including economic activity, housing tenure and car ownership. It is assumed that all adults of working age are engaged in full-time employment, with the exception of the mother who works part time. The child aged four is not at school and the child aged ten attends a primary school. The teenager is in full-time education. The households have access to a moderately priced second-hand car, and are either owner-occupiers or local authority tenants. These assumptions, and the decisions about what is included in the budget are determined usually according to the most common pattern of behaviour in the community. A 50% test has often been applied, that is, if more than 50% of a certain type of family has a particular commodity, then it is assumed that the model family has it. In line with the aim for consistent living standards across all model family types, people of like ages in different family types are assumed to have the same lifestyles. That is, the children have similar toys, leisure activities, clothing, opportunities for holidays and other activities; women of similar age in different households wear similar clothing. The budgets were priced in York to give the budget a local cultural base and, where possible, through local outlets of national chain stores to minimise geographical variation.

The FBU Budget is based on net principles which means the budget includes spending from savings, loans, credit and net income. Intra-family transfers of money, such as family gifts, loans and pocket money are not identified as such, but are represented by items of expenditure in the commodity groups. The FBU Budget Standard for three family types from which child costs are derived are shown in Table 2.1. The budgets include the cost of maintaining and running a second-hand car and vary according to the housing situation of each household.

Table 2.1
FBU budgets for three family types, October 1991 prices, £ per week.

a. Tenants	2 Adults	2 Adults, Girl 4, Boy 10	2 Adults, Boy 10, Girl 16
Housing	33.08	43.99	43.99
Food	38.35	57.17	67.82
Fuel	7.23	14.84	15.15
Alcohol	12.72	12.72	12.72
Clothing	14.92	29.64	31.61
Household goods	16.81	29.24	30.10
Household services	8.12	8.05	9.71
Personal care	8.35	10.31	12.96
Motoring	32.49	35.13	34.63
Fares	5.02	9.88	12.29
Leisure goods	8.41	15.33	15.64
Leisure services	19.00	16.13	20.62
Child care/baby-sitting	-	25.34	6.21
Total	**204.50**	**307.77**	**313.45**

b. Owner occupiers			
Housing	59.46	77.57	77.83
Food	38.35	57.17	67.82
Fuel	9.75	11.21	11.38
Alcohol	12.72	12.72	12.72
Clothing	14.92	29.64	31.61
Household goods	18.34	28.79	29.65
Household services	8.35	8.05	9.71
Personal care	8.35	10.31	12.96
Motoring	32.49	35.13	34.63
Fares	5.02	9.88	12.29
Leisure goods	8.41	15.33	15.64
Leisure services	19.00	16.13	20.62
Child care/baby-sitting	-	25.34	6.21
Total	**235.16**	**337.27**	**343.07**

Source: Bradshaw, Hicks, Parker (1992).

Methods of deriving child costs from family budgets

One way of deriving the cost of a child from a family budget is to deduct the budget of the childless couple from that of the couple with children. The balance represents the sum cost of the children. The advantage of this method is its simplicity. It fails, however, to distinguish between the costs of children of different ages or sexes in households with more than one child.

A more sophisticated deductive method is to isolate all individual and shared items in the budget which can be ascribed to the child. This enables the overall cost of each child by age and sex in the household to be calculated. This study has produced a comprehensive basket of goods and services to meet the needs of boys and girls aged four, 10 and 16 years of age, and explores economies of scale for one and two child families.

A number of processes are used to derive the child's itemised budget from the consumption of the family as a whole. First those items owned or used entirely by a particular child, such as clothing or public transport fares, are set aside. Second one of the following processes are used to cost items shared with other members of the household:

- per capita estimates
- differential calculation
- normative judgements on what items relate to the children.

The per capita method is useful for estimating consumption which is shared by all family members and where the distribution of the consumption for individuals is unknown. It provides a simple and effective method of allocating particular expenditure equally to all family members who might gain equally from such consumption. Up to a point the per capita method gives a sliding scale of costs per child as family size increases. A disadvantage of the per capita approach is that it treats children as if they are simply other adults. The result of this is generally to underestimate the adult proportion of cost and overestimate the child's.

The differential method takes the difference in spending on an item between the couple family and a family with children as the extra cost of children. This extra cost is shared equally among the children in a family. The child's housing standard, for example, is the difference between the cost of a house suitable for two adults and a family-sized house. This approach is useful because it excludes the bulk of the fixed or shared family costs from the child's budget standard. The method is only useful, however, where the different family types own similar goods.

Normative judgement is used to establish the inclusion of items in the child's basket of goods or to set the proportion of the child's commodities. An advantage of using this technique is the level of detail it achieves. This process allows for higher or lower proportions of costs to be assigned to each child's budget, for example, a higher share of internal decorating costs can be attributed to younger children. The disadvantage of the approach arises from the length of time needed to develop and update the budgets, and the subjective nature of some decision making.

The cost of children: Budget Components

Housing

Housing expenditure at the modest-but-adequate standard of living is largely determined by dwelling size and influenced by household composition. The house size and location affects levels of spending in other parts of the budget, such as household furnishings, fuel and transport.

Previous evidence of child costs: Historically, the wide range of family housing costs between regions and within housing types has created difficulties for social scientists involved in the exploration of the costs of child rearing.   Lovering (1984) and Piachaud (1979, 1981) exclude housing costs when estimating the cost of a child. The Social Planning Council of Metropolitan Toronto (1984) includes a standard housing cost in its estimate of the cost of raising children. This is calculated as the difference between the rental cost of a moderately priced one-bedroomed apartment and a similar two-bedroomed apartment. To accommodate a second or third child, the standard cost is the extra expenditure needed to rent a three-bedroomed apartment. Edwards' (1981) USDA housing budget sums housing, fuel and utilities, household operations and furnishings, service contracts, and equipment costs for households with children. The portion of housing expenditure allocated to a child's budget is a per capita share of the average total housing cost regardless of age.

The FBU standard for families: Table 2.2 summarises the FBU housing profiles for households with and without children living in rented and owner occupied housing. The choice of dwelling for each household type is judged by standards such as the General Household Survey 'bedroom standard', the Local Government and Housing Act 1989 housing 'fitness standard', and the York City Council allocation policy for local authority homes which provides three bedroomed houses to families with two children of different sexes, and one bedroomed flats to two adult households. The final considerations are the availability and affordability of dwellings in the York area.

Normative judgements and behavioural information are used to assess the purchase price, term of mortgage and level of deposit in relation to owner occupied housing. The owner occupiers are mortgage holders. The mortgages are based on 25 years repayment at two points in the housing career: for first time buyers and for those with an established ten year history of buying. Monthly repayments are net of tax relief on interest at the 25% rate and include the cost of a decreasing term mortgage protection premium. Other costs associated with borrowing are included where they exceed 75% of the purchase price.   A total of £1,000 is included to cover legal fees, survey reports and stamp duty. Additional housing costs included in the housing budget are: structure and contents insurance, water and sewerage rates, community charge, housing decoration and repair.

Table 2.2
FBU housing profiles, four household types, October 1991.

Household type	Tenure	Description
2 adults	Rented local authority	1960's flat, one bedroom, 1 mile city centre, rent £18.09 per week
	Owner occupied new mortgage or established mortgage	1890's semi-modernised brick small terraced house, two bedrooms, three-quarters of a mile city centre, purchase price £44,000
2 adults, 2 children	Rented local authority	1930's modernised brick terraced house, three bedrooms, ½ mile city centre, rent £26.30 per week
	Owner occupied new mortgage or established mortgage	1980's brick semi-detached, three bedrooms, one mile from city centre, purchase price £55,000

Source: Hicks and Ernst (1992a).

The child's standard: The differential and normative itemised method is used to estimate the housing costs of a child from the FBU housing standard. The size of the property is related to household composition and meets the criteria of suitability for comfort and personal development of all family members, and adequacy for all daily household activities.

The purchase price of the property and the level of loan repayment, given that the sum of the deposit is similar in all FBU owner occupier households, is determined by the size of the house. A measure of the direct housing costs of children is the value of the difference in size between a standard house for two adults and a standard house for two adults and two children. If the value of the extra space needed for child rearing is taken as the increased level of mortgage repayment, then the cost of the children in the same house profile will only differ according to the stage reached in the parents' housing career. The most common stage reached in owner occupied housing for the families described is the established or 10 year mortgage history, which will be referred to subsequently as a 'general' standard for analysis purposes.

The additional cost of rent for families with children is also the consequence of the increase in accommodation size. The two adult household rents a one-bedroomed flat and the family with two children rents a three-bedroomed house. The children's share of the direct housing cost in the rented sector is therefore the value of the extra rent for a larger property.

Other housing costs of children include a small amount of water and sewerage rates, and maintenance costs. The level of household decoration and DIY activities according to family type is largely an unknown factor. It is possible that a variety of cost levels apply which relate to preference and skills rather than to size or age of the property.

The FBU budgets, however, base the estimate for interior maintenance on an allowance given to all new tenants of York Housing Department. It is assumed that children increase the need for re-decoration and maintenance. Increased need relates to general wear and tear and the cost of decorating the children's bedrooms. The extra cost allowed for three bedroomed dwellings compared to one bedroomed properties is taken as the standard for children. It is assumed that the presence of children does not influence decisions on the frequency of exterior decoration.

Table 2.3 highlights the extent of the higher costs of children in owner occupied housing compared with local authority tenure. The difference in costs for the various types of owner occupation reflects the level of borrowing of the owner occupiers at different stages in their housing career. In a two child family, the average child in a family with an established mortgage incurs a cost of £8.37 or 11% of the aggregate housing expenditure. A child in rented accommodation, however, has lower actual costs of £5.32, but proportionally greater costs at 12% of the total housing costs.

In families of different sizes the costs are greatest for only children, 50% less for each child in a two child family and one third less for each child in a three child family, up to the point when the house is not big enough to suit a modest-but-adequate lifestyle.

Table 2.3
Summary housing costs of children by age and family size,
October 1991 prices, £ per week.

	New mortgage	New mortgage	Establish mortgage	Establish mortgage	Rent	Rent
Children in the family	2	1	2	1	2	1
Mortgage repayment	12.87	25.74	6.37	12.74	4.11	8.21
Water rates	0.37	0.74	0.37	0.74	0.01	0.01
Sewerage rates	0.48	0.95	0.48	0.95	0.05	0.10
Internal decoration	1.15	1.15	1.15	1.15	1.15	1.15
Total	**14.87**	**28.58**	**8.37**	**15.58**	**5.32**	**9.47**

The value of the property in relation to the presence of children is the base for the differential calculation of child housing costs. The decision to estimate housing costs for children in this way is influenced by the notion that housing is current expenditure and the mortgage contract represents the lifetime of the dwelling and the life stage of the parents. When the mortgage contract has expired, given a traditional housing market, the value of the property in theory allows at least sufficient capital to replace the dwelling. The extra capital accumulated could be viewed as resulting from a small element of investment in the repayment of the mortgage which fluctuates according to the market. The argument is whether the whole of the differential cost should be shown as child cost or whether some element should be set aside to represent parental saving.

Fuel

In general, households use fuel for space heating, water heating, cooking, lighting and to drive appliances. The aggregate fuel bill of most households, except those users of solid fuel, consists of a 'fixed' standing charge for meter rental and a charge per unit for fuel consumed. The amount of fuel used by one individual is therefore difficult to separate from the family's total fuel consumption. There are four elements which have a major effect on the variation between household fuel budgets at equivalent living standards:
- the dwelling construction
- the dwelling dimensions
- the heating system
- the number of people in the household.

The FBU standard for families: The FBU fuel standard is based on normative (expert) judgements of energy consumption. The modest-but-adequate standard is described as well above meagre spending and is based on the principle that people should be warm and comfortable in their homes. The normative decisions, however, are moderated by a number of constraints:
- the dwelling used for each household type
- the leisure and work related assumptions for each household type
- the limitations of the computer model available to calculate the household fuel standard.

The volume of the dwellings (which has a major bearing on energy consumption), however, varies considerably between the different properties, as shown in Table 2.4. As a consequence, energy usage and its cost varies significantly in different dwellings for different households.

Table 2.4
Comparison of dwelling volumes.

Household type	House type Owner occupiers	Volume (m3)	House type Local authority	Volume (m3)
Two adults with children	3 bed modern semi	179.8	3 bed 1930's end terrace	212.6
Two adults	two-bed 1890's terrace	175.2	one-bed 1930's flat	105.0

Source: Hutton and Wilkinson (1992).

All households shown above have a whole-house, balanced flue gas central heating system. The demand temperatures of dwellings to meet a criterion of comfort for household members differs according to the use of the rooms. The downstairs living accommodation (zone 1) temperature is set at 21°C, and the upstairs area (zone 2) temperature is set at 18°C during heat 'on' periods. This temperature is increased to a mean temperature in zone 2 of 19°C to give a 21°C environment in the teenager's study bedroom.

The central heating 'on' periods are determined by the household's work, leisure, and child care patterns, within a range of nine to 16 hours a day. The insulation standard includes loft insulation and lagging of the hot water tank, and the ventilation rate is taken as a middle-range value. The extent of electrical appliances included in each household is specified in the FBU household goods and services budget according to family needs, but the usage is constrained by the BREDEM computer program utilised to construct the fuel standard.

BREDEM 8 (Building Research Establishment Domestic Energy Model) bases the energy calculations on the number of people per household unit and the average fuel consumption of families in the median income range. The model estimates the energy used on space heating according to the fabric, construction and volume of a particular dwelling, and the number of people. Information is fed into the system about the dimensions of rooms, the type of heating system, the desired temperatures and the number of hours for which the heating is turned on. Water heating, lighting and average appliance rates for each household are determined by the size of the household. Cooking rates for households, however, are a constant amount irrespective of external influences. The internal heat gains from the gas water heating, cooking, electrical appliances, together with solar gains from windows and the advantages of curtain insulation are incorporated in the model as savings on the heating needs of households.

The FBU fuel budget is precise for each dwelling and type of family group. In reality however, these dwellings may contain less efficient heating systems and utilise the free energy source (internal heat gains) present to some extent in all occupied dwellings less productively. The breakdown of fuel usage for individuals within households involves subjective decisions. At present little is known about the proportion of fuel used by a child in relation to an adult.

The child's budget standard: The method for calculating the fuel cost of a child is based on the principle that the child should not be responsible for fixed fuel costs which would occur whether children were present in the household or not. Three approaches, normative, differential and a simulated BREDEM approach are considered. The 'normative' method is a list of the extra fuel usage per child at the modest-but-adequate living standard. The assumptions underlying the itemised list are based on the family work and leisure patterns of the children, and on normative decisions regarding the needs of children in families. These include, for example, additional use of the washing machine, iron, hair-dryer and television, the cost of lighting and heating the child's bedroom, and the cost of additional hot water for extra baths each week.

47

Initially a normative approach was used in creating a provisional child's fuel budget standard, which resulted in a very precise list of the estimated use of appliances in relation to age and gender. However, the standard had to be calculated manually, and it was not household specific because it took no account of the condition of the dwelling or the incidental gains from the presence of other household members.

The differential approach relies on the FBU premises that the housing type, housing volume and household composition are closely related to fuel use, and that other factors are similar across household types, for example, type of fuel. In other words the households have the same fuel standards of living. The variation in fuel use and cost between one household and another is then assumed to be the result of the presence of additional people, in this case the children. Volume variations, however, illustrated in Table 2.4, show only a trend towards bigger volumes with increased household and dwelling size. Moreover, the condition of the building insulation in older properties is poor compared with modern well insulated ones. The results of taking a simple differential approach would, therefore, lead to large variations in costs between similar aged children in different dwellings. Children living in 'old' local authority housing, for example, have almost five times the fuel cost of children in comparatively 'new' owner-occupied housing.

The simulated BREDEM approach is another differential model which aims to isolate the difference in dwelling volumes between the different properties, and assigns to children a 50% greater use of hot water and electrical appliances than the average use reported in the 1980s study by BREDEM. The BREDEM programme is adjusted as follows:

- The two adult calculation (reference base) uses the same house type as the families with children, but has a nine hour, 7.00 to 9.00 and 16.00 to 23.00, heating pattern during the week and assumes that only 50% of zone 2 is heated. The demand temperature in zone 2 for the two adults and also for the two parents with two younger children is $18°C$.
- The two parents and older children calculation uses a demand temperature of $19°C$ in zone 2 to simulate some use of the teenage child's bedroom as living space, that is $21°C$. The heating pattern for both household types with children is the same: 7.00 to 13.00 and 16.00 to 23.00 for weekdays and 7.00 to 23.00 at weekends.
- The water heating and electricity consumption for the families has been increased from 'normal' to give a consumption effect of five people in a four person house (each child has the effect of 1.5 adults). This was achieved by altering the floor areas (and adjusting the U values to keep heat losses constant) in order to ensure that the incidental gains (body heat + lights and appliances) were estimated correctly.
- The number of cooking therms used are similar in all households. Thus the households with children are assumed to use the same quantity of fuel in the preparation and cooking of food as households without children.

Table 2.5 shows the consumption of fuel in households with two adults and households with younger and older children using the simulated BREDEM method. An increase in the number of therms used for extra water heating, and in electrical appliance use in households with children, results in an increase in incidental energy gains and subsequently less therms used in space heating.

Table 2.5

Fuel consumption for three household types, by tenure, using the BREDEM simulated approach.

	Tenure (therms)	Space heating (therms)	Water heating (therms)	Cooking (therms)	Lights and appliance (kWh)
2 Adults	owner occupier	321	217	57	1367
2 Adults	local authority	603	217	57	1527
2 Adults & Child 4 & 10	owner occupier	290	313	57	2696
2 Adults & Child 4 & 10	local authority	639	313	57	3097
2 Adults & Child 10 & 16	owner occupier	309	313	57	2696
2 Adults & Child 10 & 16	local authority	674	313	57	3097

Table 2.6 above shows that in younger two child families the average child cost is £1.28 each week in new property and £2.42 in older property. This represents 11% and 16% respectively of the aggregate household fuel budget. An increase in space heating costs to heat the teenager's study room is marginal, approximately £0.09 to £0.16 per week.

Table 2.6
The cost of fuel for three household types, by tenure,
October 1991 prices, £ per week.

	Tenure	Space heat	Water heat	Cook- ing	Lights appli- cation	Year bill*	Ave. child year	Average cost week
2 Adults	owner occupier	147	100	26	105	378	----	----
2 Adults	local authority	277	100	26	118	521	----	----
2 Adults Child 4 & 10	owner occupier	133	144	26	208	511	133	1.28
2 Adults Child 4 & 10	local authority	293	144	26	310	773	252	2.42
2 Adults Child 10 & 16	owner occupier	142	144	26	208	520	142	1.37
2 Adults Child 10 & 16	local authority	309	144	26	310	789	268	2.58

* Not including standing charge or annual boiler service

Food

The amount and type of food purchased by a household is influenced not only by the composition of the household and household activities, such as work and leisure patterns, but also by food availability, buying efficiency, cultural norms, preference and knowledge of human nutrition.

Previous evidence of child costs: Experts are able to estimate the nutritional needs of children related to age, weight and sex. More than two decades ago, the DHSS (1969) published tables on the recommended daily allowances (RDAs) of energy and protein intake for good health and development, and (1979) a table of dietary reference values (DRVs). Such information serves to guide dieticians in the construction of diets for individuals or as standards for general public dietary education.

A convention in this type of calculation is to use a scale measurement of 'man-values' which are non-household specific. A 'man-value' for RNIs of nutrients and energy is equal to unity (1.00). The ratio equals the average intake of nutrients for each age/sex group divided by the average intake of nutrients of the adult male. Nelson (1986) has developed this further by creating a household-specific ratio for estimating the distribution of energy intake in particular groups of families. Nelson's scale is a ratio in terms of 'family values' of the adult male head of household which is equal to unity (1.00). Nelson studied the nutrient and energy intake in the diets of 79

Cambridge families with two adults and two or three children. Nelson (1986) found evidence of similarity in eating habits within families, for example, all family members were relatively large eaters, moderate eaters or had other common patterns in consumption. There are weaknesses, however, in using this proportional approach as families may not necessarily share food according to nutrient or energy needs. Nelson (1986) reported that men and young boys often receive more than their 'fair share' of animal protein but that the nutrient density of the diet of women and children was greater than that of the men. Nelson's scale of factors for the distribution of energy intake within households is given below:

Table 2.7
Factors ('family values') used to allocate food distribution in household of two adults and two or three children.

Adult - over 18	male	1.00
	female	0.70
Child 11 - 17	male	0.91
	female	0.81
Child 5-10	male	0.73
	female	0.61
Child < 5	male	0.51
	female	0.48

Source: Nelson (1986).

The FBU standard for families: The FBU food budgets are constructed to reflect the usual purchasing and consumption patterns of the particular household types at a modest-but-adequate standard.   The budget satisfies the requirement of all family members in food adequacy and Dietary Nutrient Intake (DNIs). Furthermore it meets the objective of a healthy diet at reasonable cost. Overall, the FBU food budget standard is determined using normative (expert) judgements about what household food consumption should be and from behavioural evidence about what household food consumption is.

The behavioural evidence is taken from the *National Food Survey (NFS)* (1983-87) which provides a diet profile of the average food consumption based on 350 food codes for households in selected bands of the income distribution scale.   A comprehensive food profile is achieved by the addition of extra foods not reported in the NFS, such as alcoholic beverages, sweets and soft drinks, and allows for foods obtained and eaten outside the household.   The *1988 Family Expenditure Survey (FES)* provides the basis for the inclusion of sweets and soft drinks while alcoholic beverages are founded on two-thirds of Health Education Authority safe levels.   There is an allowance of 6% for food wastage, 3-5% for consumption by visitors, and 8-25% for meals which are eaten out of the household.

Nutrient Conversion Factors are used to estimate the nutrient content of the food profile and adequacy is met by adjusting the diet profile to satisfy the nutrient requirements for all household members.   The original diet profile for each household is adjusted to a healthier diet by minimal substitution of healthier foods such as wholemeal bread, fish, fresh fruit and vegetables, and a reduction in the amount of fats and sugar in general. Moreover, each item is reduced to a level of 100% of dietary reference values for energy as it would be inappropriate to use the NFS or FES expenditure as the basis for budgets because households tend to over-purchase. The overall effect is to shift the household food profile towards an adequate and acceptable healthy diet which is lower in fat and sugar, higher in dietary fibre, more nutrient-dense and adequate in all other respects.

The 'reasonable cost' objective for the food budget is met by using *Sainsbury's* food database. The leading lines are assumed to reflect the usual or average household food purchasing patterns and economy goals and represent a notional estimate of the cost of the household weekly diet.

A food shopping basket is produced by converting the notional model of the household food profiles into a shopping list of items such as whole loaves of bread, packets of biscuits, pints of milk and cuts of meat. Those items which would be replaced over a longer period of time, such as tea, coffee or marmalade, are allocated a lifetime to give a weekly estimate of the cost. The cost of the commercial food basket is equivalent to the aggregate cost of the notional food budget standard for each household type.

The child's standard: A proportional approach is used to estimate the weekly food cost of a child. The FBU Food Budget Standard is a theoretical food budget standard which uses the household as the unit of analysis. Consequently, economies of scale are inherent and there is no way of knowing exactly how the household food consumption is shared among the adults and children. Nelson's family values are therefore applied to the lists of food which make up the family food profile. The unit of food is then priced and converted to a commercial food basket as previously described. A summary of the weekly food costs of children are shown in Table 2.8. The male child in all cases has higher food costs than the female child.

Table 2.8
A modest-but-adequate food budget for children,
October 1991 prices, £ per week.

		2 Adults, Children 4, 10	2 Adults, Children 10, 16
age 11-17	male	18.23	18.44
	female	16.23	16.41
age 5-10	male	14.63	14.79
	female	12.22	12.37
age 1-4	male	10.02	10.13
	female	9.61	9.73

Source: Computation by Nelson, Mayer and Manley (1992).

Clothing

The household wardrobe at the modest-but-adequate living standard is expected to meet all the clothing needs of family members. Clothing needs arise from family activities, such as leisure, relaxation, work or school attendance, and special occasions throughout the seasons.

Previous evidence of child costs: Academic surveys have provided few clues to the clothing consumption patterns of children. Wynn (1972), however, found evidence from international budget studies that older children have adult clothing costs and that girls cost more to clothe than boys. American estimates suggest adult levels of spending by the age of 12 years. German estimates suggest adult levels by the ages of 14 to 15 years and in France the clothing costs of teenagers' is substantially higher than in any other age range. Furthermore, expenditure on footwear is a major part of the child's clothing costs and Wynn believes this to be highest between the ages of 12 to 17 years.

Some budget studies imply that girls cost more to clothe than boys at almost every age level (Wynn 1972). Indeed the Social Planning Council of Toronto (1984) notes that by the age of 12 years girls' clothing costs are 40% higher than boys'. Lovering (1984) believed the low cost of clothing for Australian children especially boys was due to the cultural 'norm' of the wearing of jeans. Edwards (1981) found regional differences in children's clothing costs were significant in America, that is, urban children were more expensive and their clothing more fashionable than in rural areas.

The FBU standard for families: Clothing budgets are created for each member of the household. None of the clothes are second hand, home made, passed down to other family members or purchased in sales. On the whole, the inclusion of specific brand name clothes is supported by reference to Mintel (1987-1991) and Euromonitor (1987-1990) journals. These provide information on consumer buying patterns and the most popular outlets for pricing clothes. Occasionally, journal reports give more specific information on the ownership of garments with particular reference to age and gender. In addition, family group discussions facilitated by the FBU, with reference to the Toronto (1984) and Swedish Budget Standards (1989), aided the setting of quantities and lifetimes for clothing items.

The FBU budgets take into account a range of factors during the process of adjusting lifetimes for clothing. Consideration, for example, is given to the quality of the garment, the frequency and duration of wear, the fabric type, the manufacturing process and washing life of the garment, and the growth rate of the child. A basic clothes repair kit is included as part of the clothing standard, and the household goods and services budget includes a sewing machine for families with children.

The child's standard: The modest-but-adequate living standard sets the following criteria for clothes in relation to children:
* A choice of casual clothes for evenings and weekends

- A school uniform and PE kit for school aged children and day clothes for the child in nursery school
- Leisure clothes for indoor and outdoor activities, for example, wellington boots, training shoes and a swimsuit
- One special occasion outfit
- Sufficient clothes for all seasons.

The clothing lists, compiled by the FBU, for each child are based on the assumption that similar children in different family types have equivalent leisure, school and relaxation lifestyles, and therefore have similar clothing needs. The variation in clothing budgets between children is therefore a result of age and sex differences. The style of garments and shoes are classical so that the budget can be easily priced over a limited period of time. The lifespan calculations are determined by the growth rate of the child rather than when the clothes are worn out. The lifespan is also affected by the frequency of the family clothes wash.

Other budgets are compiled in line with the established criteria from the FBU clothing benchmark for children of specific age and sex. Table 2.9 summarises the clothing costs for children of different ages and sexes. The weekly cost increases with the child's age from £6.18 per week for a four year old to £9.17 per week for a child of 16 years. Findings from previous budgetary studies indicate that at every age level girls' costs are higher than those for boys and teenagers have greater clothing costs than adults. The FBU figures show a more complicated picture than this. At four years old girls' clothing costs more than boys. Female adults also have higher clothing costs than male adults. During the teenage years this trend is reversed: boys' garments and shoes cost significantly more than girls' of the same age. The age at which children reach adult clothing costs is also related to the gender of the child. Boys reach adult costs before their tenth birthday, girls at some time later but before their sixteenth birthday.

Table 2.9
Clothing costs of children by age and sex,
October 1991 prices, £ per week.

	Girl 4	*Boy 4*	*Girl 10*	*Boy 10*	*Girl 16*	*Boy 16*
Main items + underwear	4.93	4.60	4.60	5.33	6.64	6.05
Accessories	0.11	0.11	0.11	0.16	0.16	0.11
Footwear	1.44	1.44	2.36	2.69	1.65	2.98
Haberdashery	0.03	0.03	0.03	0.03	0.03	0.03
Total	**6.51**	**6.18**	**7.10**	**8.21**	**8.48**	**9.17**

Note: Adult female clothing costs £7.97.   Adult male clothing costs £6.98 per week.

Household goods and services

The household goods and services needs' of individual family members, at the modest-but-adequate level, are difficult to separate from the needs of the family as a whole, but may vary due to factors such as age, sex, number of siblings and family activities. Economies of scale may be evident in households where children share a bedroom and diseconomies of scale where the numbers of children increase the wear and tear on furniture, household fittings and household fabrics.

Previous evidence of child costs: Previous budget studies of children have dealt with communal goods mostly by taking a minimal approach. In the USDA estimates, for example, Edwards (1981) includes only the costs of those goods purchased during the year of the survey to which the USDA applied a per capita calculation according to household size. Lovering (1984), excludes most dwelling related cost from children's budgets. Piachaud (1979) includes a small amount of 'household provisions', for example each child is estimated to use up a pillowcase, a sheet and a towel every two years and a blanket every four years. The 1981 Social Planning Council of Toronto assigned to children's budgets the difference between the total cost of furnishings, equipment and operation for a household with children compared to the cost of similar goods in a household without children.

Household services such as child care costs are excluded because in many countries outside the UK they are provided free or subsidised by the state. The Social Planning Council of Toronto (1981), however, included an estimate for child day care costs by calculating the average cost for children of different ages in private child care centres.

The FBU standard for families: The FBU household goods budget includes: furniture, floor covering and textiles/soft furnishing; gas, electric appliances, hardware and other appliances; stationery and paper goods; cleaning products; pet food and pet accessories.

Information from surveys such as *the 1987 General Household Survey, Social Trends 1987-90*, and market research reports are used to guide the inclusion of common goods and services in the budget standard. Where statistical information is available, items are included in the budget if ownership is found in over 50% of the UK population. Where such information is unavailable normative judgements are used to include additional items. The setting of lifespans was aided by other budget standards and in consultation with consumer groups.

The lifetime calculation for each item incorporated factors such as the quality of the materials used in manufacture, the frequency of use, the manufacturer's replacement recommendations, market research findings on wear and tear, and the presence of children in the household. Quantities of furnishings and fittings are assigned according to the number and function of rooms in each type of dwelling, the composition of the family and assumptions made about the family's lifestyle.

An equivalent living standard across the different households is achieved by the inclusion of similar goods where appropriate and a similar quality of goods in each dwelling type. The furniture, carpets and floor coverings, for example, are of a similar

55

standard but vary in size to suit the dimensions of the dwellings. The gas and electrical equipment, kitchen cooking utensils, crockery, glassware and pans are sufficient to entertain visitors or additional family members. Garden tools are included where appropriate, and DIY tools are similar across all households. Quantities of household consumables such as toilet rolls are estimated according to the number of people in the household, whereas the type and quantity of stationery and the number of washloads per household relates to the ages of the children and adults. The repair of household equipment is estimated from average repair costs based on consumer behaviour. Goods are only repaired to the cost of half the value of replacement. National chains of retailers are used for pricing where they are market share leaders for particular items, other items are shown at York 1991 price levels.

The FBU household services include: postage and telephone costs; subscription fees; dry-cleaning and shoe-repairs; window cleaning; baby sitting and child care costs.

The postal and telephone costs are based on average household costs provided by the Post Office and OFTEL. An average household is assumed to be 2.55 people and weighted costs are calculated according to each FBU family. The 16 year old is considered to be an adult, and the younger children half an adult.

Subscription fees include Trade Union dues for part-time and full-time work and the cost of a ten year passport. Dry cleaning and shoe repair costs are included for adults and the child aged 16 years. A typical window cleaning cost is calculated per month for a flat and a house.

Baby sitting frequency is determined by the leisure activities of each household with children. There are three levels of frequency of three hours each, the high level is once a week, the medium level is once a fortnight, and the low level is once a month. In the case of the latter, the family is expected to rely to some extent on the baby sitting services of the 16 year old teenager. Additionally the budget standard for baby sitting contains two late-night baby sitting sessions per year which include a taxi home for the sitter.

Child care costs are based on the number of child care hours purchased, according to the number of hours the mother spends in employment and travel to work. The pre-school four year old child attends a free state nursery class at the local school during term time. The part-time working mother with children aged four and 10 years purchases a total of 2.7 hours of child care per day for 39 weeks per year, and 8.4 hours per day for 8 weeks of the year. Costs per hour are based on the minimum rate suggested by the National Childminder's Association.

The child's standard: Normative judgement and the differential method are used to estimate the child's household goods and service budget. The capital cost of a number of commodities such as a particular child's bedroom furnishings and fittings is included wholly in the child's standard. In other instances general furnishings and fittings are shared by all household members. The differential method is used to estimate the level of wear and tear on communal household furnishings, equipment and household fabrics: that is, the depreciation (replacement) cost difference of household goods in families with children compared to households without children. The extra wear on the life of an armchair when children are present, for example, is estimated at two years.

Wear and tear per week $=$

$$\frac{\sum\left(\dfrac{cost_c}{lifetime_c}\right) - \left(\dfrac{cost_a}{lifetime_a}\right)}{52} \div n_c$$

where $cost_c$ is the retail cost in a household with children, $cost_a$ is the retail cost in a two adult household, $lifetime_c$ is the lifetime in a household with children, $lifetime_a$ is the lifetime in a two adult household and n_c is the number of children.

In general the additional wear and tear and repair costs on gas and electrical equipment, kitchen and hardware goods in households with children is included in the child's standard. Some items are extra to households with children, for example, food mixers, microwaves and sewing machines. These are items which contribute towards a saving in time for parents rather than items needed by children, consequently the capital cost of purchasing the equipment is excluded from the child's budget, and a two year equivalent wear and tear cost is included. Items, such as extra paper, pens, pencils, crayons, school equipment, Christmas cards, toilet rolls, cleaning material and baby sitting are also included in the child's budget. No pet costs are assigned to the children's budgets since ownership is seen as a parental responsibility.

Table 2.10 shows the household goods and services cost of a child in a two parent and two child family. The marginal difference between children residing in houses with different forms of tenure is due to the variations in room specifications between the dwellings. The 16 year old child is treated as an adult for the cost of postage, telephone, dry cleaning and shoe repairs. The latter two costs are lower for boys than for girls. In owner occupied housing, for example, the cost of household goods and services for children aged four years is £5.04, for 10 year olds it is £5.14, and for 16 year olds it is £6.21 per week. In local authority housing the costs are only marginally lower.

Table 2.10
Household goods and services costs of children by age and tenure,
October 1991 prices, £ per week.

Child's age	4	4	10	10	16	16
	Owner	*Rent*	*Owner*	*Rent*	*Owner*	*Rent*
Furniture	0.86	0.86	0.86	0.86	0.87	0.87
Floor coverings	0.73	0.46	0.69	0.57	0.69	0.57
Textiles soft furnishings	0.47	0.50	0.47	0.57	0.47	0.57
Gas, electric appliances	0.34	0.34	0.34	0.34	0.41	0.41
Kitchen and hardware	0.32	0.32	0.32	0.32	0.32	0.32
Stationery & paper goods	0.37	0.37	0.45	0.45	1.10	1.10
Toilet rolls & cleaning	0.61	0.61	0.61	0.61	0.61	0.61
Postage	0.10	0.10	0.16	0.16	0.23	0.23
Telephone	0.00	0.00	0.00	0.00	1.06	1.06
Shoe repairs	0.00	0.00	0.00	0.00	0.19	0.19
Dry cleaning	0.00	0.00	0.00	0.00	0.22	0.22
Spare key	0.00	0.00	0.00	0.00	0.01	0.01
Passport	0.00	0.00	0.00	0.00	0.03	0.03
Baby-sitting	1.24	1.24	1.24	1.24	0.00	0.00
TOTAL	**5.04**	**4.80**	**5.14**	**5.12**	**6.21**	**6.19**

The child care standard for employed mothers: The decision to include expenditure on child care for families with working mothers in the FBU budgets gives rise to debate. Empirical evidence in the UK points to informal (non-paid) child care as the most common arrangement for working mothers of young children. The 1980 *Women and Employment Survey* cited in Cohen (1988:19) found that only a small percentage of working mothers used formal child care such as day nurseries, nannies and 'au pairs'. In the case of full-time work, it was common to use maternal grandmothers. For mothers working part-time the most common providers of child care were their husbands.

Clearly the FBU budgets have to some extent disregarded behavioural information and have included formal child care for working mothers. From a normative stance, arguments can be presented which justify the inclusion of formal child care costs in the budget standard of household types with young children and working mothers. Including formal child care gives a notion of equal opportunity for all mothers to work, whether they have an informal network of 'free' child care available to them or not and regardless of earning levels. Second, it cannot be assumed that informal child care resources are 'free', often relatives and friends are paid in cash or kind. Cohen (1988) suggests that 20% of childminders may not be registered. Adopting a formal child care standard has the advantage of using a known price base which is equally available to all family types.

The average weekly child care cost of a child of four and a child aged ten are shown in Table 2.11.

Table 2.11
The average child care costs of a child by age,
October 1991 prices, £ per week.

Work status of mother	Aged four	Aged ten	Aged sixteen
Full time work	39.36	17.18	0.00
Part time work	18.01	4.85	0.00

Transport

In general, the range of family spending on transportation can be explained in terms of different household circumstances, preferences and living standards, for example: the location of home in relation to shops, schools, work or leisure facilities; ownership of private transport; availability of an adequate public transport system; general health or attitude of the household towards other modes of travel, such as cycling, walking or private hire of transport, all affect the family's transportation choices. The distribution of public transport costs in families varies according to age and the length and frequency of journeys. The distribution of private transport costs in families is unclear, since family members share consumption on an unequal basis.

Previous evidence of child costs: The transport cost of children in other budgetary studies indicates a range which highlights patterns of travel behaviour in different countries and the impact of particular methods on an estimate of costs. The Toronto Social Planning Council (1981) provides a normative estimate of public transport costs for children in two age bands: 2 to 12 years and 13 to 17 years. The standard includes spending on travel to school and one holiday trip of limited mileage. The inclusion of a private car within the family budget estimate depends on judgements about 'necessity', for example, if public transport is unavailable or inadequate for family needs. In the UK, Piachaud's study (1979) excluded all transport costs on the grounds that children under the age of 12 would either walk to school or receive free transport and his 'modern minimum' did not include private motoring costs. In a later opinion survey of teenagers Piachaud (1981) did, however, find that older children had school transport costs and additional higher transport costs relating to their personal and leisure activities. Lovering's (1984) Australian study excludes transport costs for children of all ages because the category is 'too hard' to estimate. Lovering claims that travel costs for teenagers may be high but few private transport costs can be related to the presence of children, especially car running costs which exist regardless of whether there are children in the household. Lovering, however, acknowledges that there may be an argument for including costs when a larger car or a second car is needed in families with children.

Edwards' USDA study (1981) produces estimates of the transport costs of children in different regions at three standards of living for children in urban, rural, non-farm and farm settings. First, from the Consumer Expenditure Survey diaries of urban and rural non-farm families, the USDA study concludes that transport (public transport and the purchase and operation of private cars) is the third largest cost of a child's budget, after housing and food. The USDA study assigns to the child an equal (per capita) share of family transport expenditure. This method of estimating costs produces the greatest economies of scale for families of increasing size, the costs per child in a five child family may be one third less than in a two child family. Second, the USDA study considers the cost of transport for children in farm families. This calculation includes: public transport expenditure, current running expenses of private car ownership, and the annual consumption value of the vehicles (defined as the purchase price divided by estimates of average life of the vehicle). The cost proportions are allocated to each child according to age and sex categories: boys or girls under 14 years, boys 14 to 17 years, and girls 14 to 17 years. Under fourteen years of age, the private car costs are regarded as a share of parent expenditure. As older children can be licensed to drive in some states of America, the costs of 14 to 17 year old children refer to their own vehicles.

The FBU standard for families: The FBU transport budget includes public transport costs, bicycle costs, and private car ownership costs. Transport use reflects the location of the family residence in relation to employment, schooling and leisure facilities, and the assumptions made about modes of transport and travel behaviour for each family member. This results in budgets based largely on normative judgements informed by behavioural data from sources such as the *1985-6 National Transport Survey*.

The frequency of journeys is calculated by using three categories: work and education, personal business, and leisure. All employment and education is based locally in York. Personal business journeys include essential shopping and personal services such as visiting the doctor or hairdresser and accompanying the children to school. Leisure journeys include visits to friends or travel to places of entertainment and annual holiday mileage. The annual travel mileage for each household is estimated to be between 9,000 and 10,000 miles per year.

The FBU couple household owns a five year old car, with an engine size of between 1001 and 1500cc. A larger car is owned by the family with two parents and two children. The number of car miles assigned depends largely on assumptions made about the household travel lifestyles. For households with children, approximately 7,500 car miles are assigned per year. The vehicle running costs include petrol, oil, tyres, servicing, repairs and replacement parts. The vehicle has comprehensive insurance, a vehicle excise licence, Ministry of Transport Test Certificate and Automobile Association membership. The cost of car parking at a rate of 40 times per year is also included. Depreciation of the car is calculated over an estimated lifetime of 12 years.

The public transport standards include one long distance train fare, one local return bus fare each week, taxi fares and reduced children's fares where applicable. A

'Minster card' for adult cheap rate bus travel and a family railcard for rail journeys are included in the household budgets.

Each household with working adults has at least one bicycle, children however, have a bicycle each. The 16 year old has an adult bicycle included in the transport budget. The bicycles for younger children are included in the leisure budget. The bicycle standard includes the cost of bicycle safety equipment, depreciation on the capital cost of the bicycle and a yearly estimation of maintenance costs.

The child's standard: It is clear from the family aggregate transport costs that children incur not only public transport costs, which are relatively simple to identify, but also some costs relating to private car ownership. The transport cost of a child is estimated by the 'differential', 'per capita' and 'normative' processes.

The frequency of journeys related to the two children in the model household is calculated as a third of business and personal mileage, a third of leisure miles and a per capita share of the annual holiday mileage. This results in 1692 car miles and 210 public transport miles per year. In addition, the teenager is assigned an extra 500 miles per year to account for the extra journeys incurred by parents on their behalf, such as transporting children to and from events.

The cost of using public transport for children is dependent on the child's age. The child aged 16 years is classified as an adult fare, the child aged four travels free on train journeys but has a similar reduced fare to the child aged 10 years on local buses. The young child is assumed to travel accompanied by a parent. No school transport costs are included in the budget as the 10 year old walks to the local school, the child aged 16 cycles or walks, and the pre-school child is accompanied by the parent or a local child-minder. The standard includes a minimum of one journey on the local bus with a parent each week and one return long distance train journey (York to London) each year. The number of taxi journeys varies between different family types because it is assumed that fewer taxi journeys will be made where there are greater opportunities to travel by private car. A standard of two taxi fares per adult each year is given for adult leisure or personal business only. The remaining number of fares is shared equally between the number of siblings. In addition, two extra fares are included for the 16 year old for late night entertainment.

The bicycle owned by the 16 year old is new and valued at £149.99 (1991). The bicycle is given a 10 year lifespan. The budget includes maintenance costs, lights and batteries, and bicycle safety equipment such as a safety helmet, harness and a bicycle lock.

It is arguable whether the presence of children results in additional costs relating to car ownership. Drivers' costs are the same whether they journey alone or with passengers. The perspective taken in this study is that the presence of children leads to extra costs for car owning families in two different ways:
- If the number or presence of children is the reason for families buying a larger or additional car, then the 'differential' cost between a large and a small car (or a second car) is the direct cost of the child. The extra cost includes the differential cost of depreciation, insurance and servicing.

61

- The cost of extra mileage on child related journeys. The cost of each car mile in relation to children takes account of the capacity of the car in miles per gallon, cost of petrol, oil, tyres and servicing.

Table 2.12 gives a summary of the transport costs of a child in the two parent family.

Table 2.12
Transport costs for children by age,
October 1991 prices, £ per week.

Family expenditure	Child calculations	Aged 4	Aged 10	Aged 16
Car depreciation	Differential cost Escort-Fiesta	0.63	0.63	0.63
Car insurance	Differential cost Escort-Fiesta	0.51	0.51	0.15
Child car miles	Petrol + oil + tyre + servicing	1.11	1.11	1.76
Car safety seat	£15.00 life 2/yrs	0.14	0.00	0.00
Sub-total		**2.39**	**2.25**	**2.54**
Public transport - train	Family rail card + one fare + Apex fare	0.00	1.38	0.60
Public transport - bus	Accompanying parent-1 return wk + reduced rate child 4/10 & 16 adult fare	2.10	0.70	1.40
Taxi fares	Aged 4/10-2 year; Aged 16: 4 year	0.19	0.19	0.39
Bicycle - capital	Value 149.99 - lifespan 10 yrs	0.00	0.00	0.29
Bicycle maintenance cost	Tyres, tubes, oil, repair kit, brake blocks + lights and batteries	0.00	0.00	0.52
Bicycle safety equipment	Safety helmet life 10 yrs, safety harness life 5 yrs, bike lock life 10 yrs	0.00	0.00	0.11
Sub-total		**2.29**	**2.27**	**3.31**
TOTAL		**4.68**	**4.52**	**5.85**

The weekly transport costs for a child aged four years are £4.68, for a child aged 10 year olds the costs are £4.52 and for 16 year olds the costs are £5.85. The public transport costs relate to age groups and are therefore similar for children age four to 11 years, and significantly more for the child aged 16 years. An unexpected lower cost for the older child occurs, however, due to a car insurance differential which arises from the slight variation in drivers' ages. Economies of scale are evident in the transport budget for families of different sizes as described below in the adjustment for a one child household:

- The household with one child owns a smaller car similar to the two adult household, which results in a small saving in depreciation or insurance compared with the household with two children.
- A similar number of child related miles results in an increase in the cost per child mile due to lost opportunities for economies of scale.

The loss of economies of scale is £1.10 each week for a child aged four, 10 or 16 years.

Children's leisure activities are important for their personal development. Horna (1989) shows that the recreation and leisure activities of married couples changed when they became parents. Parents show a preference for activities that encourage intra-family communication and child socialisation. Even during later periods of parenting, Horna found that leisure is typically pursued within the family unit. Howard and Madrigal (1990) conclude that leisure is part of the parenting process, that mothers in particular play an instrumental role in shaping the leisure patterns of children and that children make decisions about their own leisure activities to a very modest degree.

Previous evidence of child costs: Little attention, however, has been given to the cost of children's leisure within family budgets. Where budget standards have included the cost of leisure, definitions of what constitutes leisure vary. The budget standard developed by Piachaud (1979) includes two separate parts for toys and presents, and entertainment. At a contemporary minimum standard of living children are expected to receive two modest gifts per year.

The amount spent on the gifts increases with the age of the child. In addition, Piachaud includes entertainment costs relating to four outings per year, and a low cost holiday-camp break for one week each year. Recreation, reading and entertainment, and other types of expenditure are included in the 'Other' category of the USDA (1981) study. A per capita share of the aggregate family expenditure was considered appropriate in this instance to assign expenses to individual family members. Lovering (1984) allocates a 'standard leisure cost' to the child's weekly expense in view of the wide range of possible entertainment options. At the 'medium' income level, Lovering's leisure standard is enough to pay for one cinema ticket, one swimming session and a game of pinball per week. Fifty per cent of the estimate would cover the cost of a football match. A two week annual holiday at the beach is included in the leisure standard cost. The Social Planning Council of Toronto (1981) developed a similar 'standard cost' for recreation. Recreation for children includes reading materials, holidays, records, entertainment, membership, toys and games, sports items, hobbies and craft lessons, postage, and pets. The standard is defined as:

> an amount permitting a balanced set of activities capable of
> addressing these (the family) needs. (SPCMT, 1984, p144)

The amount needed for children to participate in leisure activities is reported to vary by the age of the child but not by sex or family size.

The FBU standard for families: Leisure time is defined in the FBU budgets as free time after the hours spent in other activities, such as employment, domestic and personal care, child care and sleep have been excluded. The weekly time allocation for leisure is based on the Henley Centre for Leisure Forecasts 'Time Use Survey' as cited in *Social Trends* 22 (1992). The survey details time available for leisure in relation to sex, age and employment status. An adult male, for example, is estimated to have 46.6 hours free time each week, and a female 36.8 hours. This basic free time is adjusted in the FBU budgets by weighting for adults according to employment or the presence of children. The scale is then used to calculate the frequency of participation in leisure activities. Young children are given a similar weighting to their mothers. The teenage child is treated as a single adult.

Activities are selected for inclusion in the budget from behavioural data recorded in the *1986-1987 General Household Survey* using the following criteria:
- Popularity of the activity by frequency rate
- Reasonable cost of participation
- Non-specialist sport
- Inclusion of other regular activities, which do not hold a high proportional share of national participation but meet some other criteria, such as positive gender discrimination
- Exclusion of activities which are popular with a large proportion of the population but which contradict the 'healthy-life' aims of the standard, for example, smoking
- Exclusion of organised team games and those activities not available locally.

This results in approximately ten popular sports activities for individuals according to age and sex as shown in Table 2.13. The participation rate is defined over a 12 month period.

In addition, football is included as a popular spectator sport. Social or family activities include dancing, the cinema, and to a lesser degree, shows, pantomimes and exhibitions. Day trips, local trips, and holiday entertainment include visits to the Tower of London, the National Photography Museum in Bradford, York Minster and Blackpool Tower. The most popular UK holiday varies according to household type, the family with children have a seven day holiday in Blackpool at half-board rates. School activities are included, for example, an excursion to Germany, a cub-scout camp, and day trips.

64

Table 2.13
Table 2.13
FBU sporting activities, 1986-87 GHS % participation rate.

Male 16-19	%	Male 30-44	%	Female 16-19	%	Female 30-44	%
Snooker	76	Walk	71	Walk	66	Walk	67
Walk	72	Swim	50	Swim	59	Swim	48
Football	60	Snooker	46	Keep-fit	42	Keep-fit	26
Swim	58	Darts	29	Snooker	35	Cycle	18
Darts	48	Cycle	21	Badminton	28	Darts	10
Cycle	46	Running	20	Cycle	25	Badminton	10
Weight-training	38	Football	18	Running	25	Snooker	9
Running	35	Squash	14	Tennis	23	Running	7
Badminton/table tennis	26	Weight-training	12	Darts	18	Tennis	7
Tennis	25	Badminton	11	Table tennis/ice-skating	18	Tenpin bowls	6

Source: McCabe and Waddington (1992); GHS (OPCS 1989:18).

The *GHS (1987)* records the age-related average frequency for individual participation in leisure activities each year. In the case of certain individuals such as the 16 year old, this average frequency is taken to be appropriate. In other cases the frequency rate is adjusted by the FBU free-time weighted scale. The result is multiplied by the cost of the activity to provide a weekly estimate of leisure service costs for each household.

The weekly cost of leisure goods in relation to leisure activities for each household type is included in the leisure standard. The items include sports goods, audio and video equipment, books and newspapers, household and children's toys and games, photographic equipment, and horticultural goods.

The inclusion of items in the leisure goods standard is influenced by information on the market share of particular goods and the brands most commonly available. If 50% of households owns a particular leisure item then it is included in the standard.

The lifespan of goods is estimated through normative judgements, which in turn are influenced by the type of material used in manufacture, the frequency of household use, the type and size of the family, and data from other budget standards, such as those used in Sweden (1989) and Canada (1981).

The child's standard: The FBU standard for leisure activities is based on adult leisure behaviour and the following principles are adopted in order to formulate a children's leisure services standard:

- The teenage child is classed as an adult.
- The mother is assumed to accompany the younger child in all the child's leisure activities and, therefore, in certain sports, the participation rate of the child is similar to that of the mother. The criteria for including children in the parent's

leisure services is that the activities can be *either* fully shared activities with a parent, such as walking, swimming or football, *or* partly shared activities with a parent, for example, going to the cinema, which the mother and child may do together, or the mother can go alone as part of her free time. In this case an arbitrary frequency rate for a child's activity is given as 50% of a mother's rate.

- Some additional activities are included in the child's budget standard where parents are involved only at the margins, for example Cub-scouts activities and 'Tumbling Tot' sessions.

Most of the activities included in the standard for younger children have no gender bias. Activities for a four year old boy would be the same as a girl of the same age, and similar costs could be expected for the 10 year old girl, although some substitutions may arise, for example attending Brownies instead of Cub-scouts. The teenage sporting activities and frequency rates are based on the average participation of all children aged 16-19 years recorded in the GHS (see Table 2.13), and are therefore generous for children aged 16 who are at the bottom of this age range. In the FBU budgets the teenage girl's annual activity total is 41% more than that of her mother, and 15% more than that of her father. The level of activity is greater for teenage males who participate more frequently in sports than teenage females.

Leisure goods which are owned by a particular child, or where the ownership is shared between the siblings, are included in the child's standard. The 'differential' cost identifies items in households with children compared to those households without children. Gender differences are likely to be seen in the most popular goods purchased for boys and girls of the same age. The FBU, however, makes normative decisions to minimise this. The items where sex differences occur are toys, hobbies, books and magazines, cost differences, however, are small.

A summary of the leisure standard of a child is shown in Table 2.14. The overall weekly leisure standard increases with the age of the child from £5.82 for the child aged four years to £7.21 for the child aged 10 years, and finally to £9.56 for the child aged 16 years.

Few areas are found where economies of scale are evident. Entrance fees tend to vary according to age rather than the number of children. The capital cost of communally used goods such as televisions are not apportioned to the children's budget, and repairs of equipment included in the child's estimate would be less frequent when fewer children are present. Books, newspapers and magazines which have economies of scale for adults tend to be age-related for children. All toys, books and games are purchased new for particular children in the FBU modest-but-adequate budgets. A number of family games and some seasonal goods are shared, however, and would be purchased regardless of the number of children, for example, balloons, paper chains or fireworks. The extra costs for a child in a one child family are estimated at 12p per week.

Table 2.14
Table 2.14
Leisure services and goods costs for children by age,
October 1991 prices, £ per week.

	Child aged 4	Child aged 10	Child aged 16
Leisure services			
Sports expenses	0.00	0.85	1.10
Arts/entertainment/outings	0.26	0.40	1.51
School/club	1.21	0.93	0.69
Holiday expenses	0.95	1.09	2.67
Sub-total	2.42	3.27	5.97
Leisure goods			
Television, video & audio equipment and repairs	0.74	0.41	1.13
Sports goods	0.03	0.07	0.04
Books, newspapers, magazines	0.29	1.01	1.39
Toys, games and hobbies	2.06	2.04	0.27
Seasonal items	0.17	0.15	0.15
Photographic equipment and processing	0.11	0.26	0.61
Sub-total	3.40	3.94	3.59
Total	**5.82**	**7.21**	**9.56**

Personal care

Within the UK National Health Service, children below the age of 16 years old are entitled to free health care. This includes: consultations, medication and treatment, in-patient and out-patient hospital care, dental care (prevention of caries and treatment) and ophthalmic care (regular eye examination and supplying of spectacles).

Previous evidence of child costs: Piachaud's (1979) UK cost of children study excludes all medical costs. Other budgetary studies reveal that different countries interpret the principle of promoting good child health and well-being by ensuring that most standards cover the health care costs of children through a system of insurance. Lovering's (1984) Australian study also excludes all medical costs on the grounds that medium income families pay medical insurance or levies which bear no relation to the number or ages of children. Edwards' USDA (1981) study of consumption data shows that medical care represents about 5% of a child's budget costs. This estimate is based on the average medical and dental expenditure of families, and includes net expenditure for health insurance, hospital and eye care, prescription and medical supplies. Costs for medical expenditure are divided proportionately according to age and sex, whereas the family dental treatment costs are shared on a per capita basis among all family members who are over the age of two years. The Social Planning Council of Toronto (1981) adopts a standard health care cost which varies by age and sex but not by family size. Calculations are based on the Ontario Health Insurance Plan and a private drug coverage insurance plan, and include the cost of health examinations for school children as well as a comprehensive range of other health care costs, like prescription charges for drugs.

Other areas of personal care spending on children (excluding health care costs) are difficult to identify from previous studies. Piachaud (1979) includes soaps and toothpaste within the 'household provision' category of the budget for children. Lovering (1984) includes toiletries and cleaning materials in a 'household provision', estimated using an average figure derived from the case study of one family with three teenage children. Edwards (1981) in some cases includes the child's personal care cost as a per capita share of family aggregate personal care spending. In other cases, the expenditure is shared equally according to sex. The personal care expense of children is given greater prominence, however, in the Social Planning Council *Budget Guide* (1981). The inclusion of items in the budgets are based on judgements about current practices and expenditure surveys. The standard includes hair cutting, a hair brush, shampoo, soap, toothpaste, toothbrushes and tissues.

The FBU standard for families: The objective of the FBU personal care standard is to promote healthy living by preventing ill health and improving good health. The standard is in line with British Standard recommendations for health care and health promotion. The four main areas of expenditure are categorised as: health care; personal hygiene; personal accessories; and cosmetics. The health care standard includes charges for health care, such as prescriptions, but not private health care costs, eye tests for all adults, dental check-ups and a range of minor dental treatments. The first aid kit includes items for minor household emergencies and self-medication items for illnesses such as headaches, stomach upsets and colds. The personal hygiene budget is based on Health Education Authority recommendations. Hair, for example, is assumed to be washed weekly and teeth cleaned twice a day. The standard includes the cost of hair cutting and basic hygiene items for cleanliness and comfort. The budgets include a small amount of personal accessories such as travel goods, umbrellas, clocks and jewellery. Cosmetics are defined in the FBU budgets as colour cosmetics and other skin care items. Items are included for adults and the teenage girl on the basis of their socio-cultural behaviour.

Normative judgements are supported by consultation with professionals (medical experts, home economists, and beauty consultants), information gathered from market research reports, and studies of health care behaviour. Reference was made to the Toronto (1984), and Swedish (1989) budget standards, especially in support of the estimations of product lifetimes.

The child's standard: The individual itemised and differential approach is used to estimate the personal care expenditure for a child. In addition to those child costs included in the FBU personal care standard, a budget for a 16 year old boy is included in the analysis. The differential method is used to assign extra quantities of items to the child's budget. These extras are identified by the shorter lifetimes on commodities in households with two adults and two children when compared to households without children, for example, soap and toothpaste. Additional items are included which are appropriate in terms of sex, age, and price, for example, cosmetics, haircutting, and sunglasses.

Table 2.15 summarises personal care costs by age, and over the age of ten by sex. Personal hygiene items result in the highest expenditure in the personal care standard for all ages and this increases two-fold and three-fold between the ages of 10 and 16 years. Under the age of 11 years, the personal care budget does not vary according to age or sex. At 16 years however, a teenage girl costs £1.08, or 30%, more each week than a teenage boy.

Table 2.15
Personal care costs of children by age and sex,
October 1991 prices, £ per week.

	4	10	16 female	16 male
Health care	0.11	0.11	0.14	0.14
Personal hyg-iene	0.79	0.79	1.87	2.39
Accessories	0.07	0.07	0.38	0.52
Cosmetics	0.00	0.00	0.16	0.57
Total	**0.97**	**0.97**	**2.55**	**3.62**

Spending money

Previous evidence of child costs: Parents traditionally give pocket money to their children for a number of reasons. Furnham and Lewis (1986) reviewed the literature on child and adolescent understanding of the economic world and conclude that pocket money was an important issue since adult habits of using money for spending, gambling and saving are established early in childhood. Similarly, Hill (1992) found that pocket money was not simply a means of transferring resources within households but was linked to moral and educational aspects of socialisation. It was clear in Hill's study that although the children felt little direct parental control over the spending of pocket money, it was evident that they were not completely free to spend as they wished.

Hill's study (1990) of 41 Glasgow school-children aged 10 to 11 years explores the total income of children. Income is detailed from three sources: pocket money, hand-outs and earnings which may come from parents, relatives (especially grandparents) and adult friends (often neighbours). Pocket money is defined by the children as a regular and general allowance, given either unconditionally, or linked to the moral and educational socialisation of the child. It may, for example, be increased for good behaviour. Hand-outs are given to children as either a specific amount by the parent or another adult, or at the request of the child for a specific purpose or as a gift. Earnings are often received by young children, these are described as either special payments for work done, or as regular payments for work, for example, washing the car or helping older children deliver newspapers.

The Birds Eye Wall's (1991) annual survey of approximately 1,400 children aged from five to 16 years provided evidence of children's average total income related to age. Few children under the age of five years were said to receive pocket money but for older children pocket money was a substantial part of their average income as shown below.

Table 2.16
Comparison of the total income and pocket money of children by age,
£ per week.

Age (yrs)	Total income from pocket money, gifts and earnings	Average pocket money	Pocket money as a % of all income
5-7	£1.48	£0.64	43%
8-10	£2.35	£1.43	61%
11-13	£4.01	£2.16	54%
14-16	£9.20	£2.89	31%

Source: Birds Eye Wall's (1992).

A sample of 880 parents was asked how they thought their children disposed of their income. Although regional differences are evident and the replies are not age-related to the children, the main areas of spending are ranked as follows:
- Crisps/sweets/ice-cream
- Whatever they want
- Savings
- Comics/magazines
- Records/tapes
- Toys, books/stationery
- Clothes.

Spending on crisps, sweets, ice-cream, and toys, together with savings decreases with age. Children of five to seven years spend the most money on toys. Children 14 to 16 years purchase more comics, magazines, and records than other age groups. Gender differences in receiving pocket money were also identified by the Wall's survey (1992), boys received slightly more than girls on average. Much of the literature concerned with the income of children points to the unclear boundaries between pocket money, handouts and earnings (Hill 1990, 1992; Birds Eye Wall's 1991, 1992). There is little indication of the ways that age, sex and modest-but-adequate lifestyles affect expenditure from children's own income.

A number of budget standard studies of child costs have included an amount designated as pocket money based on behavioural surveys. Piachaud (1979) estimated a minimum level of pocket money for children aged five, eight and 11 years, using half the average estimated by the Wall's survey of 1977. Lovering (1984) based an estimate of the pocket money given to a child aged 2 to 11 years in the medium income family category on a range of the most common amounts of money reported by the *1983 Australian Institute of Family Studies' survey.*

The FBU standard for families: The FBU budgets view pocket money as an intra-household transfer. That is, pocket money, including children's earnings and handouts from within and outside the family, is spent as part of the total household income on items included in the existing component parts of the budget. Sweets and crisps, for example, are included in the food budget, and small games, pencils or comics in the leisure standard. Savings from children's income are treated in the same way as savings and repayments of borrowing in general in the family budget standard. It is assumed that savings are spent as items need replacing and debts are repaid on current items purchased, and this is represented in the small amounts which are calculated as the weekly equivalent of the cost of the item over its lifetime.

Income to sustain spending in the children's leisure, clothing, transport or food budget standards may be partly from the child's own earnings, gifts and pocket money. Indeed as children grow older some parents may transfer substantial amounts to the child in order that the child may begin to exercise preference and learn budgeting skills.

The child's standard: Pocket money is shown as a separate amount in the child's budget standard. A differentiation is thus made between small amounts of money that parents allow children to spend as part of household spending and money which is a sum spent without parental legitimisation. Spending money given without condition is important for a number of reasons: it allows children to learn value judgements unrestrained by accountability to the household purse; it is traditional in the UK to give a free-standing allowance to children no matter how small and whether it is earned or a gift is not relevant here. The amount allocated to the child's budget standard is based on the Walls survey (1992) and recorded in Table 2.16 as pocket money by age.

Summaries and Discussion

Comparison of methods

At the beginning of this chapter it was suggested that there were two deductive methods which could be used to derive the cost of a child from model family budgets. The itemised deductive method described below has been explored in depth in this chapter and in Table 2.17 compared with the crude deductive method. The methods are described as follows:

- Method One (crude and quick estimate) deducts the sum of the budget of a couple household from that of a couple with two children household. The result is the cost of an average child.

71

- Method Two (itemised basket of goods) extracts in detail each item which was used exclusively, or owned, by a particular child into that child's budget. Items used by all household members were assigned to children using a number of approaches - per capita, differential and normative.

Table 2.17
A comparison of two deductive methods of estimating the cost of a child from household budgets. Average cost of a child in a two child family under the age of 11 years old in two housing tenures,
October 1991 prices, £ per week.

Deductive method	Crude	Itemised	Crude	Itemised
Housing Tenure	Owned	Owned	Rented	Rented
Housing cost	8.37	9.06	5.32	5.46
Fuel	1.28	0.73	2.42	3.81
Food	12.12	9.41	12.12	9.41
Clothing	7.36	7.36	7.36	7.36
Household gds and services	5.09	6.32	4.96	7.42
Motoring	2.32	1.32	2.32	1.33
Fares	2.28	2.44	2.28	2.44
Leisure gds/activities	6.52	2.03	6.52	2.03
Personal care	0.97	0.97	0.97	0.97
Pocket money	0.87	0.00	0.87	0.00
Child care	11.43	11.43	11.43	11.43
Total	**58.61**	**51.07**	**56.57**	**51.65**

Overall the itemised method results in a higher estimate of child costs than the crude deductive method. The crude method of estimating child costs accounts for 87% of the true cost of an average child under 11 years living in owner occupied tenure. In local authority rented tenure, 91% of child costs are identified using the crude method. Commodities which are not shared by other household members such as clothing, personal care and child care costs are similar using both methods. The variations in estimates for the other components of the child's standard arise for a number of different reasons. In some cases the items included in the budget of the two adults living alone compared to the two adults who are parents are incompatible for a deductive calculation. The couple, for example, is allocated a package holiday in Spain which is considerably more expensive than a week of bed and breakfast in Blackpool for a family of four. Other differences are the result of normative decisions about what constitutes child costs in larger dwellings. Many items such as the capital costs of communal furniture and fittings are excluded from the child's budget. In other words there are some cost differences between the different household types, with and without children, which arise because of the change in lifestyle while the standard of living remains constant.

The weekly costs of boys and girls is shown in Table 2.18 at October 1991 prices. The overall weekly costs of a child in owner occupied housing at the age of four years is £60.63, at the age of 10 years £54.85, and at the age of 16 years £63.59. The reason for the drop in costs from four years to 10 years is the reduction in child care costs, which are higher for the pre-school child. If housing costs are excluded from the child's budget standard, children aged four, 10, and 16 years will have costs of £52.26, £46.48, and £55.22, respectively. The overall costs for children in local authority housing are lower. At four years a child costs £58.48, at aged 10 years £52.92 and at the age of 16 years £61.72. Excluding housing costs the children's costs are reduced to £53.16, £47.60 and £56.40 for ages four, 10, and 16 years respectively. The largest weekly expenditure in the pre-school aged child's budget regardless of tenure is for part-time child care, which accounts for more than 30% of the total, this decreases with age as the hourly need for care declines. For all children food, clothing and housing present major costs.

The cost of a child increases with age. If child care costs are excluded, a boy aged 16 years in owner occupied housing costs £12.65 more than a boy aged 10, and a boy aged 10 costs £9.10 more than a boy aged four years. Food, clothing, leisure and pocket money costs increase with the age of the child, while personal care and fuel costs are similar for younger children under 11 years, but are higher for the teenage child.

Boys are more expensive than girls. At four years old the difference is small but for older children aged 10 and 16, the cost is £3.52 a week more for a 10 year old boy than for a girl, and £1.65 more each week for a boy of 16 years old than for a girl of the same age. The original family budgets include toys, leisure goods, and some clothes that are gender neutral; however, other clothing and personal care items are found to differ in cost and quantity, according to the sex of the child. Boys aged 10 and 16 years, for example, have higher food costs than girls of the same age, £2.41, and £2,03 respectively each week, as a consequence of greater nutrient need.

Children living in owner occupied housing have higher housing costs than similar children in local authority housing. At aged four the difference is £2.15, at 10 years of age £1.93, and at 16 years £1.87 a week. Housing, fuel, and household goods are affected by different housing tenure and the age of the child. The difference in cost is probably due to the age and construction of the properties rather than the form of tenure itself. The instability of the housing market during the period the budgets are priced may account for some of the difference between renters and buyers.

Table 2.18
Commodity breakdown of the cost of a child by age and sex,
October 1991 prices, £ per week.

Owner Occupied tenure

Commodity	Boy 4	Girl 4	Boy 10	Girl 10	Boy 16	Girl 16
Housing	8.37	8.37	8.37	8.37	8.37	8.37
Fuel	1.28	1.28	1.28	1.28	1.37	1.37
Food	10.02	9.61	14.63	12.22	18.44	16.41
Clothing	6.18	6.51	8.21	7.10	9.17	8.48
Household g/s	5.04	5.04	5.14	5.14	6.21	6.21
Child care p/t	18.01	18.01	4.85	4.85	0.00	0.00
Motoring	2.39	2.39	2.25	2.25	2.54	2.54
Fares	2.29	2.29	2.27	2.27	3.31	3.31
Leisure services	2.42	2.42	3.27	3.27	5.97	5.97
Leisure goods	3.40	3.40	3.94	3.94	3.59	3.59
Pocket money	0.30	0.30	1.43	1.43	2.89	2.89
Personal care	0.97	0.97	0.97	0.97	2.55	3.62
Total	**60.67**	**60.59**	**56.61**	**53.09**	**64.41**	**62.76**
Less child care costs	42.66	42.58	51.76	48.64	64.41	62.76
Less housing costs	52.30	52.22	48.24	44.72	56.04	54.39
Less child care and housing	34.29	34.21	43.39	39.87	56.04	54.39
Rented tenure						
Total	**58.52**	**58.44**	**54.68**	**51.16**	**62.54**	**60.89**
Less housing	53.20	53.12	49.36	45.84	57.22	55.57

The cost of a child related to family size

The cost of a child varies not only according to the age and sex of the child, but also in relation to family size. The original family data from which the child costs are derived was collected for the purpose of estimating costs in two child families. But it is possible to infer the cost of a child in a one child family from this data. The term 'economies of scale' is used here to describe the difference in costs for additional children in the household. Parts of the child's budget standard such as housing, private transport, household services, leisure services and food have major elements of shared cost and so there is potential for economies of scale.

Table 2.19 shows that economies of scale are greatest in relation to housing costs for children of all ages, and substantial in baby-sitting costs for young children. Overall, economies of scale result in additional costs of £9.67 or £6.61 each week for a child in a one child family aged either four or 10 years, and £8.43 or £5.37 for the only child aged 16 in owner occupied and local authority housing respectively.

Table 2.19
Extra costs for a child in a one child family, by age and tenure,
October 1991 prices, £ per week.

Tenure	Age 4 Owner	Age 4 Rental	Age 10 Owner	Age 10 Rental	Age 16 Owner	Age 16 Rental
Housing	7.21	4.15	7.21	4.15	7.21	4.15
Baby-sitting	1.24	1.24	1.24	1.24	0.00	0.00
Leisure	0.12	0.12	0.12	0.12	0.12	0.12
Motoring	1.10	1.10	1.10	1.10	1.10	1.10
Total extra	**9.67**	**6.61**	**9.67**	**6.61**	**8.43**	**5.37**

Equivalence scales

Table 2.20 gives some examples of child ratios which can be derived from the FBU family budget standard. Ratios can be calculated for child costs in different family types, housing profiles, and combinations of sexes or ages of children. In practice, any of the component parts of the child's budget can be excluded from the summation, the child's housing cost or child care costs are used as examples. Omitting selected parts of the child's budget when setting equivalence ratios results in an increase in the share of costs assigned to parents, and a decrease in the child's proportion of the reference family budget.

Table 2.20

Child equivalence scale ratios in two parent households, living in owner occupied housing, based on estimates of boys' costs.

	Total standard	Exclude housing	Exclude child care	Exclude child care & housing
				Base couple household = 1.00
Only child aged 4	0.30	0.23	0.22	0.16
Only child aged 10	0.28	0.22	0.26	0.20
Only child aged 16	0.31	0.24	0.30	0.24
Sibling aged 4	0.26	0.22	0.18	0.15
Sibling aged 10	0.24	0.21	0.22	0.19
Sibling aged 16	0.27	0.24	0.27	0.24
2-child unit aged 4 & 10	0.50	0.43	0.40	0.33
2-child unit aged 10 & 16	0.52	0.44	0.49	0.42

Table 2.21 compares equivalence ratios for a child in a one child household and assumes that the child care costs are not treated as a child cost. Ratios vary with the age of the child, but in general the FBU ratio is higher than the other scales for younger children and lower than other scales for older children. They are very similar to the McClements scale, however, which is still the one most commonly used in analyses undertaken by the UK government such as the Households Below Average Income series.

Table 2.21
Comparison of equivalence scales, by age of the child.

		Base couple household = 1.00	
Source	*Method*	*Age*	*Ratio*
McClements 1971-2	Expenditure survey	0-4	0.18
		5-10	0.21
		11-12	0.26
		13-15	0.32
Townsend 1968-69	Deprivation index	0-10	0.17
		11-15	0.25
		16-18	0.38
Piachaud 1979	Budget standard	2	0.23
		5	0.27
		8	0.32
		11	0.35
Beveridge 1942	Budgetary	0-4	0.16
		5-9	0.22
		10-13	0.26
		14-15	0.28
Supplementary Benefit 1983	Implied scale	0-10	0.21
		11-15	0.31
		16-17	0.38
Income Support excluding Family Premium 1988	Implied scale	0-10	0.21
		11-15	0.31
		16-17	0.38
Income Support including Family Premium 1988	Implied scale	0-10	0.33
		11-15	0.43
		16-17	0.50
OECD 1982	Arbitrary		0.29
FBU - only child (excludes child care)	Budget standard	4	0.22
		10	0.26
		16	0.30

Source: Whiteford (1985: 108-111); 1988-9 IS rates, Lakhani et al (1988).

A further comparison of equivalence scales by family size is made in Table 2.22. This shows that many scales take no account of economies of scale. The McClements scale tends towards diseconomies of scale, as the extra child increases the overall cost per child. Rowntree's implied scale indicates a saving in expenditure per child of five percentage points for each child. Furthermore, the introduction of premiums in the benefit system has given an economies of scale perspective to the income support child scale rates. A disadvantage in this comparison, however, is that the ages of the children concerned are not explicitly stated on many of the scales cited. The equivalence scale derived from the FBU budget is identical to the income support scale and very close to the Whiteford geometric mean (1985).

Table 2.22
Comparison of equivalence scales by family size (excluding child care costs). Children are assumed to be under 11 years old.

				Base couple household = 1.00
Source	Date	1-child family (A)	2-child family extra child (B)	% extra (B÷A)
Rowntree	1936	1.20	0.10	8.3
Beveridge	1942	1.24	0.24	19.4
Townsend	1968-69	1.17	0.16	13.7
McClements	1971-72	1.23	0.25	20.3
Supp. Benefit basic	1987-88	1.21	0.21	17.4
Supp. Benefit long term	1987-88	1.17	0.17	14.5
Income Support + Family Premium	1988	1.31	0.21	16.0
OECD	1982	1.29	0.30	23.2
Whiteford-Geometric mean		1.20	0.18	15.0
FBU >11 years	1991	1.24	0.20	16.0

Source: Whiteford (1985:106-111); 1988-89 IS rates, Lakhani et al (1988).

The adequacy of benefits

Income support - child scale rate

Income support (IS) is a 'means tested' benefit for people who have insufficient income for their basic needs. If there are dependent children in families claiming IS, a child rate is paid for each child according to age as part of the claimant's personal allowances and a family premium in recognition of extra family costs.

Table 2.23 compares the FBU April 1992 estimate of weekly child costs before housing and child care with the IS child support rates, inclusive of a family premium. The family premium (April 1992) is £9.30 per family each week and the IS child rate is set at £14.55 for each child in the family under the age of 11 years, £21.40 for a child aged 11 to 15 years, and £25.55 for the dependent child aged 16 to 17 years. The comparison shows that the shortfall between the income support child rates and the FBU child rates increases with the age of the child. The percentage shortfall reveals, however, that the 10 year old child rate is particularly low compared to the real cost of children. In two child families the DSS child rates meet between 43% to 55% of the

78

cost of child rearing. In one child families the family premium which is payable per family and not per child results in the meeting of between 51% and 64% of costs.

Table 2.23
Comparison of the state child support rate and the FBU cost of a child in a two parent family at the modest-but-adequate level, excluding housing and child care costs, October 1991 prices uprated to April 1992, £ per week.

Age	DSS scale rate + Family Premium	FBU rate	Shortfall	Income Support as a % of FBU
2-child family				
4	19.20	34.89	15.69	55%
10	19.20	44.34	25.14	43%
16	30.20	57.34	27.14	53%
1-child family				
4	23.85	37.45	13.60	64%
10	23.85	46.90	23.05	51%
16	34.85	58.60	23.75	60%

Foster care allowances

The weekly cost of a child is of particular interest to people who provide money to meet the cost of child rearing, for example, local authorities who maintain children in foster homes. The appropriateness of the FBU derived cost of a child as an instrument for measuring the cost of children in the foster family is dependent on:
- corresponding living standards and
- the similarity of the lifestyle assumptions

from which the FBU budget is derived compared to the lifestyle of the typical foster family.

The obligation of local authorities when paying the foster care boarding out allowance is stated by the 1988 Boarding Out Regulation as:

> sufficient to care for the child placed with the foster parent as if he were a member of the foster parent's family. (Boarding Out Regulation 2184:15)

It is important that the modest-but-adequate standard of living is indeed synonymous with the standard of living of foster families in general. The assumptions made about the lifestyle and circumstances of foster families and the assumptions on which the FBU budget standard for the two parent family have been founded are compared in Table 2.24. Bebbington and Miles found that 30% of the sample of 2,694 foster parents in 13 local authorities in England in 1987 fitted the typical foster family description. The assumptions made in the FBU profiles of two parent families with children and those characteristics found in foster families identified by Bebbington and Miles appear to describe similar, though not identical, lifestyles and living conditions. Despite this the FBU-derived cost of a child at a modest-but-adequate standard of living represents an appropriate measure of the cost of a natural child in a foster family environment.

Table 2.24
Comparison of lifestyles of the FBU two parent family and the typical foster family.

Modest-but-adequate	Foster family
3 bed dwelling	3 or more bedrooms
1 parent full-time work 1 parent part-time work **Income** Within the 3rd quintile of the distribution of income in the FES	1 parent full-time work 1 part-time or not at all **Occupation** Skilled man./own account 29% Intermediate non-manual 18% semi-skill/personal service 16% employer/manager 10%
Two parent family	7 out of 8 are two parent families
Male aged 34, female aged 32	Female aged 31 -55 years
Motor vehicle ownership (5 yr old)	
Dependent own children age 4 age 10 age 16	Dependent own children 5+ Average age, youngest child 10 one child 21% } two child 25% } 46% none 37%
FBU Family Two parent, one in full-time and one in part-time work, two children 4 years +, 3 bedroom house	**Typical foster family** Two parents, one in full-time employment, dependent children 5+, 3 (or more) bedroom house

Source of foster family data: Bebbington and Miles (1989).

Two further problems remain, however:
- Should the child in the foster family be paid expenses by the Local Authority as an only child, or as a child in a larger family?
- What is a standard measure of foster care allowance, given that the 108 local authorities in England determine their own boarding out allowances?

The model used to estimate the cost of a natural child living in a family results in different costs according to the age of the child and the family size. That is, the greater the number of children, the lower the cost of the child estimate in certain major components of the budget standard. The question is whether a foster child should be maintained by the local authority as an individual separate from joint consumption or as sharing the consumption of the placement family.

The boarding out allowance is paid to all foster parents regardless of other enhancements and special payments are made in some cases. The North Yorkshire foster care rates are selected as an example of average rates paid by local authorities in England. The City of York is also the geographical centre for pricing the FBU budget, thus giving the family budgets a cultural base and setting. The basic boarding out annual allowance includes an extra week's allowance for one week's holiday, the foster child's birthday, and additional expenses for Christmas. The allowance is calculated based on 55 allowances per year, and the sum is intended to cover all the normal expenses, including certain clothing renewal costs, in respect of caring for the child. In addition to the 55 allowances, the foster parent can claim an initial clothing grant for new foster children of up to 5 boarding out allowance payments over the period of the first year and an extra two weeks holiday money if the family is away from home on holiday for three weeks each year.

Table 2.25 compares the FBU April 1992 child costs (excluding child care costs for working mothers) with the North Yorkshire boarding out allowances on April 1, 1992. The results indicate that the North Yorkshire age-related boarding out allowance is adequate to meet the day to day costs of caring for children aged four and 10 years, and is more than adequate to meet the costs of a 16 year old child. This is assuming, however, that the foster child shares the joint consumption costs of the placement household, such as housing, household durables, baby-sitting, family games, and motoring costs. To treat the foster child as an only child, the boarding out allowance would need to be increased by between 21% and 25% for the younger children.

Table 2.25
Comparison of the North Yorkshire boarding out allowances and the FBU cost of a child estimate. FBU October 1991 prices uprated by the commodity price index to April 1992, £ per week.

Age	Modest-but-adequate cost*	Basic boarding out foster care allowance	Shortfall/gain	Shortfall/gain as a % of foster care allowance
2-child family				
4	43.16	42.28	-0.88	2%
10	52.61	51.68	-0.93	2%
16	65.61	84.63	19.02	22%
1-child family				
4	52.84	42.28	-10.56	25%
10	62.29	51.68	-10.61	21%
16	73.99	84.63	10.64	13%

* excluding child care costs for employed mothers

Conclusion

The cost of a child varies with tenure and whether or not housing costs and child care costs are included. The cost of a child increases with age. Boys cost more than girls. The cost of an only child, depending on age, is between £5.37 and £9.67 more than a child in a two child family, at October 1991 prices. At a modest-but-adequate living standard, the ten year old boy in a two child family living in a local authority dwelling costs £54.68 per week. It costs £14.63 to feed this child, £8.21 for clothes, £2.42 to keep the child warm, £7.21 for entertainment, toys, leisure and holidays, and £4.52 in travel expenditure each week. On top of this is the cost of the child's share of housing, personal care expenditure and pocket money. Income support including the family premium meets only 43% of the cost of this child (excluding housing costs).

Child benefit, which subsumed child tax allowances and the family allowance, meets only 17% of the cost of a child. Child benefit is the means by which the state shares the cost of child rearing with all parents, regardless of income or social position. Average parents living at modest-but-adequate levels are having to find over £45.00 each week in addition to child benefit to meet the cost of their child.

The results show that Foster Care Allowance is adequate within 2% of meeting the cost of caring for children aged 4 and 10 years of age, and 22% greater than needed to meet the cost of a 16 year old. This estimation is inclusive of economies of scale for families with more than one child, and exclusive of the cost of child care for working parents. To consider the child as an 'only' child in a modest-but-adequate household the Foster Care Allowance would need to be increased by 21 to 25% for children aged 10 and four respectively, although it is still more than adequate to meet the costs of a 16 year old child.

The strengths of the budget standard method are that the budgets are open to scrutiny and, as a consequence, are adaptable to other circumstances such as different standards of living, different types of households and people who have different expenses such as children and adults with learning difficulties or children in crisis such as foster children.

Budget standard estimates can also complement other methods of research, they are a means of deriving equivalence scales without resorting to expenditure data, and they offer a means of identifying social indicators of living standards.

The method has some practical and theoretical limitations, however, first, the budgets assume families are able to live as budget experts think they should, ignoring tastes, customs, idiosyncrasies and habits. Second, prices based on York or national outlets will clearly not be representative of those found in London, or Northern Ireland, for example. Third, updating budgets can also be a problem, they date fairly quickly, clothing goes out of fashion, leisure activities change. The uprating by movements in prices is limited because the RPI is a national index, and the budgets include regional bias. Furthermore, the commodity mix in the RPI is not identical to that adopted in the creation of the family budgets and less appropriate to estimate increases in child costs.

Finally, it has to be acknowledged that no list of goods and services can encompass the whole range of elements which make up a standard of living for a child. No account is taken of the quality and safety of the neighbourhood that children live in, the quality of the play or school environment, or the quality of public services that children consume. In short, it does not represent the culture and political environment in which children live.

3 The extra costs of a foster child

Introduction

The previous chapter explored the costs of child rearing for a 'normal' child in a household of two adults and two children. This chapter explores the differences in cost between a foster child and a 'normal' child. It suggests that the foster child incurs costs which are common to all children at a modest-but-adequate standard of living and a range of costs which are specific to the child's fostering circumstances. The direct extra costs of a foster child are the subject of this chapter, indirect costs are explored in Chapter 4. The direct and indirect costs of a foster child are explored through a survey of 32 foster families.

The direct cost differences of 'normal' and 'foster' children are the sum of the costs of adjustment, special need, monitoring and administration of foster caring. The majority of children in care of the local authority have a combination of family factors which indicate that they tend to come from deprived backgrounds as discussed earlier. From this arises a strong argument that a child entering a foster placement for the first time will have significant costs related to health and physical deprivation, and that a child passing from one placement to another will have costs related to the change in environment. The monitoring processes of foster care may result in extra journeys, higher telephone bills, and additional activities. Special need or different needs to the natural child in the household may also result in a range of other extra costs such as higher food and heating bills, and extra wear and tear on personal and household effects.

The notion that leading a full life is more expensive for some children in special situations is not new. The costs of childhood disability have been studied by Baldwin (1985) and Graham (1987), and include both those costs arising from loss of income to the carer and extra financial expenses. Some examples of additional costs in this context are: more expensive shopping, compensatory spending on non-disabled family members, the need to pay for jobs which would normally have been completed by the household, journeys made by taxi instead of travelling by public transport and sometimes a switch to buying luxury items, for example, a larger car with the 'luxury' of spacious access, a tumble drier, an orthopaedic bed and other consumer durables. Foster children and the disabled children described by Baldwin (1985) have similarities. Some foster children fit Baldwin's broad range of disabilities. The catalogue of extra costs relating to disability can generally be applied to foster families with the addition of other costs associated with the monitoring and management of foster caring. In 1984, Baldwin found the extra expenditure for middle-income families was £12 each week which did not include the less regular costs arising from the need for housing adaptation and the purchase or replacement of household durables.

Two UK studies have monitored the actual expenditure of foster parents through diaries. The London and Regional Fostering and Adoption Group[1] in the 1990s recruited 12 volunteer families to complete a one week diary of household expenses. The foster families were dispersed across England from St. Helier, Jersey to Barnsley. The report, unfortunately was incomplete with no account given of the sample framework or summary findings. It did, however, show the wide range of living standards reported by foster parents. The spending over one week included food, fuel, travel, newspapers and an average weekly share of rent, capital goods and car costs. The total household weekly expenditure was divided by the number of people present over the week measured: adults, natural and foster children. The overall average spending per person was £115 but 7 families only spent an average of £60.75, while the two highest spending families spent £235.64 and £345.43 per person for one week. The main disadvantage of using a per capita approach to sharing household expenditure is that it assigns to children adult household expenditure which would occur regardless of the presence of children. The Camden Association for Foster Care in 1987[2] carried out a small survey of 7 foster carers who monitored the additional expenses of their own foster child. Many areas of cost were excluded, such as: toys, hospitality costs in respect of fostering related visitors, additional telephone expenses, the cost of extra journeys and others expenses. The cost of a foster child in the latter instance was found to increase with age, from £36 to £58 per week for children 0 to 18 years of age.

Outside the UK, a consensus approach was taken by Bartlet in 1980 to explore the adequacy of the Australian foster care allowances. A sample of foster parents was asked to estimate spending on the child's maintenance in selected components of the household budget. Account was also taken of any state benefits paid in respect of the foster child such as the family allowance or disability allowance. Spending on housing, household goods and services, general leisure goods such as toys, games and books with the exception of the cost of Christmas and birthday presents was excluded. The results

---

[1] Samples of the Fostering Family Expenditure Survey forwarded in correspondence from the NFCA 1991. (Unpublished)

[2] Correspondence with Camden, Greenwich and Wandsworth Foster Care Associations during Autumn 1990. (Unpublished)

indicated a 54% shortfall between allowance and expenditure over the previous year for 'non-handicapped' foster children.

Culley, Settle & Van Name (1975) in the USA sought to measure the cost of foster care to foster parents. The aim of the government funded study was to provide fostering agencies[3] in the United States with a workbook for understanding fostering costs and setting local foster care allowances. There were three elements to the research: a review of methods to measure the direct costs of a 'normal' child; a sample survey of foster parents which explored their perceptions about cost differences in rearing a natural child compared to a foster child of the same age; and a review of methods and literature on the indirect costs of child rearing. The majority of foster parents claimed that foster children had similar costs to natural children. There were, however, a substantial number of foster parents who believed they had higher costs especially in food, clothing, and housing, along with a small number reporting lower costs.

Research methods

While indicating that extra costs do exist, earlier studies have failed to give reliable and detailed enough information to assess the adequacy of the foster care allowance. This study:
- Identifies additional items in each component part of the placement household by comparing and disregarding all expenses which relate to the upkeep of a natural child in the same household.
- Constructs a budget standard estimate of the extra costs of a foster child aged 0-4 years, 5-10 years, and 11-16+ years.
- Expresses budget standard extra costs in terms of the average foster household.

The approach consists of three discrete elements:
- depth interviews with foster parents
- normative estimates of a standard cost
- statistical calculation of average cost.

Depth interviews with foster parents

This enabled foster parents to describe in what circumstances they experienced extra items of consumption and how regular these expenses occurred. The experience of Culley et al (1975) and the pilot study for this field work showed foster parents could recall items of consumption easily but not actual costs which were complicated by the age of each item. The foster parents were asked to talk about expenses which they would not expect if this foster child was their own child. Foster parents were prompted

---

[3] Recent correspondence reveals that some fostering agencies in the US are still using this survey to estimate the levels of fostering allowance today (1991).

to say whether an expense was more, less or the same as a normal child and how often the expense occurred. The framework of the discussion was the direct extra costs experienced by the foster family during the present or most recent foster placement and whether this placement was representative of others they had experienced. The interview took place at the foster parent's home and lasted approximately one hour.

Foster parents had a tendency to dismiss expenses as low compared to what they gained in 'family satisfaction'. A foster child may turn the family into an exceptionally caring unit, providing them with an opportunity to gain knowledge and skills. The balancing of costs and psychological benefits by foster parents may, therefore, inhibit the process of the exploration of expenses. Foster parents in general perceived their fostering activities as altruistic or believed that this is how others saw it. Consequently, some foster parents at times said they felt inhibited in talking about costs should their answers be misconstrued as complaining and confused about whose responsibility expenses were anyway, the local authority or their own. Many foster parents preferred to see their foster child in the light of 'normality' rather than different to other children, and as a consequence were unwilling to 'blame' the child for any unusual expense.

Normative estimates

A normative estimate of costs has been described in Chapter 2. Expert judgement was used to develop household budgets for model families at modest-but-adequate-standards of living in each component part of the household budget. Such judgement was supported by behavioural evidence where available, recommended standards, and feedback from consumers and academics in the field. The cost of a 'normal' child is derived from these family budgets. The extra cost budget standard is constructed by re-examining each basket of goods and services and increasing or decreasing the items identified by foster parents. The baskets are then priced using the original pricing mechanism. Four new budgets are included in the foster child basket of goods and services, a home security budget, a disposable nappy budget, a gift budget, and a larger car budget. The difference between the normal child budget and the foster child budget is the extra costs budget standard.

Statistical calculation of average cost

The conversion of the budget standard to actual amounts was based on the proportion of foster parents who say they have a certain item of expenditure. If, for example, 10% of foster carers reported they purchased a larger car, then 10% of the larger car extra cost budget standard was included in the foster child budget. An advantage of this method was that every item that any foster parent suggested as an extra cost was represented in the final budget.

Methodological issues

The basket of goods and services for a normal child is age specific (ages 4, 10, 16) whereas the extra costs are based on an analysis of average foster parent perceptions for children in age related bands. A normal child, aged 4 years, for example, does not have a budget estimate for infant equipment. The foster child aged 0-4 years includes a small proportion of infant costs reported by the foster mothers as extra to non-foster children of that age.

From this study inferences can be made about the extra expenses incurred by the foster family population in the particular local authority from which the sample was drawn. Compared with other regions in England, there may be some regional or local differences in the types of children fostered, aspirations of the local authority, or the price of goods and these differences will not be reflected in the budget.

Furthermore, two ideas about extra costs have been simplified in the analysis. First there is a complex relationship between the length of placement and the degree of similarity of costs to natural children. As time passes a new member of a household becomes absorbed into the family's idiosyncratic lifestyle and in doing so is considered in the long term by other household members as part of the household rather than an outsider. Culley (1975), for example, raises the issue of length of placement and quality of opportunities offered by foster parents to children. Culley found evidence that if the placement is perceived as temporary there were likely to be delays in discussion about the child's educational needs and in the willingness of foster parents to promote new social opportunities for the child. Second, the cost consequences between a 'normal' foster child and a 'disabled' foster child is disregarded. The issue about the degrees of difficulty in caring for foster children and the correlation with higher expense has been discussed in Chapter 1. In disregarding disability as a category, the problem of small cells and the need to define 'disability' is solved. The average cost in a randomly selected sample will reflect the degree of difficulty in caring for foster children in the population.

The sample of foster families

The sample population is the foster families of North Yorkshire which is the largest non-metropolitan county in England. The authority is divided into four divisional social service areas. Most areas have their own support group for foster parents affiliated to the NFCA. The first sample of seven foster parents used in the pilot study in 1990 were volunteers from the York and District Fostering Association. The main sample was drawn from the 250 active foster families on North Yorkshire's current approved list which includes a number of families who live outside North Yorkshire but foster the county's children. Approval from North Yorkshire County Council was given for the survey in November 1991, and the interviews carried out over a three month period in Spring 1992.

The initial response rate was 56%. A second attempt omitting names already approach achieved a response rate of 43%. Thirty-four foster families agreed to be interviewed and 32 interviews were subsequently carried out. The reasons for non-response are unknown as access to this group was not obtained. The location of respondent foster carers in North Yorkshire was not evenly spread. The highest response rate was in the rural area of Hambleton and Richmondshire (11). Another area with a high response rate was York and Selby (9). Scarborough and Ryedale (5), Harrogate and Craven (5) had lower response rates.

There were 32 families in the sample of which 28 were two parent families and 4 were lone parent families. The average age of the foster mother was 44 years at the time of interview. All but one family had natural children of their own (adopted or biological), the average natural family size was 2.5 although at the time of the study 28% of the families did not have dependent children. In almost all households the foster child was the youngest child in the family.

A large number of respondents (28) were owner occupiers (29% of these were outright owners), the remaining four families lived in rented accommodation. A measure of bedrooms per person (excluding foster children) revealed that 25% of families had 2 or more spare bedrooms and 47% had one spare bedroom. In 28% of households it was assumed that the foster child shared a bedroom with a dependent natural child or a foster parent. None of the families were wholly reliant on public transport as all owned at least one car. Twenty-seven foster mothers had access to a car on a full time basis, the others could arrange to use the family car on fostering business.

The head of the households were commonly skilled manual workers, self employed or managers. The heads of household were unemployed in four cases, two through loss of work and two through retirement. The individual duration of placement ranged from two to 27 years. The total experience in fostering across the sample was 243 years, an average of 8 years for each family. The sample had cared for a total of 542 children, an average of 17 children for each family. In real terms the number of children fostered per family varied from one child to over 50.

Data was collected about the extra costs of 55 foster children, two thirds of these children were boys. Fourteen children were 0 to 4 years of age, 11 children were aged 5 to 10 years, and 28 children were aged 11-16+. The age groups of the children were important in matching with children in the FBU data set. It was therefore decided not to combine the two younger age groups to give a more even distribution. The type of placement was also important in relation to costs. The majority of placements (25) were task centred by the foster parent's own definition, six families fostered on special schemes such as 'bridge to independence', and one family was the natural grandparents of the foster children. Most children at the time of the interview had been in the foster placement less than 24 months, 21 children had been in the placement for less than six months.

Perceptions of foster parents

Housing

The practical impact of providing foster placements was expressed by foster parents in relation to internal and external damage to the housing fabric and decorations, and in regard to other effects such as the need for extra security and additional bed space for foster children.

Internal damage and maintenance: Foster families reported the need for frequent re-decorating, especially the foster child's bedroom, and the repair of internal damage caused by foster children or foster visitors (siblings, parents, friends of the foster child) which they feel would not have occurred in non-fostering circumstances. Internal damage occurred more frequently in households caring for school age foster children than pre-school children, but more households reported frequent redecoration rates in placements caring for children aged 0 to four years and 11-16+ years. In younger households the most common reasons for redecoration were, a change in placement, health or hygiene reasons and a desire to improve the self esteem of the foster child. This was expressed in a number of ways by parents:

> The walls are chip paper and painted frequently, bedroom walls done between placements especially if marked by a previous child - other papers are washable for the same reason.

> We decorate and spring clean the nursery for every child.

> We decorate (the child's room) once every year now whereas we would only decorate once in two to three years if we weren't fostering.

In placement households caring for children aged five to 11 years there was a tendency to repair or patch up and clean rather than redecorate. In this type of placement, children were more destructive and redecoration was thought to be a pointless exercise until a certain point was reached during the placement or the placement drew to an end. The most common reasons for extra redecoration activity in households providing placements for children aged 11 to 16+ were, 'to freshen up between placements', 'lots of repairs so re-decorations is the best route', 'like it to look special', 'important each child individualises his/her own room'. The latter two reasons were often stated as part of the 'task' of raising the child's self esteem.

External damage to house and garden: The severity and frequency of external damage to the placement property and garden by the foster child and during access visits by natural parents, siblings and friends differed according to the age of the child. Under the age of 11 damage tended to be frequent but slight, for example, damage to fences, gates, garden walls and broken window-panes. External damage reported by parents who provided placements for children 11 to 16+ years, however, was much more serious although less frequent. In two cases vehicles were driven by the foster child damaging nearby property.

Security of the home: There were a small number of foster parents who were motivated to fit extra security locks and fire alarms. In most instances this was because of threats of violence by the child's natural parents. Parents also identified occasions of increased fire risk because of the child's sleeping pattern or covert smoking habits.

Provision of additional bed space for foster children: Foster parents described extensions to property completed to provide additional space for fostering children. The type of alteration varied but the most common reason given was to increase the capacity of the house in terms of the number of bedrooms. Four families divided a large bedroom into two single rooms, two families completed a loft conversion and two families built bedrooms as additions to their existing home. Another two families moved house to improve their fostering capacity and, in another case, the family extended the garage to store outside toys and foster children's bicycles. In most cases the foster parent's believed this would increase the net value of the property in the long term but at the present time it met a demand for extra foster child space or served as a means of providing additional foster placements. The highest proportion of home extensions were found in households providing for children of school age.

Fuel

Most foster parents believed that a foster child was the cause of additional usage of household fuel compared to the amount of usage expected by an additional natural child. Three areas of fuel consumption emerged as a common base for discussion.
- The extra use of hot water for bathing and laundering.
- The extra use of heating in the home - the home is heated for longer periods or to a higher temperature than usual.
- The extra usage of electric appliances, lights etc.

Bathing and laundering: Many foster children of school age were said to bathe more often than the natural children in the same family. Incontinence was more common in foster children than own children which resulted in daily bathing and extra washing of bed linen and clothing. Incontinence occurred in 29% of school aged foster children: 33% (2) of children aged five to 10 years, and 28% (5) of children aged 11 to 16+ years.

An additional factor was the foster parent's attitude to bathing and the role it plays in building relationships. Some children, for example, were perceived by their foster parents to be in need of extra physical care and attention and relationship development through activities such as teaching cleanliness, the provision of warmth and family 'caring'. Foster parents also pointed to the limits of the child's wardrobe and the need for frequent laundering to ensure a supply of clean dry clothes. These ideas were expressed in many different ways, the following by a carer of a pre-school child:

> The children are run down 'health wise', need pampering, I have
> nine loads of washing a week, I think one reason is (I am) more fussy

because (I feel) more responsible than if it was my own (child). (Foster) children are slower to potty-train and the crisis (coming into foster care) results in accidents... for that reason (we) have night lights on. (I) use the tumble drier because they don't have many clothes. The children bathe every day compared to our children every other day.

Carelessness or thoughtless use of hot water was also a problem.

He is very wasteful, spends hours in the bathroom, we really need to watch him the whole time, for example he will flood the bathroom when we have all gone to bed. He just fiddles like taking the top off the (toilet) system - even at school complaints come back about him playing with water, and he can't pass a light switch without turning it on even in church.

Heating: To a lesser degree carers reported an increase in the use of systems to heat their home. This was noticed especially in relation to children under the age of 5 years. There were two reasons given for extra periods of heating in the family home: visitors and access in the home, and careless use of appliances such as leaving a room without switching the heat source off. In one case the child had been expelled from school and home tutoring in the foster home resulted in a little used room being heated for approximately six hours a day, 5 days a week. The burning of additional fuel to achieve a higher temperature than usual was largely related to ill health among foster children, for example, two children in the sample had heart defects.

Appliances and lights: The extra use of lighting and appliances other than fires was considered marginal in most cases. In young children extra use was mainly due to the need for night-lights in excess of that expected for their own children and the additional use of the tumble drier because of the limited number of garments owned by the child. From five to 16+, however, the increase in use of appliances was explained in terms of carelessness and bad habits. Lights were left on, doors not closed, children regularly got up during the night and forgot to turn the television and other electrical appliances off, for example. Some foster parents believed this behaviour was a legacy of institutional care:

It is the careless use of appliances, our own children are encouraged to turn off lights from an early age the foster children don't. They have to learn to live by our standards. In institutional care they don't have to consider who is paying the bill!

Food

Foster parents suggested that additional food costs arose in four circumstances:
- Foster child's change in eating patterns in a new household

- Child's general overeating and abnormal eating behaviour
- The cost of providing hospitality for visitors in relation to fostering
- Eating out.

Foster child's change in eating patterns in a new household: Most children entering a new placement experience, at the very least, some disturbance in their eating patterns. A foster child may arrive by a single or combination of moves from a number of different locations:
i. natural home
ii. an institution (children's home, assessment centre, hospital)
iii. a planned or unplanned move from a previous foster placement.
The impact on the foster child and foster family is greatest in the initial period as the new household go through a period of adjustment in types of food provided, quantities and timetable of meals. This notion was expressed by foster parents in many ways:

> ....they had never had fruit and few vegetables, left to their choice they would have sweets and bread - it was a lot of work coaching him into the right type of eating.

> the foster child brings with him his own family's habits. Can't impose your standard on them in the short term because eating time just becomes a battleground.

> no set meal times, (and ate) only 'take aways', and tinned food - it took the children a while to adjust to proper meal times and proper meals.

It was rare that a foster parent dealt with the problem of change with no extra spending. Occasionally a foster parent put forward the suggestion they did not spend more 'on principle', the principle that all children in the household were treated the same, own or foster child.

Some changes in diet were inevitable and associated with age, for example a common reason for additional spending in respect of children under the age of two years was that the foster mothers purchased dried milk and packet baby foods whereas she breast fed and weaned her own infant with the family food. Foster children were weaned differently for a number of reasons:
i. foster household meals were no longer appropriate for very young children, forexample, the increasing popularity of oriental food, hot and spicy, pizzas and beefburgers; the family meal time was inconvenient for the very young child
ii. fostering left less time for food preparation (this aspect is discussed in Chapter 4)
iii. the responsibility for a stranger's child left the foster parents with a feeling that they needed to monitor more closely the quantity and type of feeding.

Other children under 5 years (excluding infants and babies) also incurred extra costs associated with extra milk and milk products. The reason for this was the foster parent's desire to 'build up' the child and make good earlier deprivation. Other reasons for additional expenses included:

i.   the desire to give the child a new experience,
ii. faddiness or greedy eating,
iii. the wastage of food.

Furthermore, the eating habits of a foster child could be normal to one household and expensive to another. Seven per cent of foster children were vegetarian and this often meant cooking different meals and buying additional foods as vegetarian foster children were not necessarily placed in vegetarian families.

Overeating and abnormal eating behaviour: Some foster children had serious eating abnormalities which could not be explained merely by a change in diet or living standards. The reasons given were varied but the majority caused foster parents' extra spending on food. A number of foster children (6) were described by their foster parents as 'obsessive eaters': in two cases (siblings) the children were placed with a family who described themselves as 'large eaters' so the difference was partially masked. None of the children described were medically diagnosed as having an eating disorder but the problems included:

i.   enormous appetites,
ii. hiding food, greediness,
iii. gorging food,
iv. vomiting,
v.   being manipulative with food,
vi. excessive consumption of fruit juices or pop,
vii. extreme anxiety concerning when the next meal would be.

For example:

> When he (the foster child) lived at home the kitchen door was locked, he is a compulsive eater - he goes into the garden and hides stuff. His appetite has not lessened over the years he has been with us. The child spent four days at home with his mother and she sent him back because there was nothing left to eat. Also he drinks incessantly.

> I don't like to make an issue of it...if I don't accompany her to a party et cetera she just eats until she is sick. Food is a great comforter to her.

> Enormous appetites we don't think they have been fed regularly. If there is food there they will eat it until none left. The amount they go through is phenomenal. I took a cake out of the freezer and someone ate all round the outside before it has even defrosted. The 3 year old

had two full dinners and two full puddings on Good Friday, he said he felt sick but took a handful of biscuits. This is very typical of other placements. The 14 year old would eat until he make himself sick then take any other food he found lying around, he had never had regular meals before.

He has a healthy appetite now, but for two to three years he manipulated us using food - we had to be careful what we presented him with for his meals, he could easily refuse it.

Most foster parents caring for obsessive eaters described this behaviour as a consequence of the child's background and tried to moderate it over time, however success was rarely said to be anything but 'slight' even with long term foster children.

The length of placement in relation to higher food costs is not significant, there was an overall tendency for the greatest number of higher food costs to be identified in longer term placements and older children. Table 3.1 shows the relationship between parents identifying higher cost to the length of placement and age band of the foster child. The greatest number of foster children identified as incurring extra costs in children under the age of 11 years were found in medium length placements. For foster children aged 11 to 16+ the greatest number of extra food costs reported were found in long term placements.

Table 3.1
Length of placement in relation to extra costs by age,
n=55.

Age	Length* of placement	No. of children with extra costs	% of children by placement length
0-4 (n=16)	Short	3 in 9	34
	Medium	3 in 7	43
	Long	none	none
5-10 (n=11)	Short	2 in 5	40
	Medium	3 in 3	100
	Long	2 in 3	67
11-16+ (n=28)	Short	2 in 7	29
	Medium	3 in 11	27
	Long	4 in 10	40

* Short - less than 6 months, Medium - 6 to 24 months, Long - over 24 months

Hospitality costs: Foster parents perceived that hosting visitors in connection with their foster parenting represented a cost. On average, foster parents received 1.2 visitors per foster child per week. The 0 to four year age group have the most visitors: an average of two per foster child each week. The five to 16+ age groups had on average one visitor for each foster child each week. The visitors included: natural parents, siblings, aunts, and grandparents, sometimes as often as three time a week other times very infrequently. In addition the foster child's social worker might visit once in two weeks or once in six weeks. The foster parents' link social worker visits every three to six months. There are also numerous planning and review meetings which can be as often as every six weeks and involve four to eight visitors. Occasionally there are professional visitors such as peripatetic teachers, counsellors, therapists, and GPs. Potential adoptee(s) and their natural children were another group which might visit daily for several weeks. Generally, coffee and biscuits were offered as refreshments but in a number of cases lunches were provided, especially for regular visitors such as social workers and people who travelled long distances or extended their visits over meal-times. None of this provision was obligatory, but nevertheless occurred as a result of the hospitable nature of the foster parents.

> One of the biggest additional costs is coffee and biscuits, with three teenage foster children each child has six monthly reviews often pre-meetings before this. One social worker comes every two weeks to take a child out. The foster child's mother objects to the placement so the link social worker comes especially often. In general, visitors are more frequent during the early part of the placement. Planning meetings after four to six weeks, three monthly, six monthly. Case conference can be six extra persons. I estimate on average I have one visitor each day, some days two.

> Adoptive parents plus their children arrived for a two week period and I provided one meal a day. Sometimes they are found unsuitable so the process has to be repeated over again.

> Adoptive family come for maybe six weeks and I provide food for them three days a week. It's a real intrusion because sometimes you don't like them very much but have to put that to one side because its what is right for the child. There again I have had access visits with the natural mum, a family aid worker, and a social worker three times a week for a baby. Sometimes this sort of access is elsewhere, and sometimes my link worker will use the phone instead of visiting us.

Eating out: Some eating out was perceived by foster parents as an item of expense which was over and above what they provided for their own children because, as this parent pointed out, it could be considered as part of the social education of the foster child:

> I like to think its a new experience for the foster-child and that goes for all entertainment.

The majority of foster parents suggested eating out was part of their normal family pattern of 'a whole family treat' but they ate out more often now because their natural children were older. In fact, some foster families of the under fives reported their eating out patterns were often restricted by the presence of young and short term foster children. Families providing five to 10 year old children with placements ate out infrequently at a rate of once per month or less. Eating out in the older age group occurred more often and was usually classed as therapeutic. The families ate at a wide range of places - McDonald's, Fish and Chip cafes, Chinese and Indian Restaurants, Pizza houses etc.

There were some foster parents who could estimate the actual food cost differences each week and this is shown in Table 3.2. The highest estimate was £20.00 per week extra, the lowest was for 4 pints of extra milk. The average for all ages of children was £3.42 for unusual or extra items which would not have been purchased had this child been their own child.

Table 3.2
**Foster parents' perceived extra expenditure on food by age of the child,
£ per week.**

Age	Range in £s	Average
0-4 years n=16	1.00 to 5.70	3.08
5-10 years n=11	1.00 to 7.50	3.18
11-16+ years n=28	1.50 to 20.00	3.71
Overall n=55	1.00 to 20.00	3.42

Clothing

Foster parents suggested that, unlike the clothing budgets of natural children, there were two separate parts to the clothing standard for foster children:
• an initial clothing cost
• a replacement clothing cost.
The initial cost involves the purchase of a wardrobe for a child entering a placement with an inadequate stock of clothing. The replacement clothing cost is the cost of maintaining the clothing stock.

Initial clothing cost: Natural children retain a stock of clothing suitable for different seasons, leisure activities, school and special occasions. Table 3.3 shows that a large majority of foster children have limited wardrobes on beginning a placement. The younger the child the less likely it is to arrive at the placement with adequate clothing. Overall 64% of foster children entered a placement with inadequate clothing.

Table 3.3
The condition of the foster child's wardrobe on entry to the placement by age.

Age	Limited	Adequate	Not known
All ages	(35) 64%	(9) 16%	(11) 20%
0-4 years	(11) 69%	(1) 6%	(4) 25%
5-10 years	(8) 73%	(2) 18%	(1) 9%
11-16+	(16) 57%	(6) 21%	(6) 21%

Most of the children who arrived with adequate clothing were children who had moved from one foster placement to the next. Children in the 11 to 15+ age group were perceived by foster parents to be more likely than others to have been adequately clothed by previous foster parents but also more likely than other age groups to have had previous placements or institutional care.

Foster children who arrived at the placement poorly clothed were likely to have come straight from their natural home. Foster parents described some situations as desperate and showed a reluctance in some cases to inform the authorities of the high cost of providing the child with a basic wardrobe:

They arrived with only the clothes they stood up in...

We have not had anyone come with any stock of clothes, the worst thing is they need coats and shoes.

We don't put in all our costs because we think they (the authority) will think we are being extravagant. We find parents send their children to us in the smallest of clothes because I think they know we will provide them with a new set.

Every child who has come to us has needed to be kitted out and we always have to spend 50% more than what the authorities give us. And then they will only give us something once throughout the placement no matter how long the child is with us and throughout all the seasons.

The foster parents of 44 foster children could recall the initial cost of clothing. Table 3.4 shows that foster parents spent (over the whole sample of 55 children) an average of £113.10 on each child. Younger children had a tendency towards lower costs: under five years £63.80, five to 10 years £97.01, and 11 to 16+ years £147.57. These estimates are, however, limited because some foster parents were recalling expenditure at the start of a placement which varied from a few months to six years ago.[4] The inclusion of the above estimate as the cost of initial clothing provision is problematic because first, the cost is a 'one off' for that particular child in that particular household, second, the amount of expense occurring is extremely varied as shown.

Table 3.4
Initial cost of clothing for foster children,
£.

Age	Average cost	No. of children	Range of costs
All	113.10	55	30.00 to 400.00
0-4	63.80	16	30.00 to 200.00
5-10	97.01	11	56.00 to 167.00
11-16+	147.57	28	45.00 to 400.00

Replacement of clothing cost: Patterns of replacing the clothing of foster children, foster parents suggested are dissimilar to the patterns of replacing their own children's clothing at a similar age and sex. A large number of foster parents claimed they replaced a foster child's clothing more frequently than they did their own children's clothing. A discussion emerged on certain issues which contribute to how often and why clothes were replaced more often:

- What are the reasons for a higher replacement rate of foster child clothing?
- Did the natural parent contribute to the clothing expense of their child?
- Did the foster parent use second hand clothing to reduce cost?

Shorter clothing life span: Foster parents suggested the underlying reasons for higher than 'normal' replacement rates were:

i.   Foster children are more destructive than other children which leads to more washing and repairs.
ii. Foster children lose clothes more often.
iii. Some children play the system by demanding as much as possible to use up their entitlement.
iv. Some foster children have a tendency to experience an unusual growth spurt during the early period of the placement.
v.   Appearance (good clothes) contributes to improving the child's self esteem.
vi. Foster mothers who constantly have babies to care for experience heavy wear on their own clothing.

---

[4] The Commodity Price Index re-based in 1987 to 100. 1987 to April 1993 the cost of children's outer clothing had risen by 18%, the cost of shoes for adults and children had risen by 26%. (Employment Gazette June 1993, Table 6.2)

Destructive behaviour towards clothing was evident in 64% of school age foster children. This lack of care often led to more washing, which placed more stress on the clothing fabric, and to frequent changes of clothing which led to a shortage in the number of items of clothing available. Foster children were said by foster parents to need to be taught the rudiments of clothes care often:

> Foster children can be very destructive with clothing, put knees out of trousers, scrape shoes, wear coats out by sliding up and down the wall, they sometimes do this just to get attention, you could describe this as a 'disturbed' behaviour.

> Wash clothes more often than I did my own children's clothing, but this is mainly of my making I insist on daily changes because I am still teaching them cleanliness.

> The problem is they take short cuts like clearing up their bedroom by putting clean and dirty clothes into the linen basket. One child puts lots of layers of clothing on such as two jackets, two pairs of trousers and two or more T-shirts. He complains it is because he feels the cold all the time but we think it is to do with him feeling insecure.

On the other hand, some foster children were said to take care of their clothing.

Foster children were also reported to have a greater tendency than natural children of a similar age and sex to lose clothing. Children of school age were particularly careless. Foster parents believed this happened for a number of reasons: forgetfulness, dislike of the garment, bullying at school resulting in damaged or stolen clothing, or clothes thrown away with a disregard for the worth of clothing. The latter reason was sometimes thought to be wilful and associated with the notion of institutionalisation and dependency. The child relies on a paternalistic state for its upkeep but the organisation is faceless so there is no reciprocal feeling from the foster child about 'the state' as parent. Some parents expressed this as 'playing the system'. For example:

> His attitude to clothing was because he had been in care for so long, he had no respect for possessions because someone else has had to buy it and pay for it. Some great institution paid for everything the child had no experience of the pressures of living in a family where cost is of the essence.

> In general not caring about their clothes, lose clothes especially school clothes. I suppose it's not coming out of your dad's pocket it's from social services. As young as they are they are playing the system.

Overall, about one quarter of the foster children were said to have experienced an unusual 'growth spurt' within the first few months of the placement. Abnormal growth curves were evident in 45% of children aged five to 10 years of age who also experienced rapid changes in clothing size.

> ....initially he was very undernourished, this resulted in having to replace clothes before they were worn out including shoes.

Clothes were used by a number of foster parents as a means of giving the older child a psychological lift to build pride and self esteem.

> He is not hard on clothes, but he came with no modern or fashion clothes and because he has a social problem we buy clothes which give him status.

> Not heavier on clothes but I spend more on clothes, I like to make a point of them looking nice, it makes them feel special.

> The 14 year old wants designer labels, she is more demanding than our own daughter, I expect our daughter would also like designer clothes but she knows better than to ask or expect. The foster child hasn't learned when no means no and she knows I get an allowance to clothe her.

Additionally, the high frequency of babies in certain foster households was claimed to result in additional wear in the foster mother's outer wear. Natural babies grow up and mature out of their baby habits, ailments, digestive problems and incontinence, whereas foster mothers reported the likelihood of multiple babies arriving each year resulted in the placement home always being in the infant child-rearing stage.

Natural parents' contribution to clothing: Foster parents claimed the clothes provided by natural parents were often of little use to the foster child because they were unsuitable, the wrong size, of poor quality, or second hand. Foster parents were sensitive in dealing with gifts of this sort. For example:

> If the birth parents provide clothing it is usually something for them to go home in, but most of the babies go for adoption so I treat this as a present, wash it and tag it in readiness for the child's box of memories. They can at least look back and know that their real mother gave them something.

In 78% of cases the natural parent 'never' provided any clothing for their own child in foster care. However, this largely depended on the age of the child. Foster children aged 0 to four years were more likely to receive clothes from their parents than other children. By the time the child reached five almost no clothes were forthcoming. Of those children who received clothes occasionally, almost half were from grandparents and not from parents. Children aged 11 to 16 almost never received clothes (93%), however, one child from a 'wealthy' family did and a second child did occasionally from the maternal grandmother.

Second hand clothes: Second hand clothes are defined as clothes passed on in a child's own or extended family or from friends usually with a reciprocal arrangement. No foster parents reported that they shopped in jumble sales but two parents worked in second hand shops and were able to obtain some clothing that way. One foster parent explained:

> I use pass 'ons' sometimes (but I feel I shouldn't) I work in a second hand shop so sometimes I see useful things such as jeans and play clothes, never get second hand school uniform, used second hand more so for my own (children).

The majority of carers however reported they never bought second hand, sometimes for psychological reasons such as building confidence and self esteem, and to make up for past deprivation. For example:

> Clothing tends to be all new stuff, whereas for your own children would pass down or pass from friend to friend - but with the foster child I have felt they needed their own identity their own little wardrobe ....all the clothes go with the child.

Conversely some foster parents reported they supplemented the replacement of new clothes with second hand clothes. Overall, 42% of foster children were provided with second hand clothes by their foster parents at some time during the placement.

Other clothing - disposable nappies: Foster mothers of infants had a tendency to use disposable nappies, although they generally used cloth nappies for their own children. The high use of disposable nappies for young children is not difficult to understand. First, foster parent's believed that using disposable nappies saved time, allowed for flexible and busy lifestyles, were hygienic and caused less discomfort to the child than cloth nappies. Foster parents also claimed that because of the 'trials and tribulations' of being a foster child, the children were more often than not late to toilet train so the use of nappies lasted for a longer period of time. Second, most institutions including hospitals, use and recommend disposable nappies.

Household goods

The furniture, fittings and fabrics in the placement home suffer as a result of fostering children. This is accentuated by the concentration of children in households within particular age bands. Foster parents have a tendency to foster children within a preferred age group. In addition, the heavy use of household furnishings was aggravated in many cases by the actions of children who arrive from different backgrounds and exhibit different codes of behaviour to those natural to the placement household. Foster parents described the impact of fostering on the replacement of furniture, fittings, appliances, fabrics and the extent to which damage occurred during access visits.

Damage to household goods: The range of items suffering wear and tear are shown in Table 3.5. Beds, mattresses and bed-linen were the most common items suffering extremes of wear and tear in all age groups. Furniture suffered in all age groups but this was particularly the case in the 11 to 16+ years age group where most pieces of communal furniture and personal items were affected. The comments of foster parents led to a level of consensus on the seriousness of this problem:

> Across the board foster children have no regard for our things.

> He is very tense and drops things all the time.

> They break things to demonstrate their anger... and we can't chastise them now, they are often very unhappy children.

> 'Bed-wetting' and 'soiling' is a big problem, it results in regular replacement of mattresses and heavy wear on bed-linen in general.

> The foster child has caused considerable damage, he put a hot iron on the table, left hot tongs on the carpet, he put a screwdriver in an electric plug and blew the electric circuit and put a chair through the ceiling. Overall he takes less care, he scratches furniture and misuses chairs - swinging on them until it weakens the chair legs.

> Uses our bed and his own as a trampoline, we needed to buy a new bed ... he even broke a bed in a hotel which cost us £10.00, and broke our shower door which was £200 to replace.

Many foster parents perceive that the foster child is: 'just' careless, clumsy or rough rather than wilful, for example, climbs on household items, loses items, and has low levels of responsibility for possessions owned by themselves or the household. Foster parents who provided placements regularly to children 0 to four years old suggested some damage could be attributed to the continuous stream of very young toddlers through their households.

Smoking by the foster child, friends of the foster child and natural parents, siblings and relatives also contributed to damage in many families providing for children in the 11 to 16+ year age group. Families providing places for children aged five to 10 years were more likely to report access visit damage than other age groups.

Table 3.5
The range of furnishings suffering damage as a result of fostering children by the age of the foster child.

Aged 0-4 n=8	Aged 5-10 n=6	Aged 11-16+ n=18
bed-linen furniture mattresses	bed-linen furniture beds\mattress towels crockery washer lamps ornaments TV video microwave	bed-linen furniture mattress beds toilet seat TV Video wash basin crockery shower door hotel bed wardrobe carpets curtains linen basket lamps drawer bookcase door handles glassware

Household services

Foster parents were asked to consider their use of many types of household services and consider what impact fostering a child has on service need. Need for weekly cleaning help, telephone expenses and baby sitting emerged as important issues.

Weekly cleaning help: Few foster parents reported that they bought extra weekly cleaning help specifically because of fostering needs. A substantial number (75%) however claimed they cleaned more than they would if the child had been a natural child.

Telephone: All foster families had a private telephone. One foster parent felt the need to buy a telephone answering machine which cost £80 to enable the family to cope with abusive calls from natural parents. Most frequently the reason given for extra out-going calls was those made to the child's social worker. Other reasons included contact with the child's school, G.P., natural parents, grandparents and calls made from the foster home by the visiting social worker. Most of the extra calls were local calls but some reported national calls especially in relation to the child's natural family. Most calls were made at peak pricing time. The number of calls per week varied significantly between foster parents, however two per week was a common estimate, though some stated they made as many as six calls per week. In terms of extra money per quarter, £5 to £20 was general, however, three foster parents told of their experiences of 'chat line' numbers with bills of £59, £60 and £160 a quarter more than usual. Some foster parents providing placements for children aged 11 to 16+ believed that additional calls were being made by the foster child to friends and sometimes family without their knowledge. Probably the worse case was a foster child 11 to 16+ recalled by one foster parent:

> The phone bill tripled, usually it was £85 a quarter, but the last one was £240. It took me a while to realise that when she said people were ringing her back this just wasn't true.

Baby sitting: Foster children bring special problems for their foster parents in relation to baby sitting. A problem was that almost all foster parents would ask only responsible adults, or adults who had undergone police checks, to baby sit their foster children. At times this resulted in their own older children no longer baby sitting for foster children in their own home. There was also less reporting of grandparents sitting because of the increased number of children in the household. Usual sitters were anxious about taking on the responsibility of a stranger's child because of adverse behaviour patterns and the ill-health of some foster children. The only recourse for some foster parents was to ask other foster parents to sit. Many chose to forego their own leisure and went out as a couple only during placement breaks. When the foster parents were asked if there was anything they desired for their foster children, a number of them said they would like a baby sitting service to be set up so they could enjoy some quality time away from the home.

Transport

The extra costs of transport for many foster families included private motoring costs and public transport costs.

Motoring: All placement households in this sample were car owners. Eighty-seven per cent of foster mothers had access to a car for day and evening travel for fostering purposes. Foster parents considered they incurred extra motoring costs in two ways:
- Extra journeys in respect of their present or last foster child and current fostering obligations.
- Extra car running costs overall in respect of their family need for a larger car.

The majority of these extra journeys were a mix of local and longer distance. The length of journey is important because of the rural location of many foster families. The local hospital, for example, might be 20 miles away.

The types of journeys undertaken in relation to foster children included access visits by foster children to the child's natural family or family centre. Often this involved four journeys, whatever the distance travelled. Very long journeys were infrequent but noted by some foster parents who expressed a willingness to transport the child to visit far away relatives, previous foster parents or friends. In some cases travel to panel meetings, court cases, visits to professionals such as consultants, psychiatrists, special need education, counselling, foster care support meetings and training days could involve long distances. Access visits could take place up to three or more times a week. The foster child, but not the natural child, might need to be transported to and from school or from the school bus because of truancy, lack of confidence, behavioural problems or because of the distance, danger or complexity in reaching the placement location. In most cases, foster families took responsibility for extra journeys. Many believed it was important they treated their foster children as their own.

Foster parents often had the problem of not having enough car space to carry the whole family at any one time. The average foster family had two or three dependent natural children and two foster children and needed a six-seated car. Many foster families either exchanged their car for a larger one, made two journeys or used two cars to transport the whole family. The problem was greater for families providing placements for foster children under the age of 11 years because of the children's higher levels of dependency compared to older children who could make some journeys unaccompanied.

Many foster families who changed their car for a larger car found the running costs were higher than for their previous car. Running costs included foster parent perceptions on miles per gallon, servicing, replacement of tyres and insurance differences.

Public transport: This is used little by foster families. Some foster families lived in areas where public transport either did not exist or was very limited. The common reasons for using the local bus or train services were: to travel to hospital or access visits, for leisure or educational purposes. Many families, for example, providing for children aged 11 to 16+ in particular, used public transport as an educational aid, for self-esteem and to promote independence.

> I encourage the child (11 to 16+) to travel at least some of the time on public transport, this is part of a confidence building exercise.

Leisure goods

Foster parents considered two aspects of the leisure goods budget component:
- The lifetime of toys or sports goods and the effect this has on the stock of household toys.
- The cost of gifts for the foster child and his or her natural parents or kin.

Lifetime of leisure goods: Foster children rarely arrived at a placement with their own toys or games. In the majority of cases, foster homes retained a minimum stock of toys or games which were used by foster children. These were collected from various sources including natural children, past foster children, friends, neighbours, relatives, new or sale items, and second-hand items from jumble sales.

One issue is the circumstances in which foster parents' stock is depleted and the rate at which toys, games, books, seasonal goods and sports goods are replaced. Foster parents said that leisure goods were often subject to heavy wear and tear, and replaced more frequently in foster households than in other families. The explanation for replacement included wilful play, carelessness, inability or lack of knowledge on how to play, older children playing with a younger age group's toys, loss, bullying, misuse by visitors such as siblings on access visits and in some cases items of stock were given to the foster child when the placement ended.

Gifts: The giving of gifts represented both major and minor spending for most foster families in two ways: the purchase of gifts for the foster child and the purchase of gifts for the natural family of the foster child.

All foster parents claimed to have substantial spending on gifts for the foster child at the child's birthday and Christmas although the amount of spending varied from family to family. For some foster parents (as other parents) recalling the amount spent on such occasions was a sensitive issue because of the personal and private nature of giving. Some parents tried to compare their spending to what they thought other families spent while others reported high costs:

> Birthdays and Christmas for all our family including the foster child lags behind the spending of the well to do families in this area.... most of the children around here own their own TV and video, and our foster child is the only one in his class that doesn't have a computer.

> Spend a fortune at Christmas (birthdays £100 each and I treat them to the burger bar), at Christmas I bought one a £310 music centre, they have had computers and bicycles and the one coming up 18 I have given him a car with comprehensive insurance and I pay most of the running costs.

It was, therefore, more relevant to enquire if the foster child was treated any differently to a natural child within the same family. Few foster parents claimed they spent less. The reasons for spending less were usually very specific, for example, in one particular case the natural parents retained the role of financial support for the child. Other cases generally involved very young foster infants where giving equally was not in the views of foster parents so important.

A few foster parents spent more on the foster child than their own child. The reason for doing so was reported as compensatory to make good earlier deprivation. For example:

> We do spend more on him than we do on our own children, well - we try to broaden his outlook. Helped him to pay for a motor bike ... mind you he didn't look after it... but we try to help him if he really wants something.

The vast majority of foster parents spent similar amounts on all their children including foster children, often regardless of the length of placement. The reason for this was usually claimed to be equality of giving and social justice.

Other foster parents informed all children in the household that they had a set amount of money and could spend it on what they liked. Many foster parents perceived the true expenditure at Christmas and birthdays especially high because of additional spending on parties, special teas or treats provided alongside the present. In most families however this activity was particular to the family culture and tradition and performed equally for all members.

Gifts to the foster child's natural extended family in many cases were considered as a token gesture. On the whole the amount spent on this type of gift was reported to be low and the frequency of giving limited to important events such as Christmas, birthdays, Mother's Day and Easter. Those foster parents who purchased gifts for the child's own family did so for many reasons:

- It was traditional in their own household that gifts were exchanged in a similar way (a demonstration of the foster child's position in the placement household),
- A role model for the foster child and natural family in demonstrating caring relationships,
- To acknowledge major events in the child's life or the calendar year in relation to the natural family.

The gifts included cards, small presents such as flowers, boxes of chocolates, home baked cakes and calendars.

Leisure activities

Although many foster parents commented that leisure activities were expensive, the pattern of leisure in 61% of foster families is similar to the general leisure behaviour of their particular household. Foster children on the whole are found to be given many opportunities to experience a wide range of leisure activities. The number of activities is largely by choice, some foster children are 'not sporty', others 'have a go' at many activities as shown in Table 3.6. One 13 year old boy, for example, had a highly structured programme of activities:

> Mondays is cricket practice, Tuesday he goes to a boy's club, Wednesday he goes swimming and diving, Thursday was orienteering, Friday a disco, Saturday he goes with his foster father to a football match and on Sunday he usually plays football.

Table 3.6
The leisure activities of foster children by the age of the child.

Age 0-4 years	Age 5-10 years	Age 11-16+
peer play, parties, playgroup, nursery, visiting, swimming	brownies, twilight club, music, judo, dancing, hockey, bowling, cinema, visiting	youth club, scouts, football, disco, horse-riding, dancing, theatre, cricket, orienteering, swimming, clubs, videos, cinema, bowling

A number of questions arose about foster children's leisure activities:
- Did the foster child restrict foster family leisure?
- Did the foster family have a positive attitude of social integration through leisure in relation to the foster child?
- What impact did the foster child have on the family holiday?
- Did the foster child's pattern of leisure differ from that of the natural child in the same household?

The question of whether foster children restricted the family activity was an important one because of the policy of placing children in families with older children. Some evidence was found of this. In the age group 0 to four years it occurred most frequently for two reasons, age and disruptive behaviour.

The way in which teenagers restrict the foster family activities is largely the result of unacceptable behaviour, for example, a 14 year old girl restricted the families activities thus:

> because she cannot be trusted to be left, the first time we left her she drank all the alcohol she could find and ended up in hospital. The second time which was during the day she took a car and drove it around the field and into a fence causing some damage. When we have friends around she acts so badly we have almost stopped entertaining anyone.

Many foster parents had a positive attitude towards the integration of foster children in their new community. The foster parent of a young child, for example, commented:

> As soon as a new foster child arrives we throw a party for the whole street to meet her.

The length of placement for some parents had some bearing on the decision to positively integrate the child:

The longer the child stays the more we try to integrate them into the new community... we like to give the children something they haven't had and I don't like to say no to everything the child wants to do. She would like to try many things but sometimes its not worth starting these things off as we don't know how long she will be here. Task centred placements are not meant to go on forever. She would like to go horse riding - own her own pony - try piano lessons!

The disturbed behaviour of other foster children also resulted in a cautionary reluctance to socially integrate the child without careful planning for the event and only when the responsibility for the child could be passed to another willing adult.

Some foster children can be very aggressive and often bullish... need to carefully brief the parent of the children they are going to play with - on the whole people are very good.

The majority of foster parents, especially in the teenage age group, find a positive plan of social integration in the new community unnecessary. Older teenagers would sometimes travel back to their place of origin for social events or integrate in their new community at their own pace.

Overall, 64% of foster families took their foster children on an annual holiday during the placement but none of those foster parents could identify any costs additional to that of taking just one extra child of their own. Generally, the types of holidays experienced by foster children with their foster families are modest holidays, a common type is camping or caravanning. Holidays for teenagers, however, had a tendency to be more varied than those with younger children. Teenage holidays included those taken with the foster family at home and abroad, and independent of the foster family but financed by them, such as school trips and adventure holidays.

Personal care

The discussion among foster parents about personal care conveyed patterns of usage of individual items and the health of foster children in general, and whether this (or hygiene problems) led to extra cost in any way.

Patterns in the usage of personal care items: A small number of foster children in the 11 to 16+ age range were perceived by foster parents to use additional amounts of personal care products because of their destructive, careless or extravagant behaviour. This situation rarely occurred in younger children aged 0 to 10 years of age because the foster parents found greater opportunity to monitor usage. A carer of an 11 to 16+ child pondered the issue of usage:

Shampoo, just poured it over his head, Initially very wasteful, now we give him a measured amount as the child has no idea about quantities, he spends ages under the shower. His behaviour is strange could be part of his general naughtiness. You see by the time he came to us he had, had as many different homes as he'd had years to his life. Now each home or institution would have a different set of rules, a different set of allocations, and the household different priorities, so he was perpetually for a long time testing the limits of our household. Our children would just accept the family norms, he didn't. We could have dealt with this particular behaviour but we were coping with so many problems it wasn't one of the major problems.

Few foster children demanded brand named or individual personal care items, however, when this did occur, the child's choice was generally respected (within reason) by foster parents who viewed this, especially in teenage foster children as a step towards independence.

I would buy the boy skin creams because he had acne but he didn't use them, the girl has vitamin tablets because she is a vegetarian, both children wanted brand named toiletries... The social worker said I should encourage this because it gives the children a greater sense of autonomy - whereas I buy economy packs of things for the family to use.

Many foster parents of older children, however, viewed any deviation from the normal personal care family purchases as something children bought from their pocket money allowance or Saturday job earnings.

Health and hygiene: A large number of foster children overall were perceived by foster parents to be in poor health although this did not always lead to extra costs:
- 64% of children aged 0-4,
- 25% of children aged 5-10,
- 54% of children aged 11-16+.

Poor health in younger children was more likely to be medically diagnosed and treated and foster parents had a greater propensity not to self medicate the child than in older age groups. Reasons given for poor health in young children included, allergies, digestive problems, chest infections and frequent colds, hair lice and worms, spots and eczema. Two children were monitored closely by the hospital for more serious problems. A number of foster parents mentioned problems which they associated with being 'run-down' which resulted in some expense for the whole family, for example, head lice, athlete's foot, worms and skin conditions.

A larger number of older foster children suffered poor health through a range of minor but persistent psychosomatic or physical illnesses. The range included, complaints of feeling ill a lot, frequent colds, throat infections and stomach upsets, nasal problems, athlete's foot, bouts of impetigo, frequent headaches, eczema, etc. Hygiene problems were perceived by foster parents in a few cases to be the result of poor education, in other cases it was related to incontinence. In one case, pressure came from the natural parents for the foster parent to sort out the child's persistent complaints of headaches and stomach aches. Other foster parents highlighted the foster child's regular demands for analgesics as abnormal. Table 3.7 highlights a list of common items bought by foster parents over the counter which were additional to what they would expect to buy for their own child.

Table 3.7
Table of extra personal care items by age of child.

Age	Additional items* or items where additional amounts are used compared with that expected for a natural child
0-4	Herbal tablets, gripe water, tissues, Calpol, head lice shampoo and tablets for worms for the whole family, extra toothbrushes.
5-10	Head lice shampoo and tablets for worms for the whole family, extra toothbrushes.
11-16+	Paracetamol, cream for dry skin, treatment of spots, vitamin tablets, cough mixture, throat lozenges, Sudafed, brand name personal care items, extra toothbrushes.

* Not including items obtained by prescription from the child's G.P.

Pocket money

The foster parents' views on the meaning and definition of pocket money in relation to foster children varied, for example, some parents related it to earnings and education. Half of all foster parents treated the foster child similar to their own child when providing pocket money. Foster children aged 11-16+, however, in 65% of cases received considerably more than parents gave to their own child of a similar age. The conditions on which payment was made and the amount of money some foster parents gave to older children was set by local authority 'regulations'. This meant the authority stipulated how much and what budget category of spending pocket money should cover, for example, clothing and personal items. Despite this, the majority of foster parents maintained similar levels of spending on the weekly budget as previously because the foster child lacked the budgeting skills to provide for itself.

Misdemeanours

The definition of a misdemeanour was left to the foster parents resulting in the inclusion of incidents, reported and unreported to the police, of behaviour which had cost implications for the foster parents. The misdemeanours most reported by foster parents were stealing and vandalism by the foster child. Other kinds of deviant behaviour of lesser or greater severity which resulted in no cost to the foster parent was not discussed.

The severity of each case varied, as expressed in the individuality of the comments below: A child five to 10 years was said to:

> take things, sneaks things out of the house and then gives them away at school.

Another child stole from foster siblings and parents. Foster children aged over 11 in one household earned a reputation for vandalism. Children of this age were also caught stealing from shops. Many misdemeanours were dealt with informally. Occasionally the actions of a foster child required the intervention of the Police:

> He shot next door's booster aerial with his air rifle and I had to pay £65 to replace it. Then he went on a Trident course and worked in a travel agent and stole £240 which I repaid and he continues to steal. He stole £300 from my bank account because I let him go to the cash point with my cash card. He has been involved with the police because he stole hundreds of car badges and was selling them.

Misdemeanours by foster children are an expensive problem for up to 60% of foster families. The cost to some foster parents is substantial. Children aged 11 to 16+ have a greater propensity to commit misdemeanours which affect their placement family than other age groups. None of the foster parents professed to have natural children who had similar histories, therefore any costs arising are assumed additional to the cost of a natural child.

Summary of foster parents' perception of costs

Inclusion of items in the budget standard is based on the perceptions of foster families interviewed in the spring of 1992. When asked to compare the direct cost of a foster child to a normal child in their own family the majority of foster parent's claimed foster children incurred higher costs. Conversely, a few families found the expenses for a foster child were less and some families believed the expenses were similar although this depended largely on the part of the budget under examination.

Foster families were given the opportunity to contribute further by considering if there was any item or service they felt they should provide, needed to provide but did not do so or desired to provide for their foster child. Carers of foster children in the 0 to four age group, produced two ideas. The first concerned the urgency of a request for psychiatric help for a child and the desire to 'cut the red tape' by purchasing a private consultation. The second was a regret that the foster family could not afford a new bike rather than a second hand one, for a foster child. Foster parents caring for older foster children desired mostly to provide the children with new experiences and increased activities. The lack of adequate transport, however, was said by many foster parents to constrain their activities. Also, the need to take time off through a supply of baby sitters was expressed by foster parents. Extra curricular activities such as, music, dancing lessons, school subject tuition, trips and holidays abroad, a computer and horse riding lessons were suggested by foster parents as desirable when providing placements for older children. The only conclusion drawn from these replies was that no important categories were omitted from the budget standard and that, from a foster parent perspective, most expenditure equates to needs as defined by them.

Table 3.8 shows the proportion of foster families who perceived they had higher costs than they would have had if the foster child had been their own child (accounting for age and sex differences). Over 90% of placement families claimed telephone and extra travel costs. In relation to the age of the child, more than 90% of foster parents of a child aged 0 to four years believed telephone and baby-sitting to be in excess of normal child costs. Foster parents of a child five to 10 suggested fuel, food, wear and tear on household goods, telephone and extra mileage was more expensive, and fuel and extra mileage higher for a foster child aged 11 to 16+.

Table 3.8
Proportion of foster parents who perceive foster children costs are higher than natural children of the same age/sex and in the same household.

	0-4 % high	5-10 % high	11-16+ % high	All % high
Housing - decorating &				
- internal repairs	63	67	89	78
- external repairs	50	83	39	50
- security	13	50	22	25
- extensions	25	50	39	38
Fuel	75	100	100	88
Food	81	91	71	78
Clothing - replacement	50	55	79	65
Household goods				
- wear/tear	50	100	72	72
- smoking damage	0	17	50	28
- access damage	13	83	17	28
Household services				
- cleaning	63	83	78	75
- postage	0	0	11	6
- telephone	100	100	83	94
- baby sitting	100	83	56	72
Transport				
- mileage	75	100	94	91
- larger car	63	71	41	53
- public transport	38	29	41	38
Leisure goods				
- wear/tear	56	73	50	56
- gifts internal	38	0	22	22
- gifts external	63	50	39	47
Leisure activities	11	9	17	11
Personal care	36	13	46	38
Pocket money	13	0	65	38
Misdemeanours	0	43	59	54
Initial clothing	69	73	57	64

Normative estimate of extra costs

Additional housing costs

The extra cost housing budget is shown in Table 3.9. The budget includes the extra cost of re-decorating an additional room, and in the case of the teenage child an extra 1.5 rooms each year. The external decoration cost of a 'normal' child budget is increased by 5% each year.

Table 3.9
Base for costing housing in relation to the FBU assumptions and pricing.

Category	Description	Age of child	Cost year
Internal damage	Re-decorate		
	1 extra room	0-4	40.00
	1.5 rooms	5-16	60.00
External damage	5% increase	0-16	22.54
Home Security	New budget	0-16	25.00

Home security budget

Smoke alarm, Index, 3, cost £6.75 (20.25) Life 2 year - 10.12 year.
Sensor night light, Index, cost £7.99 Life 1 year   - 7.99 year.
Window locks, Barnetts, 13, cost £2.65, life 5 year   - 6.89 year.
Total cost per year   **£25.00**

Home extensions

The cost of servicing an appropriate loan is assigned to the extra cost budget for foster children. The capital cost of the extension is not included as a child cost. Table 3.10 shows the average cost of extensions or alterations to property incurred by the foster family.

Table 3.10
Average cost of extensions or alterations to home.

Child 0-4 years n=8	Child 5-10 years n=6	Child 11-16+ years n=18	All n=32
£300	£1845	£1361	£1186.56

Personal loans are the most straightforward type of loan for borrowing small amounts for home extensions. The Midland Personal Loan facility offers short term loans repaid in 12 to 60 months. The current rate of interest (April 1993) for loans below £3,000 is 21.4%. Table 3.11 shows the results of calculating the interest and repayment on a loan of £500 over a 12 month period for foster parents providing for children aged 0 to four years and £2,000 loan over a period of 36 months for families providing for older children.

Table 3.11
Midland Personal Short Term, Low value loans, £.

Amount of loan £	Insurance premium	Monthly repayment	Total repayment	Total to service the loan	Weekly interest
500	41.59	49.91	598.88	98.88	1.90
2000	276.57	83.85	3018.28	1018.28	2.36

Additional fuel budget

The budget standard for fuel is shown in Table 3.12. The estimate for placement households was the result of increasing the family fuel bill in specific areas of fuel consumption by the following standard. The increases were arbitrary percentages but fit the magnitude and order expressed in pragmatic terms by foster parents.

Table 3.12
Base for costing fuel in relation to FBU assumptions and pricing.

Category	Description	Cost year Age 4 and 10	Cost year Age 16
Water heating	increase by 25%	36.00	36.00
Space heating	increase by 15%	19.95	21.30
Lights/appliances	increase by 10%	20.80	31.00

Additional food budget

The distribution of food in households is based on the energy needs of children and adults as described more fully in Chapter 2. The method used to estimate the extra costs of foster children bases the increase on the amount of energy used by a child in a higher age group. That is a child aged 0 to four years has food expense which is equivalent to the needs of a child aged five to 10 years, a child aged five to 10 years has needs which are similar to a children aged 11 to 16+ and a child aged 11 to 16+ has needs over and above those of an adult. Table 3.13 shows that the extra food costs of a foster child ranged from £3.61 each week for a child 0 to four years, to £4.00 and £4.39 for a child aged five to 10 years and 11-16+ years respectively.

Table 3.13
The extra food costs of children, 1991 prices, £ per week.

Age	Natural child	Increase	Foster child	% change
0-4	9.82	3.61	13.43	37
5-10	13.43	4.00	17.43	30
11-15+	17.43	4.39	21.82	25

Additional initial clothes budget

The average perceived cost of clothing is taken as a good estimate of probable expense. On average foster children 0-4 years cost their foster parents the sum of £63.80 for a basic starter wardrobe. At 5-16 years and 11-16+ years the sum is £97.01 and £147.57 respectively. The sum of the initial clothing budget is shown separately in the summary tables as a one off payment at the start of a placement.

Additional replacement clothing budget

The higher clothing replacement costs are calculated for children by reducing the life-span of clothing and shoes by one third on each item included in the data set for a modest-but-adequate clothing standard for natural children. This budget assumes no second hand clothes are used, no sale clothes are purchased and the foster child's natural parent makes no contribution. The results are shown in Table 3.14. The extra cost of replacing clothes more often for foster children is given for boys and girls. An average weekly cost for boys or girls aged 0 to four years is £2.91, five to 10 years of age is £3.21 and £4.33 for children aged 11 to 16+.

Table 3.14
The extra replacement costs of clothing, 1991 prices, £ per week.

Age	Sex	Main items	Accessories	Footwear	Total
0-4	girl	2.11	0.05	0.62	2.78
	boy	2.28	0.05	0.71	3.04
5-10	girl	2.01	0.05	1.01	3.07
	boy	2.25	0.06	1.03	3.34
11-16+	girl	3.80	0.09	0.77	4.66
	boy	2.65	0.06	1.28	3.99

Additional nappy budget

Disposable nappies were used in 88% of families providing for children in the 0 to four age group. There is no allowance for this expense in the natural child budget. However, based on the strong argument in favour of using this type of product, a budget is included as an extra fostering cost for young children.

Nappy budget = micro to junior in size (birth to 3+ years), Pampers, outlet Tony's Textiles, Average number per year is 52 packets, 6.99 each packet = **£363.48 each year**

Additional household goods budget

Wear and tear: The method used to take into account the additional damage to household furniture, fittings and fabrics reduces the life of each item by approximately one third. Furniture includes communal furniture and the foster child's bedroom furniture. In families with natural children communal furniture is estimated to last 15 years and bedroom furniture 20 years, in foster homes this is reduced to 10 and 13 years respectively. An example of the calculation is shown in the diagram below:

	Item = 3-seater settee.		
	2 Adult H/H (a)	*2 Adult/2 child H/H* (b)	*Foster H/H* (c)
Price	499.95	499.95	499.95
Lifetime	17 yrs	15 yrs	10 yrs
Cost/year	29.41	33.33	50.00
Child's share/year		(b-a) 3.92	(c-a) 20.59
Extra foster cost/year			(c-b) 16.67
Extra cost/week			**0.32**

Fitted carpets, underlay and fitting for communal spaces and a child's bedroom are treated in a similar fashion. The lifetimes of nine years for carpets and 18 years for underlay in homes with natural children are reduced to six and 12 years respectively for foster homes. Bathroom and kitchen coverings' lifetimes are reduced pro rata.

Household textiles and soft furnishings such as bed-linen, quilts, towels, the child's bedroom curtains and linings have similar reductions in lifetimes. The washing machine, iron, vacuum cleaner and facilities to hire carpet cleaning equipment have lifetimes reduced to seven years, six years, eight years and one year respectively for homes with foster children. In addition, the frequency of repair of these items is increased from approximately twice in 11 years to twice in seven years. Extra washing powder and carpet shampoo are included in the weekly estimate of costs. Additional

Christmas and special occasion cards are also included. Table 3.15 shows the additional household goods budget for foster children.

Table 3.15
Household goods budget by the age of the child.

	Age 0-10 yrs	Age 11+yrs
Communal furniture and child's bedroom furniture	1.38	1.42
Communal floor coverings and child's bedroom carpets	1.14	1.18
Soft furnishings and textiles	0.28	0.28
Electrical appliances and repairs	0.92	0.92
Additional greeting cards and cleaning materials	0.18	0.18
Miscellaneous consumables	0.19	0.19
Total	**4.09**	**4.17**

Smoking: The level of damage caused by cigarettes is estimated using normative judgement at £70 once in three years based on the limited number of carers reporting the degree of minor damage caused. This amount covers the call out charge of a craftsman for wood repair or repair of curtains and fabric. The weekly figure is calculated at £0.45 each week.

Access visit damage: Other damage caused by siblings, natural parents or the foster child's friends tends to be slight in terms of the costs of repair. The budget estimate includes the extra hire of cleaning equipment at £16.00 each year and an additional electrical repair of £50 once in three years. This budget equates to a sum of £0.63 each week.

Additional household services

Cleaning help: Contracting regular cleaning help was outside the financial constraints of most foster parents although for many the need was evident and desired. A normative estimate of one hour every two weeks at £3.50 an hour is included as a token cost.

Postage: Postage costs are increased by £0.50, equivalent to two extra letters per foster child each week.

Telephone: The extra telephone expenditure for foster families is based on the residential quarterly telephone expenditure for households published by Oftel 1989 for local and national calls. Oftel prices are increased by British Telecom price rises to bring the figures up to 1990/91 level. Table 3.16 shows the effect of adding to the median FBU household bill, 50% extra local calls and 30% extra national calls for foster households. The extra cost does not include any part of fixed telephone charges such as exchange line rental, connection charges or estimates of international calls. The extra telephone cost in respect of a foster child under 11 years of age is estimated at £40.04 a year or £0.77 per week. For a child aged over 11 years, the extra cost is £60.32 each year or £1.16 each week.

Table 3.16
Summary of the extra telephone expenditure incurred by foster parents.

Age	National calls	Local calls	+30% national calls	+50% local calls	VAT on calls	per 1/4 yr	per year
under 11	9.19	11.63	2.76	5.81	1.50	10.07	40.28
11 and over	13.78	17.44	4.13	8.72	2.25	15.10	60.40

Baby sitting: The budget for baby sitting is one sit every two weeks of three hours duration at £1.50 an hour and two late sits a year at £2.50 an hour. The extra cost of sitting is increased to £2.00 hour before midnight and £3.00 an hour after midnight in fostering households. This equates to an extra £41.00 each year.

Additional motoring budget

Car miles: The number of average car miles each week in relation to natural children is estimated previously (Chapter 2) as approximately 23 miles for children aged 4 and 10, and 33 miles each week for children aged 16 years. The cost of an additional 25 miles per week (1300 miles each year) are calculated to account for the extra journeys in relation to the fostering circumstances.

Larger car: There is considerable evidence from foster parents of additional costs in the provision of a suitable vehicle to transport children when the family becomes a placement family. The additional costs arose from the purchase of a larger car and higher running costs.

The larger car may have extra costs in miles per gallon, servicing, insurance, larger tyres and the initial cost of exchange from small to large. There are other costs which cannot be ignored because they relate to the change in car. The initial cash outlay at the point of exchange is taken into account as the differential between an exchange for a small size family car and a larger family. In 1987, the Transport Statistics Great Britain 1978-1988, Table 2.24 reported that 49.7% of cars have a life of 12 years.

The problems foster parents experience in the provision of a six to seven seater car are numerous. Alternatives to a larger car such as a mini-bus or converted van are disregarded in estimating a standard because of unacceptable safety ratings. Three examples of larger cars manufactured in 1987 are selected from the Which? 'Guide to new and used cars' (1991) and their vital statistics, ratings and price detailed below, in order to select one for comparison with the average family car.

The criteria set for a comparison between a family car of 4 seats suitable for a family of '2 adults and 2 children' and a foster family car suitable for '2 adults and 4 children' is as follows:

- The vehicle is 5 years old with a life of approximately 7 years.
- The vehicle is no bigger than a family estate car with seating capacity for 6 people.
- The price is modest-but-adequate.
- The three budgets for larger cars represent choice and availability.

Table 3.17 highlights some of the difficulties foster parent may find in locating a 6 seater car. There are no such 'non-luxury' cars produced as standard on the British market, and those manufacturers from abroad producing a large seater car had a small share of the UK market, limiting choice and availability. The engine capacity of foster family cars are rated higher than the average family car which may imply higher consumption of fuel, oil, servicing and tyres - perhaps offset by lower depreciation rates towards the end of its life-span. The larger cars in the comparison below are similar in chassis size to the average family car albeit slightly longer which implies they can be managed by the average car driver.

Table 3.17
Vital statistics of larger cars.

Age yrs	Make	Market share	Model cc	Size L x W in m.	1987 new-cost 1991	Seats
5	Ford	25.25	Escort 1400	4.04 1.88	3600	4
5	Mazda	1.21	626 2.0 GLX	4.59 1.69	3980	6 (2-rear face) Standard
5	Volvo	3.29	240 GL 1966	4.79 1.71	4900	6 (2-rear face) optional
5	Mitsu-bishi	0.65	Space wagon 1800 GLX	4.30 1.64	5360	6-7(front face) standard

Table 3.18 shows where some of the extra motoring costs lay for foster families compared to families with natural children. Measured in miles per gallon, the foster families averaged 25% less miles per gallon of fuel and slightly less miles per pint of oil. The tyre ratings per car are an indication of higher cost in the replacement of tyres for two of the three larger cars. The larger cars, however. have a tendency towards better security ratings although safety ratings are similar to the smaller family car. Insurance is likely to be more expensive, between two and three 'car groups' more for drivers of the 6 seater cars shown below, than for a small car.

Table 3.18
Ratings of larger cars.

	Ford	Mazda	Volvo	Mitsubishi
MPG	36	26.6	24.8	29.2
MPP oil	3800	none	3200	1100
Tyres	175-70-R13	195-60-R15	185-70-R14	165-R13
Security rate	3	4	4	4
Safety rate	5	5	7	d.k.
Insurance group	4	6	7	6

The extra cost of motoring for a foster child is calculated as the difference between the motoring costs of a Ford Escort 1400cc and a Volvo Estate 1966cc selected as an example of a middle range modest 6 seater car. The Volvo has a high safety rating, is mid priced and the manufacture holds a larger share of the British market. The cost of an additional 25 miles travel is included each week for families providing for children of all ages. The differential motoring costs include comprehensive insurance which is based on a quote with maximum no claims bonus, inclusive of legal protection costs and a £50 excess fee. The lifetime of the 1986 Escort and Volvo car in 1991 is estimated as 7 years. The price of petrol is £1.96p per gallon for unleaded petrol and the price of oil £3.29 per litre at October 1991 prices. Tyres are replaced at a rate of two each year and for all vehicles a major and interim service is included every 12,000 miles. Any other costs included in the transport budget for a family car such as car wash, car parking and replacement of parts are assumed to be similar for both vehicles. Table 3.19 shows the extra motoring cost for foster families. The transport standard is £8.79 each week which includes the cost of an extra 25 miles motoring in a larger car and the differential costs between the purchasing and running of the Escort and Volvo (including the everyday differential cost of mileage by the whole family).

Table 3.19
The extra costs of motoring for foster families taking account of extra mileage, the differential cost between a Volvo and Escort, 1991 prices in £ per week.

Extra miles	25mls-Petrol	1.96	
	25mls-Oil	0.07	
	25mls-tyre	0.23	
	25mls-servicing	0.28	**2.54**
Larger car	Extra cost over seven years	3.57	
	Insurance differential	2.07	
	Family petrol differential	0.55	
	Family oil differential	0.02	
	Family tyre differential	0.02	
	Family service differential	0.02	**6.25**
Total			**8.79**

Additional public transport

Public transport journeys are increased by one extra return journey each week and the budget for a child under 11 years includes an accompanying parent. In addition, two extra taxi journeys are included each year for a child under 11 years and 4 extra for a child 11 to 16+ years. Table 3.20 shows that the extra cost for a foster parent of a child under 11 years is £2.29 and £1.78 for a child 11-16+ years of age.

Table 3.20
The extra cost of public transport by the age of the child.

	0-4 years	5-10 years	11-16+
Bus journeys	2.10	2.10	1.40
Taxi journeys	0.19	0.19	0.38
Total	2.29	2.29	1.78

Additional leisure goods

Wear and tear: Estimating the life time of an item is one way of establishing the level of wear and tear. The wear and tear of a natural child has already been estimated in Chapter 2 by reducing the lifetimes of communal goods in families without children by 2 years (approximately 18%), for example, a radio cassette is replaced every 12 years in a family without children and every 10 years when children are present. The lifetimes of goods in relation to a foster child are reduced by 50%. The leisure goods budget is shown in table 3.21.

Table 3.21
The leisure goods budget by the age of the child, £ per week.

	0-4 year	5-10 years	11-16+ years
TV,Video, Audio equip	0.94	0.61	1.25
Sports goods	0.03	0.08	0.04
Books, etc.	0.28	0.44	0.75
Toys, games, hobbies	1.56	1.12	0.55
Total	**2.81**	**2.25**	**2.58**

Gifts: A new budget for gifts to the foster child's natural parent is included in the extra costs of foster care.

Cut flowers £3.60, Houseplant £0.99, Chocolates £4.00 = each year £8.59 (0.17 week)

Other gifts such as spending by foster parents on the Christmas or birthday presents of their foster child is already accounted for in the FBU leisure standard.

Additional leisure activities

A leisure activities standard is estimated by upgrading the FBU budgets. Table 3.22 shows a child aged 0 to four years has one extra cinema trip and 12 extra swimming sessions each year. A school age child has two extra cinema visits and 12 extra swimming sessions, two extra football matches and an extra trip a year.

Table 3.22
The additional activities of foster children each year.

Activity	Unit cost £s	0-4 years	5-10 years	11-16+ years
Cinema	2.00	2.00	4.00	0.00
	Off peak £2.50			4.50
Swimming	0.66	7.92	7.92	7.92
Football	3.50	0.00	7.00	7.00
Trips	5.00 and 10.00	0.00	5.00	10.00
Total		**9.92**	**23.92**	**29.42**

Additional personal care

The method used to include extra personal care items in the foster child budget standard was to create a list of items foster parents claimed to buy more often, attaching lifetimes to items and deducing weekly costs from this. The results are shown in Table 3.23.

Table 3.23

Table 3.23
Extra personal care items for foster children.

Item	Cost	No.	£s year	0-4 year	5-10 years	11-16+ year
Jnr toothbrush	0.89	2	1.78	0.03	0.00	0.00
Adult toothbrush	0.89	2	1.78	0.00	0.03	0.03
Shampoo 300ml	2.59	2	5.18	0.10	0.10	0.10
Comb	0.35	2	0.70	0.01	0.01	0.01
Comb	0.65	2	1.30	0.03	0.03	0.03
Conditioner 350ml	2.19	2	4.38	0.08	0.08	0.08
Toothpaste 125 ml	1.29	2	2.58	0.05	0.05	0.05
First Aid Kit refill 5 items	6.02	1	6.02	0.12	0.12	0.12
Paracetamol 24	1.33	4	5.32	0.00	0.10	0.10
Jnr Calpol	1.27	2	2.54	0.05	0.00	0.00
Cough Mixture	2.34	2	4.68	0.00	0.00	0.09
Cotton Wool	0.75	4	3.00	0.06	0.00	0.00
Tissues	1.00	4	4.00	0.08	0.00	0.00
Gripe water	1.80	4	7.20	0.14	0.00	0.00
Infracol	2.00	4	8.00	0.15	0.00	0.00
Total				**0.90**	**0.52**	**0.61**

Additional pocket money

Pocket money is included as cost for a natural child in the family budget with little expectation that the child takes seriously budgeting for items previously bought by their parents.

Foster children are expected by the authorities to become independent of families sooner than natural children. At the age of 16 years old the foster child is given a substantial allowance for budgeting and the foster care allowance is in effect reduced pro rata. Foster parents, however, claimed that their spending on foster children did not reduce because the child had not enough skills to spend wisely.

An additional pocket money standard for older foster children is a notional estimate of spending on clothing, food, leisure activities, leisure goods, household goods, personal care and transport. The objective of such a standard is that the foster child budget includes a provision to fund the gradual and individual movement towards independence.

Table 3.24
A notional spending money estimate for older foster children in £ per week.

Budget component	Total average weekly cost
Food	1.08
Clothing	5.78
Household goods	0.16
Transport	1.40
Leisure goods	1.57
Leisure activities	2.23
Personal care	0.51
Total	**12.73**

Misdemeanours, cost implications for foster parents

There is no standard set in this budget for the loss to foster parents though their foster child's potential to commit misdemeanours. From the views of foster parents there is no consensus on the amounts of money involved.

Table 3.25 summaries the normative estimate of the extra costs of a foster child as perceived by foster parents.

Table 3.25
A normative estimate of the extra costs of a foster child by age,
£ per week 1991 prices.

	0-4 years	5-10 years	11-16+ years
Housing			
Internal maintenance	0.77	1.15	1.15
External maintenance	0.43	0.43	0.43
Security	0.48	0.48	0.48
Home extensions loan interest	1.90	2.36	2.36
Fuel			
Water heating	0.69	0.69	0.69
Space heating	0.38	0.38	0.41
Lights/appliances	0.40	0.40	0.60
Food	3.61	4.00	4.39
Replacement clothing	2.91	3.21	4.33
Nappy budget	6.99		
Household goods			
Wear and tear	4.09	4.09	4.17
Smoking damage	0.45	0.45	0.45
Access visit damage	0.63	0.63	0.63
Household Services			
Cleaning help	1.75	1.75	1.75
Postage	0.50	0.50	0.50
Telephone	0.77	0.77	1.16
Baby sitting	0.79	0.79	0.79
Motoring			
Extra journeys	2.54	2.54	2.54
Larger car	6.25	6.25	6.25
Public transport	2.29	2.29	1.78
Leisure goods			
Goods	2.81	2.25	2.58
Gifts to outside family	0.17	0.17	0.17
Leisure activities	0.19	0.46	0.57
Personal care	0.90	0.52	0.61
Pocket money			12.73
Total	**42.69**	**36.56**	**51.52**
Extra initial clothing - ad hoc	63.80	97.01	147.57

Calculation of average costs

The proportion of foster parents who perceive they have higher costs is applied to the foster child extra costs budget standard shown above. Every type of cost perceived by foster parents is consequently included in the extra cost according to the number of families who had experienced that cost. Table 3.26 shows the extra costs of fostering are considerably more for older children. A child aged 0 to four has additional costs of £26.40 each week, a child aged five to 10 years additional costs of £26.75, and a child of 11 to 16+ incur extra costs of £32.28 above those of a 'non foster' child in the family.

Table 3.26
The extra costs of a foster child by age,
£ per week 1991 prices.

	0-4 years	5-10 years	11-16+ years
Housing			
Internal maintenance	0.48	0.77	1.02
External maintenance	0.22	0.36	0.17
Security	0.06	0.24	0.11
Home extensions loan interest	0.48	1.18	0.92
Fuel	1.10	1.70	1.70
Food	2.92	3.64	3.12
Replacement clothing	1.46	1.77	3.42
Nappy budget	6.15	0	0
Household goods			
Wear and tear	2.05	4.09	3.00
Smoking damage	0	0.08	0.23
Access visit damage	0.08	0.53	0.11
Household Services			
Cleaning help	1.10	1.45	1.37
Postage	0	0	0.06
Telephone	0.77	0.77	0.96
Baby sitting	0.79	0.65	0.44
Motoring			
Extra journeys	1.91	2.54	2.39
Larger car	3.94	4.44	2.56
Public transport	0.87	0.66	0.73
Leisure goods			
Goods	1.57	1.64	1.29
Gifts to outside family	0.11	0.09	0.07
Leisure activities	0.02	0.08	0.06
Personal care	0.32	0.07	0.28
Pocket money	0	0	8.27
Total	**26.40**	**26.75**	**32.28**
Extra initial clothing - ad hoc	44.02	70.82	84.11

The total cost of a foster child

Table 3.27 shows the cost of a normal child and the extra costs which make up the aggregate direct costs of a foster child. At aged four, the cost of a foster child is £69.02, at the age of 10 the cost is £76.75 and at the age of 16 the child incurs expenses amounting to £95.87 each week. The extra costs of fostering represent 62%, 54% and 51% (for ages 4, 10, and 16 years respectively) more than the cost of a normal child. The basic foster care allowance would need to be increased by 71%, 56%, and 19% for ages 4, 10, and 16 years to meet the cost of foster children.

Table 3.27
Comparison of the total costs of a foster child and the foster child allowance by the age of the child,
October 1991 prices, £ per week.

	0-4 years	% cost	5-10 years	% cost	11-16+ years	% costs
Extra costs	26.40		26.75		32.28	
Normal costs *	42.62		50.00		63.59	
Total costs	69.02	62	76.75	54	95.87	51
Foster care allowance	40.28		49.24		80.63	
Shortfall	28.74	71	27.51	56	15.24	19

* Excluding child care costs

Equivalence scales

Table 3.28 shows the ratio of the cost of a natural child and that of a foster child at a similar modest-but-adequate living standard in respect of a couple household. Housing costs are included but child minding is excluded. The normal child scale is most similar to McClements and this has been discussed in Chapter 2. McClement's scale is also the scale used by the NFCA to assess the cost of a child in relation to average household expenditure. The ratio derived from this research indicates that a foster child scale will need to be significantly higher than McClement's scale to represent the real costs of a foster child.

Table 3.28
Implied equivalence scale for foster children.

1.00 = Couple household (FBU estimate £235.15) including housing

Normal child	Ratio	Foster Child	Ratio
Child age 4	0.18	Child age 4	0.29
Child age 10	0.21	Child age 10	0.33
Child age 16	0.27	Child age 16	0.41

130

Sensitivity of the study to other measures

Foster parents in this study were asked to comment on the situation of their present or last foster child and to make some judgement about how common these particular costs were in relation to other placements they had experienced. A majority of placements (59%) were claimed to be typical of others encountered. Under the age of 11 years, 67% of families believed the placement typical, 53% were reported typical in the 11 to 16+ age group. Atypical placements were found to have little in common. Some reasons for believing a placement atypical were as follows:

- unusually high number of access obligations to meet each week;
- a particularly ill foster child;
- a 'shared' placement - residential school and natural family;
- child's natural family particularly affluent resulting in shared financing of maintenance;
- child less, or more, destructive than usual.

Five foster parents answered that they did not know or had no means of comparison as this was their first experience.

A number of other measures of the cost of a foster child have been described at the beginning of the chapter. Table 3:29 shows, at 1992 prices, that the extra cost of a foster child is approximately £10 greater than Baldwin's extra cost of disability. Also, the Camden Association estimate including owner occupied housing is within £3 (approximately) of the estimate for an average child between 0 to 16 years. Moreover the NFCA who believe the extra cost of a foster child is approximately 50% more than the cost of a natural child is similar to the middle age range of this study. Allowing for inflation this study is validated by others who use different methods.

Table 3.29
Sensitivity of the cost of a foster child to other estimates, prices held constant 1992. Average child.

Study	Method	Amount
Extra Cost		
Baldwin (1985)	Expenditure survey disability	18.33
Oldfield (1992)	Normative	28.48
Oldfield (1992)	% of normal child	54%
NFCA (1988)	% of normal child	50%
Full Cost		
Camden Ass (1987)	Expenditure survey	77.15
Oldfield (1992)	Normative	80.55

Conclusion

This chapter has shown that foster children do incur substantially higher direct costs than normal children of a similar age and sex. The extra costs are greatest for a child 11 to 16+ (£32.28), and similar for children under the age of 11 years (approximately £26.50) each week. The greatest shortfall between the foster care allowance and estimated costs of a foster child is in younger children. To reimburse the direct cost of foster children the foster care allowance would need to be increased by 71%, 56%, and 19% for children aged 4, 10, and 16 years respectively in order to meet the adequacy criteria.

Foster parents proved to be perceptive about costs and able to make complex comparisons when asked. To what extent this study highlights a measure of local problems, however, is not possible to say and how typical the sample of foster families was compared with those found elsewhere is unknown.

4 The indirect costs of fostering

Introduction

This chapter explores the indirect costs to the foster parent of fostering a child. No part of the basic foster care allowance is designated to meet indirect costs, therefore, this chapter poses the question: what would be the level of costs that might be reimbursed if indirect costs were included?

The indirect costs for foster parents of a foster child includes both financial and non-financial costs. Although not explored in this study, the non financial indirect costs of child rearing suggested by Espenshade (1977) for natural child-parent relationships might be similar in foster child-parent relationships, for example, the emotional and psychological burden of parents caring for children in terms of feelings of responsibility, anxiety about the child's health and future welfare, and child development. Foster parents might also claim additional stress unique to the fostering situation caused by their often ambiguous working relationship with natural parents, the effect of foster caring on the rest of the family and specific foster care problems (Orlin 1977, Southon 1986, George 1970. Berridge et al 1987 and others).

The financial indirect costs of rearing non-foster children are hard to define. A contemporary concept might include earnings foregone, the value of the service of child rearing and parents' leisure activities foregone. It is usually the mother, rather than the father, who bears this burden. Children tend to require most attention in their early years. There are economies of scale for families caring for more than one child, that is; caring for two children does not take twice the amount of time spent caring for one child. Furthermore the service to children by the mother is only marginally reduced if she starts paid employment. (Piachaud 1984, Henley 1991 to 1992, Bittman 1991, Walker and Wood 1967, Szalai 1972 et al). Gershuny (1983) addressed the issue of time scarcity for mothers with children. Time scarcity arises when the accumulation of hours spent in different activities equates to more than the 24 hours in a day. Gershuny suggests time given to employment, without decreasing the value of time lost to other activities in a 24 hour day, may be achieved, in some cases, by balancing the purchasing

133

of goods and services from the formal economy with household production: buying in help to do the housework, or buying convenience foods rather than spending time preparing dishes or doing the ironing, for example. Chapter 3 has already explored some costs relating to the provision of more goods and services from the formal economy instead of from home production as a result of time scarcity, for example, buying convenience foods, and using a car rather than public transport. Earnings foregone encapsulates a range of factors resulting from the loss or reduced participation of mothers in the labour force. Factors such as the loss of earnings from time out of employment, lost promotions, downward mobility in occupational status, shorter working hours, lost financial benefits, such as reduced pension rights, reduced eligibility for paid leave and sick pay. This has been well documented by Joshi (1984, 1987, 1992), Ginn and Arber (1992), Humphries et al (1991), Martin (1986) and others. The notion of the indirect cost of leisure foregone for mothers and carers is drawn from time budget studies such as Henley (1991-2), Robinson (1987), Humphries et al (1991), Nissel & Bonnerjea (1982), who suggest a depletion in the carer's free time rather than in time spent in employment.

The additional indirect costs incurred by a foster mother as opposed to a non-foster mother may arise for a number of reasons, assuming the foster child is a younger member of a family and not an only child. The mother may delay her return to employment or work less hours than she would otherwise do because the presence of foster children has increased the size or age range of her family. Furthermore, as discussed in Chapter 1, she may consider fostering an altruistic activity legitimating the foregoing of her leisure time. If foster parents were to be paid for their additional time spent in caring for a foster child the first step would be to define the amount of time spent in fostering tasks which are outside those normally expected in child rearing. The second step would be to attach a monetary value to the time spent in caring for an extra child in the household who has additional needs associated with fostering.

Time spent on fostering tasks

No previous studies have attempted to measure the time spent on fostering tasks by foster parents. Culley's American study in 1975, however, suggests the value of the time spent rearing a foster child was the difference between time spent in household tasks for a couple without a child and the time spent in household and child care tasks for a foster family. To estimate time spent by non-foster families in child care tasks, Culley utilized Walker and Wood's (1967-68) quantitative time study of households in New York which categorised time spent in the following activities:
- Food related activities
- House care related activities
- Care of clothing related activities
- Marketing and management related activities
- Family care related activities.

134

Walker and Wood's study indicated that family size was the most influential factor in estimates of time spent in caring for children. The time spent in tasks caring for non-foster children under school age was greater for an only child than the average time in a family with more than one child. By asking the following question of fostering agencies, Culley suggested the normal child time could be weighted to give an estimate of the cost in time to parents of fostering a child either as a first or subsequent child in the household:

> Does the change in time family members devote to households and child care activities with the addition of a natural child to the family differ significantly from the time they would spend on such activities with the addition of a foster child of the same age and sex to the family? (Culley 1975 5-80)

As Culley's contribution to estimating fostering costs was a workbook for agencies, the second part of the calculation was not tested empirically.

Attempts to measure the time spent in non-foster child rearing, however, have been made. The most common method of estimating the time spent on different activities in a day is by averages of activities. Traditionally studies took account of a single time attribute of human activities. Proponents of time budgets, however, believe traditional time data lacks the necessary depth of analysis: the frequency of an activity and its duration and who did it was just as important as the average time taken on a specified activity in 24 hours. To produce time budgets in which the total duration is 24 hours, assumptions are made about which activities are counted when several (secondary) activities are carried out simultaneously. Some activities such as employment or eating, represent the structure for the day. This brings about the notion of time order reporting of first and secondary activities through 24 hour diaries. Activities are checked at close intervals throughout. Dimensions other than the temporal ones mentioned are also important, such as, contextual dimensions of spatial or locational aspects of everyday activities.

Another method is to use depth interviews, diaries and recall. Piachaud (1984) focused his study exclusively on the time spent by parents on child caring tasks in 55 families with a pre-school child. Although enquiry was also made about spells of time free of all child care and the effort of the caring activity. The aim of the study was to provide some indication of the burden of parental child care in addition to how much time was spent on caring. Establishing the period of time spent in a child caring activity was the result of a discussion between respondent and interviewer which attempted to divide the activity into smaller segments in order to construct the amount of time taken to complete it from the bottom up.

A major problem of previous studies is that few, with the exception of Piachaud, have focused on time spent on child care. The primary focus of the survey may be leisure (Henley 1992) or employment (Gershuny 1979, Bittman 1991), and the age of the children and socio-economic structure of the family is ignored. Child care is complex, the tasks often spontaneous, unnoticed among other less common tasks and reported with cultural, social and personal bias. Several studies of the diary approach have established the validity and reliability of the time budget method (Gershuny 1979) yet time diaries give incoherent and inconsistent estimates of time spent by parents on child care activities. Table 4.1 gives examples to emphasise this point. Where studies have focused on parental time spent in child rearing there is a tendency to explore time spent in the caring of pre-school children. In comparison, little importance has been attached to a holistic view of child rearing to adulthood. Pre-school children use between 21 and 56 hours of parental time each week. The extra time spent on an additional child in a household with more than one child is small, between 6 and 14 hours each week, because of economies of scale.

Table 4.1
Parental time spent on child care in hours each week.

Study		Focus of study	Age > 5	Age 6-16	All age	2nd child
Wood & Walker USA*	1975	Household	21.0	-	-	9.1
Szalai Europe	1972	Household	56.0	-	-	14.0
Bittman Australia	1991	Employment	33.4	16-10#	-	5.7
Henley Centre UK	1992	Leisure	-	-	34.8	-
Piachaud UK	1984	Child care	49.4	-	-	-

* Culley
# time decreasing as child's age increases towards independence

Research design

This study is designed to explore what constitutes the difference in parental child care time between a foster child and a natural child in the same household. The objectives were to:
- Identify and describe the activities and tasks which constitute the difference in time.
- Estimate a time budget for the extra tasks.

The method used was semi-structured interviews with 32 foster families who were asked to describe why extra time was needed to care for the foster child and to estimate this amount of time through a reactive process between interviewer and interviewee. The unit of analysis was the child regardless of the number of placements, and whether the time was given directly to the child or indirectly in support of the placement. The framework for discussion was set by reference to the present or last foster child. Information was collected on 47 foster children and the recorded interviews lasted approximately 30 minutes. The questions were set in the following context:

- Personal care
- General household care
- Travel
- Therapeutic care
- Administration
- Emotional care.

The unit of analysis was time spent over a one week period. Information was collected per weekday and weekend day. Less frequent and one off activities were counted over a period of a year and averaged to give a weekly estimate. Personal care, general household care, travel, therapeutic care and administrative were all counted as primary time. Emotional care was time spent counselling foster children, often done at the same time as primary tasks and therefore, included as secondary time.

The cases were sorted into three age groups (0 to four years, five to 10 years and 11 to 16+ years). Aggregates for each age group and average time spent per case were estimated. For each age group in each category two further calculations were made. First the range of estimates was identified and then the proportion of interviewees in each age group who believed they spent no more time than they would expect for a normal child was estimated.

Methodological issues

The reliability of recalling time periods in activities for the 'last' foster child is inevitably less reliable than recalling time spent in caring for the 'present' child. Most parents kept diaries of events and these improved accuracy of recall.

In caring for foster children or natural children, some of the time spent in child rearing is by other household members, often there was no differentiation made between which time belonged to whom. Also families occasionally do tasks together, however, there is no doubt that most of the time recalled is that spent by the foster or natural mother. Generally all time reported is analysed in terms of the mother's time with no separate analysis of time spent by the father.

In this survey the difference in time spent in caring for a foster child and caring for a non-foster child is measured. Unfortunately, the results do not measure the quality or quantity of time given to foster care (only the extra effort made by the average foster parent to spend more time with foster children than they would with their own child). Some parents give a large amount of time to children per se so the difference in the extra time given to foster children may be marginal. A parent with a natural child who has special needs, for example, or a parent who gives high priority to play sessions to all children may give a high input of time from which all children in the household will benefit. Consequently, the amount of extra time the foster child receives will give no indication of the amount of time that the foster parent actually spent, and the extra time reported will give no indication of the quality of placement.

Finally, it is inevitable in studies of time that there will be some double counting. No account has been taken of foster parents doing other tasks in the household whilst caring out essential foster child tasks. Some attempt is made to distinguish between essential and secondary 'extra' time by defining for foster parents 'emotional care' as secondary time. Essential time is that time spent primarily with a particular foster child. Nevertheless, some emotional time will inevitably be primary time in instances where the foster parent tackles some situations on a one to one basis.

Foster parent perceptions

Additional time spent in personal care

Foster parents reported extra tasks associated with the personal caring of the foster child. These tasks were in addition to those performed in caring for normal children. Largely the tasks were a result of:
- the change in lifestyle for the foster child,
- life skills training by foster parents and
- needs which arose through psychological and physical disorders such as learning difficulties, poor behaviour and physical disabilities.

Changes in lifestyle. The impact of a change in lifestyle mostly depends on the closeness of the matching of the placement family with the foster child's natural environment. Sometimes the difference is not great but the child still has an adjustment to make in taste and preference to fit in with the placement lifestyle. Extra tasks associated with a change in lifestyle were said to diminish over a long term placement:

> With my own I know what they like, it takes much longer with foster children.

> Every meal time I have to supervise the foster children for lots of reasons. I am worried that my own children would pick up bad habits - don't want my own starting to use a fork as a shovel or eating with their fingers...I also have to act as a referee... this is every evening meal and extra at weekends...

In some families foster children are expected to 'fit in'. That is, the amount of extra time is all relevant to the attitude and standards of the foster family. For example:

> No extra time really, at meal times we just let her get on with it, don't think it makes much difference. Its not our policy to prepare or cook differently for her even if she doesn't like what we are having. She does make more mess at meal-times but it takes no more time to mop

up 6 baked beans than a handful... and you can gather we don't like housework, the foster child is just as untidy as my own kids are. The laundry is just the same heap as my own children I suppose because they are not much older...

Some foster families accommodate foster children by adjusting their own lifestyle to meet the foster child's expectations.

> We do packed lunches for the foster children I have never done this for my own children.

> I always have to make his supper whereas my own children always made their own from a very young age.

Life skills training. Many parents said that training the children in life skills was of paramount importance in the role of foster parent. Some foster children would need a similar amount of input to the foster parent's own children, others a great deal more. In some cases the foster children are described as 'slow learners', 'immature' or 'retarded in their early development':

> She does have extra supervision than mine would have needed at her age in personal hygiene. When she arrived at 5 years of age we had to start from scratch, how to wash, clean teeth, brush hair everything.

> Most of the time I would sit with him one to one on my own, I found this best so that I could try and teach him to eat in an acceptable way. This would take 30 minutes one or two times a day.

> Extra time is spent because this child is not able to do things for himself at an age when you know your own were able. For example I wouldn't normally have to supervise a 13 year old boy when bathing.

Some children find learning difficult because the change in standards is rapid. For example:

> They don't like it so I have to stand over them when they wash or clean their teeth, and make sure they wash their hands after going to the toilet.

> I don't tell her how much money the authorities will allow me to spend which is quite generous because she is pregnant. But we go

139

from shop to shop comparing prices and deciding what she needs and what can be bought later.

Psychological and physical need. There are many different psychological and physical disorders found in foster children which manifest in poor behaviour and 'special needs'. Few foster parents had 'natural' children who displayed similar needs:

> I supervise baths and wash hair twice a week, checking her all the time, teaching her all the time, especially need to take care with cleanliness during menstruation times. The other foster child is similar to my own. (Down's Syndrome Child)

> I have to supervise him dressing, otherwise he just sits on the bed and does nothing. It takes 40 minutes in all to persuade him to dress for school.

> He gives me orders in a very aggressive adult male manner - 'fetch me this woman'. Now we have got as far as persuading him to get his own snacks between meals - its taken a long time but we are proud of that achievement.

> He has a fetish for water, loves this, I can hear him running backwards and forwards playing with a cup pouring it down the toilet, bath or basin. Plays with the toilet brush, has extra time in the bathroom and wastes hot water. I have to listen and wait then go and persuade him to come out.

> Used to have to spend a much longer time (at meal times and) it caused the foster father to have indigestion problems, initially it was an on-going situation every meal-time. Now we spend about 10 minutes extra (at meal times) but initially it was double the length of the meal, his behaviour was so bad, sometimes he would burst out into a rousing song and it would take 10 minutes to calm him down.

Sometimes the reasons for additional time spent on tasks performed by foster parents are subtle, for example, building relationships, building confidence and status.

> He likes to be supervised he doesn't have to be. I help him with his hair other 12 year olds could do this themselves.

> Spend more time once every so often when we 'clothes' shop, he is so disadvantaged because he is so small and I have to be careful he doesn't lose his confidence.

Other children exhibited serious displays of unreasonable behaviour which included testing the limits of the foster parent's patience and endurance. These children were not always defined by parents as having 'special needs'.

> They need continuous supervision and are very demanding. They cause a lot of damage even though they are now 16 and 18 years they have special needs. I have to be here the whole time they are in the house they can't be left ever on their own.

Time spent by foster parents in the personal care of foster children emerged as the extra time spent at meal-times in supervision not extended to the rest of the household, the preparation of special or additional foods not provided for others in the family, personal hygiene care at an age or degree that other children do not need, and extra time in combining shopping and personal development of the child. Table 4.2 shows that the average extra time each week in personal care of the foster child is 2.6 hours for a child aged 0 to four years, and 2.9 hours for a child of five to 16+ years. The estimates varied within a range of none to 10 hours. Most foster mothers of teenagers experienced extra personal care time. Only about two thirds of foster parents caring for children under 11 years claimed they spent more time than they would otherwise expect in non-fostering situations.

Table 4.2

The average time spent by foster parents in the extra personal care of foster children by the age of the child per week in minutes.

	n=14 *0-4*	*n=9* *5-10*	*n=24* *11-16+*
Extra time spent supervising and preparation of meals, special meals, extra tasks, hygiene supervision, shopping	155	175	174
% foster parents reporting no extra time	36%	33%	8%
Range of estimates	0-630	0-525	0-545
Average total hours each week	2.6	2.9	2.9

Additional time spent in general household chores

Many foster parents claim they spent more time on general household chores than they would expect if the foster child was their own child. Four reasons were given:
- the medical conditions of foster children,
- teaching foster children housekeeping skills,
- the behaviour of some foster children and
- the increased flow of visitors in relation to foster children.

Medical conditions of some foster children. Almost one in three school age foster children suffered problems with incontinence. There were instances of other disturbed behaviour, such as head banging, rocking, picking at fabrics, wild play and destructiveness. Allergies and chest conditions were also mentioned by a number of foster parents. The results were extra chores such as heavy and light cleaning, repairing and laundering.

> He has an allergy to dust so I change his bed more often, dust daily, have to thoroughly clean his bedroom like a spring clean each week otherwise he starts to wheeze although he is not a bad asthmatic.

Teaching independent living skills. This is crucial for teenage children who were expected to become self reliant at an earlier age than other children. Some foster parents stressed teaching skills and counselling the child as the primary task rather than as a means of completing chores.

> I try to get them to clean up themselves but its hard work and frustrating and takes more time.

> Spend time showing her how to be independent, cooking, caring, washing, because of the need to get her to that stage sooner than you need to with your own.

> We have massive arguments about whether he should wash up. He is very lazy he won't even clear his plate away or anything like that unless we remind him he is responsible. It takes us 10 minutes of standing over him before he does anything - he has so many problems it goes on and on. Its not indulgence on my part that he does not do things but he doesn't respond as most children will - he's ruthless.

> I spend more time doing his laundry about one hour a week longer. Our own children did this for themselves at his age, however the foster child now does his own ironing.

Destructive behaviour. Boisterous play, wilful damage, carelessness and mischievousness were the reasons given for extra time spent in household chores: for example, continuous clearing up, breakages, re-making beds used as trampolines, putting clothes back in drawers, extra laundry and repairs.

One foster parent said she went through periods of compromising over the child's poor behaviour, protecting the child from external criticism and influences which could undo previous hard work, for example:

142

Spend more time doing everything for him, he is not allowed to go to school with dirty football boots and as he won't clean them I have to - its a sort of covering for him. He doesn't think about other people, selfish, we have the pretence of living a normal life, but we don't really he is being propped up much more so than other children need. So does take an enormous amount of time - can't explain it. He is beginning to share more responsibility in the family now. Hard battle to get him to dry a few pots. When I ask why I have it to do and not him he says 'because your a woman'. We understand his background and the effect his father's behaviour has had on him. He was very badly damaged and it's taking a lot of undoing.

In one household the foster father acknowledged the time and effort of the foster mother in coping efficiently with so many extra tasks:

I find it impossible to do what she does because I am not used to doing it but my wife can be hoovering, washing, cooking a meal and goodness knows what else all in one go whereas I have to do one job at a time. If she goes anywhere and I have to run the house I cannot get through what she does in a day.

The increased flow of visitors, children and adults is the cause of some extra work for foster parents. In particular, the siblings of foster children, especially young children, take their toll on household furniture and fittings. A flow of social worker visits and regular meetings frequently takes place at the foster parents home and some time is spent before and after the event putting the house back in order:

I spend more time cleaning up in general because of the fostering circumstances such as visits from social workers. I just feel more obliged to clean up than if we weren't fostering - we can get visitors anytime and sometimes without warning so I like to be prepared. The child is quite tidy in himself. About 3 hours more each week I would say.

Table 4.3 shows the extra time spent by foster families in extra general household chores. An average family providing for children aged 11 to 16+ incurs almost 3 hours extra time in general household chores each week. Families providing for children under 11 years of age spend under two hours extra each week. The range of estimates was wide across the sample from nothing to five or eight hours each week. Approximately 22% of families of children under 11 years reported no extra chores, whereas all those fostering teenagers reported some additional time within the range of half to eight hours each week.

Table 4.3

The average time spent by foster parents in the extra general household care of foster children by the age of the child per week in minutes.

Task	$n=14$ 0-4	$n=9$ 5-10	$n=24$ 11-16+
Extra time spent clearing up, repairing, laundry	107	111	175
% foster parents reporting no extra time	21%	22%	0%
Range of estimates	0-489	0-309	30-495
Average total time in hours each week	1.8	1.9	2.9

Additional time spent in travelling

Most foster parents used the family car for fostering business, rarely did they resort to public transport. Reasons for journeys generally fell into two areas:
- official meetings including access and statutory obligations and
- health and leisure travel.

Official commitments. Access visits take place in a variety of places, for example, the foster parents home, the family centre or the home of the extended natural family. The onus of meeting the child's access demands falls on the social services who arrange where and when they take place and whether they need to be supervised. At times the social worker will arrange to collect the child from the placement household, at other times the foster parents act as chauffeur. The distance travelled and the time spent in travelling may be substantial as one foster parent expressed:

> The contact visit with the foster child's parents is in Leeds each Saturday, this takes 4 hours time from start to finish.

Meetings such as reviews and planning meetings are regular events in the foster child's calendar, other meetings such as panel meetings are rare. Meetings are held outside the foster family home for many reasons: the wish of the natural parents or the foster family, or the desire by social services to find neutral ground. Support meetings for foster families are held every four or six weeks in addition to a number of training days each year. The distance from each meeting point may be significant for some foster families resulting in very individual travelling times:

> There are special activities I take him to, and then I have to travel some distance for support meetings - Harrogate, Ripon, and York is

2 hours return drive. That's why I try and arrange other meetings such as planning meetings and access here at the farm.

Health and leisure travel. Travel to medical appointments, GPs, hospitals and clinics tends to occur more regularly than these parents experienced with normal children. Statutory health checks are carried out at the beginning of each placement and annually throughout the placement. Foster parents also tend to visit the GP or call at the hospital sooner compared with a normal child should a problem arise.

Other travel may include leisure activities which are often ad hoc or annual events which are offered to the foster child and not to other members of the placement household such as Christmas parties, trips to the seaside and picnics.

Table 4.4 shows the average time spent by foster parents transporting their present or last foster child each week. The time spent in hours travelling each week is greatest for children of 11 to 16+, an average of one and a half hours. The 0 to four years age group tend to spend the lowest average time in travelling approximately one hour a week. This reflects the greater probability of home meetings and access visits (21% report no extra travel time at all). Estimates of the range of travel times in the younger age bands are similar whereas foster parents of teenage children report between nothing, in 8% of cases, to five hours more than normal each week.

Table 4.4

The average time spent by foster parents in the extra travel needs of foster children by the age of the child each week in minutes.

	n=14 0-4	n=9 5-10	n=24 11-16+
Travel to meetings, reviews etc, access, therapy, school events, hospital	61	83	88
% foster parents reporting no extra travel time	21%	0%	8%
Range of estimates	0-190	3-184	0-302
Average total hours each week	1.0	1.4	1.5

Additional time spent in therapeutic activity

The time spent in therapeutic activities varied a great deal between households. The variation was due to the individual and special needs of foster children and the attitude of their foster parents to home teaching. Tasks included helping with school and home work, playing educational games and therapeutic play, often under the instruction of an educationalist, speech or play therapist:

> Homework is a nightmare. Can sit over his maths for an hour. Very bright but presentation of his work is appalling. We know he is intelligent he has a terrific facility for number work but gets worked up when presented with tasks at school. He has a support teacher to help him at school. We have to supervise him the whole time, it

145

takes two hours and then the evenings gone, but we can't give up when we know we are making progress.

No more time than my own as my own child has special needs.

I spend a lot of time about an hour each day in which I do an activity with him. Sometimes we go to the pictures, swimming or bowling. This is more time than I spent with my own daughter.

Initially we did spend a lot of time with her, the whole family encouraged her to play because she found it difficult, she still can't play apart from drawing and doing a jigsaw she cannot play by herself. She can't watch half an hour of children's programs unless she is nursed. My own children at this age would watch one and a half hours of TV and be engrossed. If I put a children's film on, one she has chosen for herself, within 10 minutes she is behind me in the kitchen - whether this is because of her previous home circumstances or the type of child she is I don't know. Personal individual time I would say she needs a good hour every day, two hours at weekend and provided I can give her this she is no problem.

Table 4.5 shows foster parents caring for teenage children spent an average of three hours a week on therapeutic activities. The amount of time spent is also substantial for younger children, an average of two and a half hours for a child aged five to 10 years and two hours each week for a child aged 0 to four years. The range of estimates indicates, however, that some parents have reported extremely high inputs of time compared to others, especially in the case of teenagers. The number of parents reporting no extra time spent is substantial, between one third and over one half of all foster parents.

Table 4.5
The average time spent by foster parents in the extra therapeutic needs of foster children by the age of the child per week in minutes.

Task	n=14 0-4	n=9 5-10	n=24 11-16+
Educational time, school work, play therapy, reading	128	152	190
% of foster parents reporting no extra time	43%	33%	58%
Range of estimates	0-420	0-388	0-960
Average total time in hours each week	2.1	2.5	3.2

Time spent by foster parents on the administration of the foster placement makes up the largest proportion of extra time. The time spent, unique to the fostering situation, is broadly classified as:

- meetings and
- paperwork,

with time taken up in social worker or link worker assessments, supervising some access visits, communications, writing diaries, reports and contributing to 'life-books'.

Meetings. The foster child has a program of statutory and formal meetings as part of the inspection, monitoring and planning of the placement. In general, foster parents said planning meetings and reviews were held at the start and finish of the placement, six monthly during the placement and lasted from 1½ to 2 hours. Additionally, there were home visits by the foster child's social worker. The frequency varied between children but some respondents reported two-weekly visits, 6-weekly visits or 3-monthly visits. Occasionally these visits were substituted in stable or long term placements by telephone calls. In multi-child placements, especially when the children were non-siblings, each child had a separate social worker and programme of meetings and visits.

The monitoring of the foster parent was a separate system of usually six-monthly meetings with a personal link worker allocated by the social services department. Difficult placements were monitored more often and disruption of a placement was followed by a re-assessment of the needs of all parties concerned. Other meetings which were less regular included adoption panel meetings, foster family recruitment panels and support meetings. Support group meetings were held four or six-weekly and lasted about two hours. The frequency of meetings depended to some extent on the particular location of the foster home. Training days tended to be held at venues which covered more than one area, usually in York, about four times a year for full or half days. Inevitably, some foster parents became further involved in the support of their colleagues by taking on voluntary official positions in the structure of the support organisation. The time spent in such cases was two or three times that of other members and often included large amounts of time in telephone counselling.

Access visits were not always a source of foster parent time spent. Many were unsupervised, especially for older children. Some difficult access visits were held at a family centre and the foster parent's task was to prepare the child for the visit and await the child's return. For a small number of foster parents, however, facilitating access took a great deal of time. Sometimes the foster parent took on the role of supervisor. At other times the time given involved travelling with the child to a place of access which resulted in waiting around or making twice the number of journeys. One family reported daily access obligations which accumulated to about 10 hours a week.

Paperwork. Diaries and other paperwork were also an important feature of fostering administration. A daily diary was kept by most foster parents to monitor the child's behaviour and events. Instances of writing diaries and reports, for example, to adoption panels or case conferences were reported. The time taken was highly individual but 10 minutes was usual for diary entries whereas reports could take several evenings.

The nature of the type of tasks involved in the administration of a fostering placement from the perspective of the foster parent was expressed in vivid terms by the following foster parents:

> I do daily diaries and probably once a week look at a life book or do some other paper work. My telephone calls take a lot of time because I give support to other foster carers as well as contact with social workers.

> I spend about two hours a week doing something about him, diaries, reports and I often chat about him on the phone. When he rings his mother I have to stand with him because he needs prompting and then I have to also ring his mother to make arrangements but those are short calls.

> Yes a lot of administrative time, we each spend 2 evenings each every 3 or 6 months, and then pool ideas. Keep an enormous file on him, initially everyday writing notes and a lot of letters, keep a diary and a life story book with photos, up dates, old birthday cards etc., recorded language and days he didn't swear for psychiatric treatment. We have been asked to do an evening with support groups, and Banardos' help us a lot - but its quite involved when you take a child through Banardos not only keeping up with their requirements but also North Yorkshire requirements. We do reports for a quarterly journal.

> Really none, at one time a new social worker decided to do a life book but the child found it so upsetting I asked them to stop. We have never had social work support and few phone calls, not been involved in meetings - hospitals are the only thing which may fit in here and a medical with the GP every year.

> A lot of paperwork, especially if reviews or adoptions are coming up, reports, weekly play sheet for one child, and I do a diary of events each night.

> I spent a lot of time on the telephone, much more than one call a day, and sometimes they were lengthy I would say about one and half hours a day. This particular child played truant. Normally I would get a call each day from the social worker to see if she had left home

to go to school. Then the social worker would be in touch with school and ring me back to say she wasn't in school, then I would get a call from the headmaster or form teacher, later we would get a call from the policeman or someone else because she would give our name, eventually it got too much so I would ring Social Services to say where she was and let them deal with it.

With a young child often need to be in touch with the social worker and they are difficult to get hold of. You end up leaving messages to ring back and then hang around waiting for a return call. If its important you keep trying. For example left a message that I needed help with a problem at 8.30 am, it wasn't until 5.30 p.m. that I actually got the problem sorted out which involved the hospital. I couldn't be away from the phone all day - things like that are really annoying.

Table 4.6 shows that foster parents providing for children in the youngest age group of 0 to four years invest the greatest time in administrating the placement, although for all ages the amount of time spent was substantial. A child aged 0 to four took up more than five and a half hours of foster parents time in administration of the placement each week; a child aged five to 10 took up almost five hours of foster parents' time and for children aged 11 to 16+ the amount of time was five hours each week. The range of estimates shows the differences in foster parent's perceptions of time spent but also that all foster families incur administrative costs to some degree regardless of age of foster child or any other factor.

Table 4.6
The average time spent by foster parents in the administration of foster children by the age of the child per week in minutes.

Tasks	n=14 0-4	n=9 5-10	n=24 11-16+
Reports, diaries, life-book, time in meetings, reviews etc., social worker/ link worker, telephone time	341	287	244
% foster parents reporting no extra costs	0%	0%	0%
Range of estimates	132-709	44-688	17-1025
Average total time in hours	5.7	4.8	4.1

Additional time spent in the emotional support of foster children

How ever good the fostering experience, there were problems to overcome, emotional adjustments to make and relationships to develop.   In general foster children live traumatic lives. The processes of the care system exposes and evaluates all the normally private spheres of the child's family life. Decisions are usually made on behalf of the child by professionals (strangers) about where he/she will live, often away from the community and the family the child knows and understands. The results even in the best cases of regular contact with the natural family can be difficult in terms of psychological adjustment.

The foster child inevitably turns to the foster parent for the majority of its emotional support:

> Probably once a month I get complaints about the child which can take sometime to sort out. Apologising, replacing things, seeing people - you see he is very disruptive and an anti-social child.

> Sometimes he has nightmares and then it takes me three hours to settle him.

> At bedtime especially, about 2 hours a day I would say, he used to sit on the stairs and cry instead of sleeping. He still calls out in his sleep but we tend not to hear him as much now.

> Sometimes the children quite young are distressed when they have had an access visit. Mostly access visits you have to supervise, with this last one I haven't had to sit in all the time can be in and out. You spend time with the parents trying to help them and teach them how to look after children. Sometimes the access is arranged but the parent doesn't turn up. If the child is going for adoption several afternoons spent with potential adoptee.

> We talk everything through although I have to wait for the opportunity. Just lately its been more intensive as he has been going home and we have to talk through the happenings and how he can cope with them - what his reactions are and what they should be. He follows me round the house, always with me in the kitchen and when I go into my bedroom he waits outside the door for me to come out. It can be 2-3 hours a day at weekends or holidays.

Some foster children cope by demanding endless foster parent time, some are incessant talkers, others are opportunist in their approach. It is usual for the child to demand and the foster parents to respond to the child's emotional needs:

> She is now more confident but I am available at any time of the day she decides she wants to talk usually when there is a problem. I try other times but always I am speaking to the back of her head, most frustrating... I speak to her the whole time and receive nothing back at all - very hard. I try to explain to the Social Worker but she just doesn't accept there is a problem, just changes the topic. The Social Worker was here for 3 hours and all she spoke about was her own family, the cat, and the garden. Mind you the age of the social worker makes a difference the older ones are best.

> One hour in the morning, and five in the evening every day, we talk the whole time usually about the child's problems and what the future holds and sometimes his parents. Sometimes I have to sit with the child until he falls asleep.

The pressure on the foster parent to be always available places a strain on the family relations and, at times leads to disruption of the placement:

> First thing on a morning, she gets up at 7.00 with me and during the next half hour she talks through her worries and anxieties.

> I spend most of the time while they are in the house dealing with them in ways I wouldn't have to do with my own children. For example, if I was doing something else, watching TV - I would ask my own children to let me watch the TV, leave me alone and I'll talk later. But with a foster child always have to stop and pay attention to their comments, its our role to encourage conversation and discourse. Never know when the child is going to give you information you need or just wants to involve you in conversation or just wants attention. This is the largest time drain - that and meetings.

> 24 hours a day, I can assure you that is 24 hours a day if anyone tells you different that is a lie - that is 24 hours a day. Even through the night, one or another has nightmares or is just pacing around. Most counselling is in the evening, after tea time during early evening. Getting them to go to bed is awful and then we can't wind down. I spend a lot longer with one child on a stress level - sometimes he takes it out on the other children, he can start on a morning until early the following morning. Our own children do suffer because

151

you are obliged to give time to the foster child. You need a degree in psychology, I have had a child 8 hours in the hall-way just biting and kicking - the other children do help at these time. Never relax, constantly thinking about what the children are doing and thinking. (Foster parents with three teenage foster children)

How much time depends on the age of the child, if the child is at school then its more intensive when it comes home. Different things show at different times and its a case of dealing with it at the time. Spend a lot of time preparing the child for adoption, we still have contact with some parents who have adopted our foster children. This is valuable for the child because they realise although they have moved on they have not cut the ties of their former life. Some parents however won't keep the ties, prepared to say that it is finished. One couple said these children's lives will not start until we get them home - not happy at all about this.

Hardest thing is giving time to everyone, foster children and own children, but the foster child needed a lot of extra time initially but he was so independent he couldn't accept it. Now he is learning to be cared for so at this point he is getting a large share.

Emotional caring is usually more intensive in the early weeks and months of the placement. Some fears do, however, remain throughout as recalled by these foster parents:

She is just like my own child now, although she is still worried that they (her and her brother) might be taken away and we talk that through. The child can't wait to be 18 and rid of the threat even though I reassure her, even when she knew you were coming she said can't they leave us alone. Initially when there were access visits they were traumatic and sometimes the parents would not turn up so it caused a great deal of anxiety.

I don't really know how much time I spend talking to him not as much as I did when he first arrived, he doesn't need a lot of reassurance now.

Time spent in emotional counselling by foster parents appears often to be time already being used for other essential tasks. Sometimes it helps the child to talk when attention is on another task, at other times it is a coping mechanism used by foster parents to ameliorate the pressure and intensity of the task:

152

Well, listening continuously to them, when you are alone with her, have to move away sometimes, perhaps spend an hour a day. If you are on your own she will off load her problems, I do other things while she is talking.

The foster parent's perceptions of the amount of time spent in boosting the child's confidence, befriending and counselling the child is substantial. This time is largely already spent in other essential activities, however, and therefore, categorised as secondary time. Table 4.7 shows that time spent in this activity increases with the age of the child. For all children this is substantial, approximately eight and a half hours for children 0 to four years, 14 hours for children aged five to 10, and 19 hours for children aged 11 to 16+ each week. The range of estimates indicates some foster parents did no more extra counselling than they would for their natural children, others did from 21 to 56 hours per week. Thirty-six per cent of the parents of children aged 0 to four years gave no extra time but this was a reflection of the number of infants and age of the children in this group. Parents of teenage foster children gave greater amounts of time than they would expect to give to normal children.

Table 4.7
Extra time spent in the emotional counselling of foster children by age of the child in minutes each week.

| Time | $n=14$ | $n=9$ | $n=23$ |
	0-4	5-10	11-16+
Minutes	513	824	1148
% foster parents reporting no extra time	36%	11%	0%
Range of estimates	0-1260	0-1260	30-3360
Average total hours each week	8.6	13.7	19.1

A summary of the extra effort of caring for foster children

It was very common to find that foster parents spent a considerable amount of extra time with their foster child compared to the time given to a natural child of a similar age and sex. Table 4.8 shows the majority of carers spent extra time with the foster child on almost all activities. All carers spent extra time on administering the placement, that is on paper work, meetings and assessment work. In general, the proportion of carers spending extra time increased by the age of the child. Approximately 65% of carers of foster children under the age of 11 years spent more time on the personal care of the child than they would expect to do with their own child (of similar age and sex). Ninety-two per cent of foster parents of 11 to 16+ foster children spent extra time in personal care and a 100% gave extra time in general care. The extra time given in emotional caring of teenage foster children was greater than in the case of children of five to 10 years and of those less than five years of age. The giving of extra time in therapeutic activities, however, occurred less often in older children than younger ones. These foster parents referred to the extra effort they made for foster children rather than indicated the quality or quantity of hours spent in child rearing.

Table 4.8
Foster parents' perceptions of extra time spent with foster children in caring activities, by the age of the foster child, % of the sample reporting extra time.

Age	Personal care	General care	Travel	Therapeutic time	Admin.	Emotional counselling
0-4	64	79	79	57	100	64
5-10	67	78	100	67	100	89
11-16+	92	100	92	42	100	100

The extra time spent in fostering tasks

Table 4.9 shows a summary of the extra time spent by foster parents in caring for a foster child each week. Foster parent's perceptions showed that time spent in extra tasks increased with the age of the child. About 13 hours was spent in primary tasks for a child aged 0 to four, 14 hours spent caring for a child aged five to 10 and 15 hours for a child aged 11 to 16+. Time spent on secondary tasks followed a similar trend, it increased by the age of the child from 9 hours, 14 hours and 19 hours each week respectively for children 0 to four, five to 10, and 11 to 16+ years of age.

Table 4.9
Summary of extra time spent in essential and secondary foster care tasks. Weekly in minutes by age of child.

Primary time	0-4 years	5-10 years	11-16+ years	all ages
Personal care	155	175	174	169
General care	107	111	175	143
Travel	61	83	88	79
Therapeutic	128	152	190	164
Administration	341	287	243	280
Total	**792 (13.2hrs)**	**808 (13.5hrs)**	**870 (14.5hrs)**	**835 (13.9hrs)**
Secondary time				
Emotional care	513 (8.6hrs)	824 (13.7hrs)	1148 (19.1hrs)	891 (14.9hrs)

The value of foster parent time

The value of foster parent time is a contentious issue. The interviews with foster parents explored their present labour market value. In the case of foster mothers, however, it became apparent that fostering affected the wage they were able to earn from other paid employment. In view of this, it may be appropriate to value the time spent in fostering work with a pay scale which reflects the tasks of child care undertaken rather than by the market value of current employment.

The majority of fostering tasks were claimed to be completed by foster mothers although the responsibility of the placement was shared. The youngest mother was aged 31 years and the average age was 44 years. One foster mother was 60 years old and considered herself retired from employment. A higher proportion (75 per cent) of foster mothers have some educational qualification compared to (64 per cent) of mothers in general (OPCS, GHS 1992 Table 8.7). Thirty eight per cent of mothers caring for teenage foster children were in intermediate and professional occupations.

Some foster mothers claimed that fostering had an impact on the type of work they did and their employment status. Approximately 75% of foster mothers of children under the age of 11 years said fostering affected the type of work they did (39% of the foster parents of older children). Those foster parents who worked tended to be employed in part time work so they could meet their fostering commitments. Most foster mothers desired a higher income through working more hours in employment in order to maintain their family activities. There was a consensus of opinion in all groups but especially in the group fostering teenage foster children where, in almost 90% of cases, mothers desired to have more hours in employment.

Average hourly earnings of foster mothers

The average earnings were based on the hourly rate, before tax, of the foster mother's present job in each household. The hourly rate for foster mothers who were not presently employed was based on the General Household Survey estimates of average women's rates by educational attainment. A foster mother caring for a foster child had average hourly earnings of £4.30 per hour in 1992. The rates reported, however, were very varied and the majority reflected their already disadvantaged position compared to other mothers, of reduced hours available for work and low paid jobs such as child minding despite their overall above average level of education. An appropriate alternative hourly rate would be a residential care worker rate of £5.01 per hour in 1992.

The indirect cost of fostering

Table 4.10 shows the indirect costs for a foster mother of a foster child by the age of the foster child. The indirect costs are based on the number of hours allocated to caring for a second child in the family and the extra hours needed to meet the special circumstances of a child who is also a foster child. The estimate of 9.6 hours needed for an additional child in the household is based on research by Walker & Wood (1967), Szalai (1972) and Bittman (1991) illustrated in Table 4.1 (and not verified by this study).

The extra hours needed to care for a foster child aged 0 to four years is estimated at 22.8 hours per week. In the case of a child aged five to 10 years the mother spent approximately 23.1 hours each week and for households caring for a teenage foster child, the mother's spent approximately 24 hours per week in foster child related and fostering placement related activities. The value of time spent in caring for each foster child at aged 0 to four years, five to 10 years and 11 to 16+ years in 1992 is estimated at £114, £116 and £120 per week respectively. In households with more than one foster child there may well be further economies of scale both in the essential foster care tasks and the time allocated to the raising of an additional child in the household.

Table 4.10
The indirect costs for a foster mother of a foster child by the age of the foster child.

Years	0-4	5-10	11-16+
Hours spent in essential fostering tasks	13.2	13.5	14.4
Hours spent in child care of an additional child	9.6	9.6	9.6
Total hours	**22.8**	**23.1**	**24.0**
£5.01 per hour	£114.23	£115.73	£120.24

Residential care worker rate 1992.

Conclusion

This chapter has attempted to identify the indirect costs for foster parents of fostering children. The concept of scarcity of time means that time spent on fostering activities may be traded off against other activities. The trade off is likely to be a reduction in time normally spent on leisure activities and employment outside the home.

This chapter explored the time spent by foster parents on foster caring tasks, tasks that would not occur in non fostering households. Foster parents described their experiences in essential or primary foster child care, such as personal care of foster children, general household care, travel time, therapeutic time and time spent in administering the placement. In addition, they described time spent on the emotional care of their foster children, that is counselling, talking and reassuring. The latter task is mostly done at the same time as other tasks and is treated as secondary time in the analysis. A minority of foster parents suggested that no extra time was spent on foster children than they would expect to spend on an additional child of their own of the same age and sex. Almost no foster parents reported they spent less time on foster children than they would on their natural child. The method of averaging the perceived time spent on caring for the foster child (including those who reported no extra time and those who reported on foster children with 'special needs') allowed for all views and a range of fostering circumstances to be reflected in the final analysis. Foster parents indicated prime time spent specifically on caring for foster children was in the order of 13.2 hours a week on children aged 0 to four years, 13.5 hours on children aged five to 10 years and 14.5 hours each week on teenage children. The time spent on secondary tasks by foster parents on their teenage foster child was estimated at 19.1 hours each week. What has been measured in this study is the extra effort made by the foster mother in the care of her foster child rather than the quality or quantity of hours spent in child rearing.

Ultimately, the total time (time spent in bringing up an additional child in the household and the extra time spent in fostering tasks) can be valued in terms of an appropriate hourly rate of pay. At a residential care worker rate the value of time spent in care for a foster child is £114 to £120 per week according to the age of the child. No account in the cost analysis has been taken of the substantial amount of time spent on secondary tasks such as counselling the foster child.

5 The comparative cost of a foster child: a survey of fifteen countries

Introduction

The objective of this chapter is to compare the state support of foster children in fifteen countries. That is to evaluate the cash or transfer payments made to foster families in support of their foster child directly or indirectly through an agency. The foster child support package is defined as: the basic state paid allowances; foster wage; guaranteed costs such as education fees, health fees, and taxation on allowances; and benefits which mitigate foster care expenses, such as family allowance and tax credits. Provision for special or exceptional needs payments to foster parents are also compared. The variation in the level of support is explored between children of different ages within countries and related to internal wages and prices. The countries compared are the twelve member states of the European Union (Belgium, Denmark, France, Germany, Greece, Ireland, Italy, Luxembourg, Netherlands, Portugal, Spain, UK), Australia, Norway and the USA. The information on national and local foster care policies was provided by national informants who were simultaneously contributing to a large and complex cross-national survey on child support reported by Bradshaw, Ditch, Holmes and Whiteford (1993).

Why comparative research?

The reason for undertaking a cross-national comparative study of foster care allowances was to evaluate the adequacy of foster care allowances in the UK. The study, however, presents a number of other opportunities. It provides a chance to:
* Examine how other countries compensate or remunerate foster parents for the cost of fostering.
* Learn lessons from abroad (Higgins (1986) referred to this as 'policy borrowing').

- Examine similarities and differences between countries (Hill 1991, Spicker 1992, Le Grand 1991, Ditch 1993).
- Try to explain those differences.
- Examine the financial consequences of those differences for foster caring.

Limitation of comparative research

Despite these benefits the study has many limitations, some are inherent in comparative research, others are specific to this study. The problems are:
- Comparing like with like: Ginsberg in 1932 warned about too much reliance on generalisations from international comparisons (Rodgers, Doron, Jones 1979).
- Countries are better understood from a case study rather than a statistical snapshot (Rodgers et al 1979, Kamerman 1983).
- Language and interpretation of questions by national informants communicating in a second language is problematic (Jones 1985, Hantrais, Mangen, O'Brien 1985). Cultural bias can be reduced by pre-testing and back translations.
- The number of countries compared, compounded by the use of regional information instead of national averages, contribute to difficulties in data handling.
- Reliability of the survey especially when breaking new ground in an area where knowledge has the potential to become cumulative.

The need for a systematic, standardised and analytic structure in general is stressed. As Bolderson (1988) warns, however, there are instances where concepts are closely specified and comparable, but analysis proves capable of generalisations only with many qualifications. The 'profile' methods (who receives what and how much) are strong on standardisation, need caveats and tend to loose sight of the actual, for example: Bradshaw and Piachaud (1980), and Bradshaw, Ditch, Holmes, and Whiteford (1993). At the start of this study there was no other comparative research about foster care payments on a similar scale. Since then Colton and Hellinckx (1993) have published a guide to foster and residential care in the EC. The authors of each country specific chapter were indigenous to the country concerned. Each was asked to prepare a descriptive chapter according to a standard structure in order that some common developments in the field of residential and foster care might be highlighted. The nature of residential and foster care provision was outlined with the historical antecedents of the service, the legal and administrative framework of services, recent trends, and research on residential and foster care. No attempt was made at any type of economic analysis across countries although some countries gave examples of basic foster care allowances. Colton and Hellinckz's research provides a rich source of contextual material to the financial analysis attempted in this chapter.

Research methods

Theoretically, one way of collecting statistics on foster care payments and numbers is through national accounts. National accounts are less developed, however, in some countries than in others and even in those which produce detailed statistical data, foster care expenditure is rarely featured as a separate item. In Britain, for example, foster care allowances are determined at local authority level and do not appear in national accounts although returns from local authorities provide aggregate totals of spending on particular services.

Another approach would be to survey the income and situation of actual families in each country to find out what they receive in support of their foster children. The problems with this are: this type of study does not exist across the different countries; the numbers of foster carers are too small to be identified in secondary analysis of large data sets; generating such a study in each country would be expensive and time consuming. The results would indicate what parents have rather than what is available to them.

This study used a national informant to seek out what was available to foster parents and to simulate the way in which the foster child support package helped an archetypal foster family. The advantage of this method is that it describes how the system should work rather than how in practice it does work. There are two drawbacks. First the extent that foster parents 'take up' their entitlements and the effectiveness of the system in directing money to foster parents is unknown. Second, the model foster family (average earning capacity couple and two children) is based on perceptions of a UK foster family which may not be typical elsewhere.

The Bradshaw et al (1993) survey was already available to provide data on earnings, employment, benefits and costs, and the survey's national informants were prepared to collect foster care information. The focus of Bradshaw's study was to compare the ways in which a number of model families were treated by the tax and benefit system.

Design of the foster care survey

In the first instance, the foster payment survey was designed to be answered quickly by a telephone call to a fostering agency in the respective countries. In the second instance, the subsequent country profile was to be returned to the national informant for verification of interpretation. Accepting that culture free language is not possible, a common definition of foster care was agreed by all informants:

> We (UK) define foster care as substitute family care for a planned
> period for a child when his/her own family cannot care for him/her
> for a temporary or extended period and when adoption is neither
> desirable nor possible. Fostering generally involves the placement of

children with families with monitoring by some kind of recognised authority.

The questionnaire and analysis refer specifically to May 1992 figures and prices. The following categories were used:

- Standard sum at ages four, ten, and 16 years. (Minimum amount paid to reimburse direct costs.)
- Additional payments at ages four, ten and 16 years. (One off payments or sums paid irregularly.)
- Exceptional payments at ages four, ten and 16 years. (Usually paid for a disabled or disruptive foster child, additional to the standard/additional payments.)
- Salary or reward payment at ages four, ten and 16 years. (Additions for exceptional cases.)
- State transfer benefits - family allowance, disability allowance, tax credits.
- State transfer costs - tax on allowance, education, health.
- Any debate on the supply of foster carers and the adequacy of allowances.

Currency conversion

There were a number of possible indicators that could be used to convert the value of foster care support into a common monetary denominator: exchange rates; purchasing power parities (PPPs); or as a proportion of average earnings.

The exchange rate conversions, perhaps the most traditional measure of monetary values between countries were found unreliable for this particular measurement for a number of reasons. Exchange rates are inclined to be volatile as they relate to equilibrium in foreign transactions and as such are not good indicators of the relative value of within country purchasing power. Although all the countries in the sample keep national accounts from which exchange rates are calculated there was some concern that not all were reliable (Beckerman 1966).

The PPPs of a currency were, however, a useful indicator of comparative value. PPP scales are determined by the amount of goods and services that may be purchased with one unit of that currency. This provides a means of adjusting different countries' currencies to a common standard or equivalence scale. The base rate in 1992 is set in Sterling, thus £1 purchasing power in the UK has the same purchasing power as 1.03 Irish Pounds or 1.54 American Dollars and so on. Purchasing power parities are estimated by Eurostat and the OECD in a joint project. A major drawback of this measure is the length of time before publication of each year's scale. The PPPs scales used in this analysis for May 1992 are calculated by Whiteford (Bradshaw et al, 1993) using changes in consumer prices from the 1991 OECD estimates. Despite their seeming appropriateness as a common denominator, PPPs are a rough estimate of

161

equivalent spending power. Though representative of a similar baskets of goods in each country, they do not fully take account of all cultural and social differences.

The second useful indicator of relative spending power in the respective countries is gross and net disposable income from average earnings. The average family income of a typical family likely to foster was taken as a benchmark. The disadvantage of this simplification was that it excluded from the comparison the low income, unemployed, or even affluent households who may have the opportunity to offer themselves as a placement family. In addition the assumption was upheld that income is derived entirely from earnings which is not necessarily the case. It is assumed that the family has two children aged seven for the calculation of the household net disposable income. The household's gross and net disposable income figure is used as a reference in two examples of households.

- One average male earner, female non earner.
- One average male earner, +66% average female earner.

The average gross earnings, tax and national insurance levels are derived from Bradshaw et al (1993). The earnings data is based on OECD (1989) estimates, adjusted by OECD published percentage changes in earnings to 1991. The final adjustment for 1991-2 was then estimated by internal changes in prices. The female average earnings estimate uses ILO statistics which provide ratios of male to female earnings. All the earnings estimates were checked by the child support informants mainly through their own national accounts and verified to be within plus or minus five per cent with the exception of the Nordic, Benelux countries and France whose statistical departments lacked the relevant information. The weekly disposable net income is calculated as gross wage less personal tax and national insurance.

Transfer benefits and costs

The foster child support package includes the value of subsidies and services in kind and costs for average income families. For the sake of statistical consistency, the foster child was counted as a first child where benefits or costs were adjusted for family size. The calculation of common arrangements were as follows:

Family allowance: The family allowance applicable for natural children was included if foster parents received this in addition to their foster care allowance.

Disability allowance: A general disability allowance was included in the disabled foster child support package if this was received by foster parents in addition to the foster care allowance.

Tax credits: If the foster child was counted as a dependent child in the tax assessment of the foster family, the amount for one extra child was taken as an addition to the foster care allowance.

Tax: If the foster care allowances or foster wage was counted as income in the tax assessment of the foster mother, an estimate of tax (based on the income of the model family) was deducted from the total.

Education: The baseline was that no school costs were paid with the exception of school meals. Differences for regular payments to schools for school books, trips or other items were counted as a cost, whereas grants given to moderate the cost of school books etc. for foster children reduced the normal education cost to none.

Health costs: The baseline was established as health care free at the point of demand, available to all regardless of means and of similar quality across countries. Differences were estimated as costs for the foster parent. A standard amount was derived from Bradshaw's (1993) health package which was adjusted to reflect child rather than adult costs: the cost of one visit to the GP and the equivalent of one child's antibiotic each month, for example.

Demographic context

The differences and similarities in the numbers and proportions of needy children looked after by public funds in the different countries is shown in Table 5.1. Relatively speaking, a greater number of children in Belgium and Denmark are supported by the state, approximately 1.5% of children. The reasons for this are not explored here, but demographic, economic, and socio-political factors as well as ideological considerations will feature in the equation. At the other end of the scale less than 0.5% of children under the age of majority in Greece, Ireland, Italy, Portugal, Spain and Australia are in the care of the state, whereas, Luxembourg, West Germany, France, Netherlands, the UK, Norway and the US support almost 1% of children.

The proportion of children in care of the authorities accommodated in foster care also varies significantly from approximately 8% in Spain to 76% in Norway. France, West Germany, Ireland, Netherlands, UK, US and Norway all support half or more of children in state care in foster placements.

Foster care rates are nationally determined in Belgium, Denmark, Germany, Ireland, Luxembourg, Netherlands, Portugal, Australia, Norway, and USA, although most retain a small amount of local autonomy. Where no national fostering rates are available regional rates are compared, for example: Athens (Greece), Turin (Italy), Meuse (France), Catalan (Spain) and North Yorkshire (UK). In these latter countries the relationship of local rates to national averages is unknown with the exception of the UK. In Australia, the state rate applies to Western Australia, and in the USA to New York State, Germany refers to former West Germany, and Belgium refers to the Flemish Community of Flanders.

Table 5.1
National Statistics 1990-1991.

Country	Child pop <18 in millions	Children in care of the state	% of children in care	No. in foster care	% in care children fostered
Belgium (Flanders)	1.2	17,448	1.5	2,697	15
Denmark	0.9	14,710	1.6	5,613	38
France	13.7	116,557	0.9	60,000	50
Germany	11.2	87,437	0.8	42,673	49
Greece	2.3	4,049	0.2	517	13
Ireland	1.1	2,614	0.2	1,830	70
Italy	14.6	3,939	0.3	1,062	27
Luxembourg	0.1	677	0.7	229	34
Netherlands	3.3	20,000	0.6	10,000	50
Portugal	2.4	11,055	0.5	1,782	16
Spain	9.0	11,000	0.1	825	8
UK	12.8	70,561	0.6	39,308	56
Australia	4.5	14,908	0.3	5,316	36
Norway	1.0	6,917	0.7	5,282	76
US	67.3	429,000	0.6	306,306	71

Source: National informants.

Basic foster care allowance

Almost all countries pay approved foster parents a minimum standard allowance for the basic costs of the child's board and lodgings. The rates (converted to PPPs) are shown in Table 5.2. The exceptions are Italy where payment is not universal, and to some extent Greece where payment schemes are in the early stages of development. The basic foster care allowance includes a set sum and additional expenses (the amount that all carers receive relative to the age of their foster child). The Southern European countries in general make no differentiation in payment by age. The other countries recognise that older children cost more to keep than younger children. Allowances vary with age in different ways, sometimes only in the case of the teenage child, other times by school rather than age related status. The UK increases the 10 year old child allowance by 64% for a child aged 16 years; and, a child aged 10 years receives 22% more than a child aged four years. All other countries allow smaller age related increases for teenage children. Reducing the age groups to an average estimate in each country shows that the countries of Southern Europe tend to pay the lowest amounts. Australia, although a proportionally higher user of foster care, reimburses foster parents at one of the lowest levels. The US pay more than other countries. Nevertheless, there are a lot of similarities across countries. The UK pays most in the EU largely due to its generosity to older children. Germany, Belgium, France and Norway pay within £5 of the UK age related average.

Table 5.2
The basic Foster Care Allowance by Country in PPPs, £ per week.
Rates refer to May 1992.

Country	age 4	age 10	age 16	average
Belgium	56	56	60	57
Denmark	46	48	48	48
France	53	56	60	56
Germany	47	57	68	57
Greece	41	41	41	41
Ireland	42	42	53	46
Italy	51	51	51	51
Luxembourg	35	35	35	35
Netherlands	32	36	51	40
Portugal	19	21	19	20
Spain	40	40	40	40
UK	42	52	85	60
Australia	29	34	42	35
Norway	46	58	65	56
US	62	73	89	74

Caveat: There are a number of allowances paid to all carers in countries which are not taken into account in this table. These are discretionary allowances, too vague or individual to be used in the analysis. Belgium pays pocket money, holiday and savings extra. Denmark pays clothing, special diets and child care for children over 10 years. Greece pay capital costs of beds, bed-linen, underwear and holiday expenses extra. Ireland pays holiday costs. The UK and Australia pay an initial clothing grant at the start of placements.

State transfers of costs and benefits to foster parents

The basic foster care allowance does not take into account other benefits or costs that foster parents receive or pay in respect of their foster child.

Family allowances

In Belgium, Ireland, Luxembourg, Netherlands, Portugal, Australia and Norway the family allowance is paid in addition to the foster care allowance. In Germany the family allowance paid to foster children is tapered but the extent of the disregard is not known. The family allowance, where paid in fostering situations, varies by the age of the child and by family size. In the case of the latter the amount counted is for a first child. In other countries the otherwise universal child benefit is either not paid to foster children or the fostering allowance replaces other government child support.

Tax credits

In Belgium, Ireland, Italy, Luxembourg, Portugal and Norway the tax system includes a child allowance or child credit, and foster children are counted as an extra child in the placement household. The basic foster care maintenance allowance does not count as income for tax assessment purposes in any of the fifteen countries explored.

School costs

In Belgium, Luxembourg and Portugal there are some compulsory school costs (school books, materials, etc.) for foster children. In Italy these costs apply to older foster children. Luxembourg, however, offsets some costs for some families with an annual school grant. France and Ireland pay additions to the fostering allowance for school expenses. In other countries, UK, Denmark, Germany, Greece, Spain, Australia, Norway and the US, such school expenses are waived to all children.

Health costs

In the US and Luxembourg children have health costs such as dentistry, hospital and GP charges, and medicines. In other countries such as Denmark, Greece and Norway all charges for foster children are reimbursed. The remaining countries (Belgium, France, Germany, Ireland, Italy, Netherlands, Portugal, Spain, UK and Australia) operate free health care for foster children and in some cases for all children.

Table 5.3 shows the adjusted foster care allowances taking into account transfers of benefits and costs. In Denmark, France, Germany, Greece and the UK there are no such costs or benefits to mitigate additional costs. In Spain and the US additional costs reduce the value of the basic allowance. Transfers in some countries make significant increases to the allowance, for example, in Luxembourg and Belgium, representing an increase of £13.00 each week, in Norway approximately £12 a week. In the Netherlands, Ireland, Italy and Australia the amount equates to a rise of between £5 to £9, and in Portugal an increase of £2.38 each week.

Table 5.3
The foster care support package in PPPs per week, May 1992.

Country	Age 4	Age 10	Age 16	Average	Average increase	Rank
Belgium	68	69	73	70	13	2
Denmark	46	48	48	48	0	11
France	53	56	60	56	0	7
Germany	47	57	68	57	0	5
Greece	41	41	41	41	0	12
Ireland	48	49	60	52	7	8
Italy	58	58	54	57	6	6
Luxembourg	50	50	45	48	13	10
Netherlands	39	46	62	49	9	9
Portugal	22	24	20	22	2	15
Spain	40	39	39	39	-0.5	14
UK	42	52	85	60	0	4
Australia	35	39	47	40	5	13
Norway	62	75	67	68	12	3
US	58	70	85	71	-3	1

Comparisons across countries have taken account of the differences in prices through the use of PPPs. Table 5.4 shows the foster care package as a percentage of average earnings after tax and insurance for a household of a couple and two children (one male earner, average wage). The foster care allowance in Belgium is 33% of the disposable income of the family and the UK allowance is 28% of the disposable income of an average family. The foster care allowances in Australia are 17% of a similar family's income. Most countries (within plus or minus two decimal places) show similar ranking using indicators of average wage and PPPs, however, there is some disparity. Greek foster parents receive a higher proportion of foster care allowance to disposable income than foster parents in the UK. The US foster parents receive a similar proportion of foster care allowance to average earnings as UK foster parents.

Table 5.4
Foster Care Support Package as a proportion of average disposable income in national currency per week.

Country	Foster care support package	Average disposable income one earner	% of average wage	Rank	PPP rank	Differ- ence
Belgium	4229.62	12743.48	33	1	2	+1
Denmark	669.66	2709.25	25	7=	11	+4
France	566.24	1797.40	32	2=	7	+5
Germany	187.69	739.52	25	7=	5	-2
Greece	11384.62	36258.08	31	4	12	+8
Ireland	53.98	214.87	25	7=	8	+1
Italy	130187.55	443306.61	29	5	6	+1
Luxembourg	2937.85	15957.54	18	14	10	-4
Netherlands	164.49	685.44	24	11	9	-2
Portugal	4021.53	17675.35	23	12	15	+3
Spain	7294.87	35669.71	20	13	14	+1
UK	59.53	214.62	28	6	4	-2
Australia	82.90	480.13	17	15	13	-2
Norway	967.16	3051.83	32	2=	3	+1
US	109.65	442.10	25	7=	1	-6

Foster wage

Table 5.5 shows that six countries (Denmark, France, Germany, Luxembourg, Portugal and Norway) pay foster wages in addition to maintenance payments, as a reward or salary for caring. Germany and Denmark do not pay the wage separately but estimate it as an approximate proportion of the whole allowance. The amount paid is constant across all age related foster child groups. In Denmark and Norway it is taxed as earned income. In France the tax is at a much lower level than ordinary wages. In Germany, Luxembourg and Portugal it is non taxable. The wage levels range from the equivalent of £13 in Portugal to £51 per week in Luxembourg. The mean amount is £35.62 for the six countries. There is no foster wage paid to foster parents in normal circumstances in the UK. The value of the foster wage in national currency as a proportion of the female gross average weekly wage (full time) and female 66% average (part time) gives some indication of its nearness to a replacement wage. Luxembourg pay the nearest to a replacement wage, 29% of full time and 41% of a part time wage. Germany's foster wage is equal to 10% of the full time female average and 14% of a part time wage.

Table 5.5

Foster wages in PPPs and as a proportion of the gross average female wages and 0.66 female average wage, per week, May 1992.

Country	Wage National currency	Tax	PPPs	Average female wage	%	0.66 Average female wage	%
Denmark	497	yes	33	3769	13	2488	20
France	455	yes low level	45	1754	26	1299	35
Germany	69	no	21	719	10	488	14
Luxembourg	3136	no	51	10846	29	7704	41
Portugal	2316	no	13	17559	13	11589	20
Norway	683	yes	48	3423	20	2259	30

Total financial support to foster parents

It is evident that the difference between the allowance paid for the daily upkeep of the child and the reward (foster wage) paid for looking after the child is not so clearly defined in some countries as in others. In addition, in financial terms the amount paid in wages is insufficient in any country to be viewed as an alternative to work in the labour market. To complicate matters, in some countries such as the US, the term 'stipend' is applied to describe the allowance which suggests a general allowance involving some element of profit. In view of this, the total foster child support package includes both maintenance and wage elements.

Table 5.6 compares the total foster child support package in PPPs and as a proportion of the disposable income of a model 2 adult, 2 child family. In most cases these measures gave similar rankings, but in Portugal and Greece the foster care allowance as a proportion of average family disposable income compared to the UK is more generous than that shown in relation to internal prices.

In relation to prices (PPPs), the greatest financial effort to support the age related average foster child is found in Norway, France, Luxembourg, Denmark and Germany. The UK is found to be within a group of middle countries in terms of effort. The least effort to support foster children is seen in Australia, Spain and Portugal.

In relation to average wages, the proportion that foster care allowances meet them gives an indicator of how 'well off' foster parents would feel with an extra child in the household. In de la Meuse in France the placement family of four receive the equivalent of 56% of their net disposable income to care for one extra child. In Norway the situation is similar. A family receives the equivalent of 54% of their disposable income for one extra child. At the other end of the scale, Australia comes out relatively poorly, it supports its foster children up to a rate of 17% of a similar family's net income. The UK provides support for an extra child in a placement family to the value of 28% of the family's net disposable income. Countries such as Italy, Ireland and the US are similar to the UK in their overall effort.

Table 5.6

A comparison of the total Foster Child Support Package in relation to prices and wages in fifteen countries, PPPs per week (equivalent £s), May 1992.

Country	Foster Child Package	Foster Wage	Total	Rank	% disposable income one average earner family	Rank
Belgium	70	0	70	6	33	7
Denmark	48	33	81	4	42	3
France	56	45	101	2	56	1
Germany	57	21	78	5	34	6
Greece	41	0	41	12	32	8
Ireland	52	0	52	10	25	11=
Italy	57	0	57	9	29	9
Luxembourg	48	51	99	3	38	4
Netherlands	49	0	49	11	24	13
Portugal	22	13	35	15	36	5
Spain	39	0	39	14	20	14
UK	60	0	60	8	28	10
Australia	40	0	40	13	17	15
Norway	68	48	116	1	54	2
US	71	0	71	7	25	11=

Disability

The way that countries cope with special needs in foster placements is found to be very individual and difficult to quantify and compare.

All countries with the exception of Italy, Luxembourg and Norway recognise that fostering a disabled child results in higher costs. Australia, Netherlands, Ireland and Denmark reimbursed additional expenses on a discretionary basis. Other countries (Belgium, France, Germany, Greece, UK and the US) set a minimum and maximum level of enhancement to the basic foster care allowance. Spain and Portugal give a supplement for the 'worst' cases of need only.

Denmark, France, Germany, Portugal and Norway reward carers for looking after a 'disabled' foster child by a supplement to the basic wage. The UK and Ireland introduced fee paying schemes specifically for teenage children who were 'disabled' or difficult to place in some way. Only in Denmark and Norway did the highest disability wage supplement plus basic wage come within 20% of the average female wage.

In seven of the fifteen countries the state disability allowance for children living within their natural homes was available to be claimed by foster parents of disabled foster children. In Italy, Luxembourg, Netherlands and Australia the state disability benefit was the only certain, non discretionary supplement that foster parents received in addition to their basic foster care allowance. In Belgium, Luxembourg, Portugal, Netherlands and Australia the disability state benefit was a supplement to the child benefit or family allowance. In Italy the foster parent was eligible for an 'Accompanying Person Allowance', and in the UK the Disability Living Allowance can be claimed for a disabled foster child.

Table 5.7 shows the varieties in additional financial support a foster parent could receive in respect of the foster child's disability as a supplement to the foster child support package indicated previously. The final column compares the disabled child package of *supplements* in the most extreme case possible for each country. In Italy, Luxembourg, Netherlands and Australia, foster parents receive little extra than a normal family with a disabled child. The range of state support for a disabled child is £7 to £14 each week. At the other end of the scale, the UK has the potential to support a severely disabled teenage foster child, for example, with up to £215 a week. This includes a comparatively generous state disability living allowance that all disabled children receive regardless of their family circumstances, a 100% enhancement on the basic maintenance allowance for 'normal' foster children and a special scheme 'fee'. Denmark, US and Norway also support a severely disabled foster child comparatively well.

Table 5.7

Disability Supplement by age (average of three age related groups) and degree of severity in PPPs (rounded to the nearest £), May 1992.

Country	Special Need supplement	Exceptional supplement	Wage or wage supplement	State disability benefits or benefit supplement	Total maximum supplement
Belgium	10	13-17	None	Child Benefit supp. based on scale of difficulty £42-£49	66
Denmark	Discretionary	Means test of foster parents	66-197#	None	197
France	3	12	11-45#	None	57
Germany	12	13-57	21	None	78
Greece	6	88 HIV etc.	None	None	88
Ireland	Discretionary		98*	None	98
Italy	-	-	None	Accompanying person allowance	0
Luxembourg	-	-	None	Child benefit supplement £8	8
Netherlands	Discretionary		None	Disabled child supplement £7	7
Portugal	-	13	13	Child benefit supplement £7	33
Spain	-	10	None	None	10
UK	11	56	86*#	DLA care £12-£43, mobility £12-£30 child over 5yrs	215
Australia	School costs, day care, health costs	Above scale subsidy	None	Disability benefit £14	14
Norway	-	-	148#	None	148
US	127	192	Salary for a few	None	192

* Special scheme older teenager   # taxed
Source: National respondents.

Adequacy of payment and the supply of foster parents

The respondents were asked to comment on the adequacy of payment to foster parents. In Germany, Greece, Ireland, Netherlands, Spain, Portugal, UK, Australia, the US and France the foster care allowances were claimed to be insufficient to meet the costs of the

172

foster child. In Luxembourg debate on adequacy was mixed leading to an unclear overall opinion. In Australia the problem of adequacy was seen as particularly acute for teenage foster children. In France this was also the case despite the policy to select only families with adequate income to avoid the possibility of the allowance serving the family and not the foster child. In Portugal the onus is on the foster parent to apply for payment. Greece believes that the adequacy debate arises because foster care is not enacted which leaves the allowance based on private agreement and not all foster parents receive it. The Netherlands reported the inadequacy to cover the child's costs to be so serious it led to a government enquiry. Ireland believe the value of the foster care allowance has in real terms (relative to cost of living indices and wages) lost ground during the 1980s. Germany supports a similar view that the willingness of foster parents is not dependent on the level of foster care allowance but has to be seen relative to the present forms of living and structure of society. The issue of adequacy of allowance has recently been redressed in France with a 50% increase from July 1992 and a move towards a monthly guarantee of pay regardless of placement; in Greece from October 1993 there has been a 10% increase; Portugal also reports a recent increase. The impact of these changes are not known.

At times the debate on the adequacy of foster care allowances focused on other aspects of payment, such as:

- The within region and between region inequalities in amounts paid to different carers, for example, in Denmark the debate is about actual amounts paid and not about adequacy (Danish municipalities pay discretionary amounts for quality of care). In Belgium, Ireland, Australia and the UK the debate concerns variations in discretionary payments for additional expenses (Flemish foster parents desire a move towards standardisation by a lump sum for additions to all carers regardless of need).

  The governments' lack of resources to pay more because of the relationship between payment and national budget; Germany argues that the allowance should be relevant to the overall federal government budget and resources are insufficient to pay a higher rate. A similar argument is found in the UK as authorities claim rises would be at the expense of other services.

- Loss of benefits received by non foster parents but which foster parents are not eligible to claim on behalf of their foster child is an issue debated in Italy.

- There is a trend towards small community accommodation instead of foster family placements in Italy, therefore, the impact of foster care allowances is not the key issue.

- Long delays in the authorities' processing of additional expenses incurred during the foster placement was mentioned by Australia and the UK as a problem.

- Concern about foster care run by private organisations arises in the UK, Norway and US.

- The UK and the US put forward similar arguments about paying foster parents a fostering wage. In the US the 'special needs' foster care allowance has become larger and a taxable para-professional salary in some cities.

Supply of foster parents was not identified as a problem in Denmark, France, and Italy. Six countries (Belgium, Germany, Ireland, Spain, Australia and the UK) mentioned demand for foster parents to foster disabled and teenage children was not met (although finding foster parents was less of a problem for children under the age of 12 years). Norway claim shortages in Oslo and the US in some large cities. Spain have many applicants who foster with a view to adoption. The UK claims apparent shortages exacerbated by recent changes in child care law which limit the number of children placed with a foster family to three with few exceptions. Additionally, the UK claims the emphasis on racial matching has caused some problems in supply of foster parents. The Netherlands, Greece, Luxembourg and Portugal state simply that supply is insufficient although Portugal reports that the shortages may be related to the inefficiency of the bureaucracy and the co-ordinating processes rather than the willingness of families to apply.

Other issues raised concerning the supply of foster parents included the trend in France, Australia and the UK towards placing children in foster homes near their natural home to maintain family links: this was causing some problems in supply. The US further highlighted two problems of interest to the UK: first, the impact of community care policies which make high demands on families to care for their elderly at the expense of the family's engagement in work such as fostering. Second, the impact of the recent trend towards foster caring by kin appears to have (for reasons as yet unknown) led to a rise in the abuse of fostered children.

Reasons for the differences in payments to foster parents

Table 5.8 shows the relationship between the levels of allowance and other factors. No correlation was found between a country's generosity to its foster parents and the percentage of children in care of the authorities or the percentage of children in care and fostered. The affluence of the country measured in terms of GDP per head of population showed a slight tendency for richer countries such as Norway and Luxembourg to be more generous to their foster parents than poorer countries with the US as a notable exception. There was, however, a clear relationship between the generosity of the country and claims of adequacy of the foster care allowance.

Table 5.8
Relationship between levels of allowance and other factors.

Most generous = 1	Country	1989 GDP rounded to nearest thousand	% of children in care of authorities	% of children in care & fostered	Adequate *
1	France	9	0.9	50	no
2	Norway	10	0.7	76	yes
3	Denmark	9	1.6	38	yes
4	Luxembourg	10	0.7	34	yes
5	Portugal	5	0.5	16	no
6	Germany	9	0.8	49	no
7	Belgium	8	1.5	15	yes
8	Greece	5	0.2	13	no
9	Italy	9	0.3	27	yes
10	UK	9	0.6	56	no
11	US	12	0.6	71	no
12	Ireland	6	0.2	70	no
13	Netherlands	9	0.6	50	no
14	Spain	6	0.1	8	no
15	Australia	9	0.3	36	no

* Respondent's perception of adequacy

Conclusion

The objective of this chapter was to compare the UK allowances with other state financial support of foster children in the European Union and three other countries. The information was collected by English speaking national academic informants. In two cases, Ireland and Australia, the academic input was backed by direct contact with fostering support groups who supplied information on current rates. The economic analysis utilised an average earning model family to simulate the way in which foster care allowances interacted with other state benefits and costs. The two comparative indicators were foster care allowances converted to purchasing power parities (Stirling), and foster care allowances as a proportion of mean earning family income in different countries.

Allowances paid in normal circumstances to all foster parents were considered at a number of levels: the basic amount paid (including non-discretionary expenses paid to all carers in relation to the child's age); basic allowances plus other costs and benefits; fostering wages; and the combined foster child support package. In addition, levels of payment by states to disabled foster children were compared.

The Southern European countries in general did not differentiate allowances by age, other countries recognised that older children cost more. The differences tended to be small except in the UK where teenage children received proportionally more compared to children aged 10 years old.

An initial comparison of the basic foster care allowance in the 15 countries indicated that the US made the greatest effort in terms of direct money transfer. The UK made the greatest effort within the European Union along with Germany, Belgium and France. The UK, however, does not pay any additional general child support benefits to foster parents to support foster children in normal circumstances. Additional state benefits and costs in other countries made a difference of about £13 extra a week in Belgium, Norway and Luxembourg. The value of the UK state effort to reimburse the cost of the foster child was less than the US, Belgium and Norway.

Six countries, Denmark, France, Germany, Luxembourg, Portugal, and Norway paid a foster wage to all foster parents in addition to the amount paid for the child's maintenance. The highest amount paid was £51 each week, the lowest was £13. In no country was the wage component of the allowance sufficient to be considered as an alternative to earnings in the labour market. There was evidence in some countries that the wage component subsidised the sum allocated for the child's daily upkeep.

A final analysis of the total support of foster children by public funds in the fifteen countries put the UK in a middle position. In terms of the proportion of average disposable income for a family with children, however, which may be a better indicator of how 'well off' the foster family feel than the basket of goods (purchasing power parities) approach, the UK is less generous than some of the poorer countries of the EU: countries such as Greece and Portugal do considerably better than the UK, and the UK drops to a position in the lower middle range of the countries overall.

The support of foster children with special or exceptional need was shown as a supplement to the basic allowance and wages. Estimating the 'worse' case, the UK makes considerable effort to compensate foster parents caring for a disabled foster child. The US, Denmark, Norway and Ireland are also generous in their support of disabled foster children.

An attempt to discover the reasons for the differences between the amount of financial support received by foster parents in the UK and other countries was inconclusive. Little correlation was found between levels of foster child allowance and the percentage of children in care and the percentage in foster care accommodation. There was only a slight tendency for richer countries, measured in terms of GDP, to pay more in allowances than poorer countries. There was, however, a correlation between those countries who perceived that their allowances were adequate and their position in comparison to other countries. In conclusion, there are likely to be other ideological factors in the policy making process to account for the differences between levels of foster care allowances in different countries.

This chapter has indicated that the UK foster care allowances are not generous to foster parents in normal circumstances in comparison to the state support of foster children elsewhere. The UK is placed in eighth and tenth positions, ranked with some of the economically poorer countries of the EC. Moreover, the reasons for differences in allowances between countries are not explained by countries' access to wealth or the amount of use they make of the fostering service.

Conclusion

Summary

The objective of this research was to explore the adequacy of the foster care allowances paid by local authorities for the upkeep of a foster child. This is important because there is evidence of a change in the nature of fostering and a need for payment policy to reflect that change. The degree of difficulty in caring for the average foster child is greater than before and the tasks of foster parents more demanding and skilful. Local authorities have at times had to compete with each other to maintain their supply of carers and pressure group campaigns for increased allowances have been influential in some areas.

The principle on which the foster care allowance rests is that it should pay for the foster child's upkeep at a socially recognised and approved standard of living. This principle has not changed since foster care was first covered by legislation in 1870. This research has used an analytical framework to measure historically and in modern time the adequacy of the allowance to meet its key policy objective. Five criteria were set to evaluate the adequacy of the foster care allowance:

- The extent that foster care allowances have maintained their value over time.
- The extent that allowances meet the normal costs of child rearing.
- The extent that allowances meet the extra costs of fostering.
- The extent that the indirect costs of foster parents are compensated by the foster care allowance.
- The extent that the UK foster care allowances are comparable with those paid elsewhere.

The traditional barometer of foster care allowances has been welfare payment levels. At the turn of the century (1900) foster care allowances were three and four times higher than a child's 'outdoor' relief. During the 1960s and 1970s the allowances fell to twice the supplementary benefit scale rates, increasing to approximately three times the income support child scale rates in the early 1990s. Welfare payments, however, have not remained constant over time as an indicator of basic needs.

Two further measures have been used to assess the extent that the foster care allowance has maintained its value over time. The retail price index from 1945 to 1992 has been used to measure the degree that the foster care allowance has increased in line with price inflation. The results showed that the value compared with price inflation had not only maintained its level but there was evidence of an increase in the real value of the allowance especially in relation to older children. The real percentage increase during the last decade averaged 6% per annum. The foster care allowance has also been measured as a proportion of the male average production worker's weekly gross wage over the same period in time. In 1945 the foster care allowance for the average foster child represented 13% of the average wage, by 1992 this proportion had risen to 24%.

The first test of whether foster care allowances were adequate in terms of their value over time showed that they were more than adequate.

Exploring the value of the foster care allowance over time, however, tells us little about how adequate the allowance is to cover the costs of a child in a placement household. Budget standards methodology has been used in Chapter Two to estimate the living costs of a 'non-foster' child with the aim of judging to what extent foster care allowances meet all the normal costs of child rearing. A characteristic of budget standards methodology is that normative (expert) judgement is used to create a 'basket of goods' which when priced represents a living standard for a particular type of family. The family budgets from which the cost of a child have been derived were created by the FBU to represent a modest-but-adequate living standard. The process of itemising a basket of goods and services for each child from the family budgets included identifying individual child items and sharing the joint household consumption appropriately. To this end, per capita, differential approaches and normative judgement were employed.

To achieve a modest-but-adequate standard of living in 1991, a child aged four, ten, and 16 would need £42.62, £50.00, and £63.59 respectively for their weekly upkeep, excluding the cost of day care for children of working mothers, and assuming they lived in owner occupied housing. Local authority housing produced costs which were approximately £2.00 per week lower than owner costs. For all children food, clothing and housing represented major costs.

The cost of a child has been found to increase with age. A boy aged 16 costs about £13 a week more than a boy aged 10, and a boy aged 10 costs about £10 more than a boy aged four years. Food, clothing, leisure and pocket money costs increase with the age of the child. Personal care and fuel are similar for younger children but increase for teenage children.

Boys cost more than girls although the costs according to sex are similar for pre-school children. At ten years a boy costs £3.50 more than a girl of the same age and at 16 years the difference is approximately £2.00 each week. Boys are found to have higher food cost and higher clothing costs (especially footwear) than girls which is offset slightly by higher personal care costs for girls of 16 years.

The sharing of accommodation, transport, baby-sitting and other household items with other children in the household results in economies of scale. It costs less per child in two child families than for the same child in a one child family: approximately £10 less for a child under 11 years and £8 less for a young adult aged 16 years in owner occupied housing.

The foster care allowances (1992), assuming the foster child shares the joint consumption of the family and the family is in owner occupied accommodation, meet within 2% or £1 the normal costs of the child aged under 11 years and are 22% or £19 more than the amount needed to meet the normal costs of a teenage child. Assuming the child is an 'only' child in the household, however, results in high cost estimates because of loss of economies of scale, and consequently a shortfall in the foster care allowance of £11 a week for a child under 11 years, although the teenage child's allowance remains more than adequate (£11 each week surplus). These calculations assume the mother does not have child care costs.

The second test of whether the foster care allowance is adequate to meet the normal costs of child rearing concludes that it is adequate to meet the needs of a child under 11 years old and more than adequate for an older child.

Evidence shows that foster children have greater costs than other children and this has been tested empirically in Chapter Three. The perceptions of foster parents provided an average profile of the extra items to be included in the budgets for foster children. The budgets have been priced through the FBU data set at 1991 prices.

The extra items in the foster child's weekly budget have been estimated at approximately £26.50 for a child aged 0 to four and five to 10 years, and £32 for a child aged 11 to 16+ years old. The extra food, wear and tear on household goods, motoring expenses, pocket money for the teenager, and disposable nappies for young children represented significant differences in cost between a non-foster child and a foster child. The aggregate cost of a foster child increases with the age of the child. At aged 0 to four years the cost is approximately £69 each week, at five to 10 years it is £77 each week, and for a teenage foster child £96 each week. The shortfall in the foster care allowance for North Yorkshire is £29 a week for a child aged 0 to four, £28 for a child aged five to 10 years, and £15 for a teenage child, in 1991.

The equivalence ratios of a foster child have been found to be considerably more than a normal child. For a normal child aged four, ten and 16 years the equivalence scales are 0.18, 0.22, and 0.27 as a ratio of a two adult household; and similarly as a ratio of the same two adult household, 0.29, 0.33, and 0.41 for a foster child of the same respective age.

The third test of adequacy of the foster care allowances to meet the aggregate direct costs of maintaining the foster child concludes there is evidence of a shortfall for all ages of foster child but especially for children under the age of 11 years.

No part of the basic foster care allowance is designated to meet the indirect costs of fostering. This research, however, has explored what they might be if it was decided that it was desirable in order to bring about and retain an adequate supply of foster parents. The financial indirect costs of foster parents has been conceptualised as the value of the time given to raising foster children. Some time is dedicated to fostering tasks outside the normal tasks of child rearing.

The tasks of fostering have been explored through empirical investigation. Foster parents described the activities and tasks which constituted the difference in time caring for a natural child and foster child. The elements of time were placed in a framework of additional personal care of the foster child, general household care, travel time, time spent on therapeutic exercises, and administration. Time spent in the emotional care of foster children was counted as secondary time. The opinions of those that found no extra time spent on the care of foster children were reflected in the average sum.

The older the foster child the more time was spent on specific foster caring tasks by the foster mother. Under the age of 11 years, the foster mother spent approximately 13 hours extra a week, for teenage foster children the time spent was 14.5 hours a week on essential foster child rearing activities. The amount of secondary time spent by the foster mother was between nine and 19 hours each week. A value of extra time spent in essential tasks has been given at £66, £68, and £73 each week for foster children aged 0 to four years, five to 10 years and 11 to 16+ years old, respectively in 1992. This is in addition to the normal task of raising an extra child in the family.

The fourth test of adequacy of the foster care allowance to cover the indirect costs to foster parents of fostering concludes that hours spent on additional tasks to those expected, were this a natural child in the household, were substantial and no part of this was included in the allowance.

Should a fostering wage become a policy objective for foster carers some consideration might be given to the extra hours spent in raising a foster child. On average foster parents spent 13.5 hours per week meeting the additional needs of a foster placement. The total time spent in caring for a foster child, provided this child was a second or subsequent child in the household, is estimated at an average of 23.3 hours per week. In terms of a value based on the residential care worker rate in 1992, foster parents could expect to earn £114 to £120 per week.

Other countries make different arrangements to pay foster parents a fostering allowance which sometimes includes benefits in kind and fostering wages. A comparative analysis has been attempted in Chapter five with the aim of reflecting the appropriateness of the UK payment system. National informants collected information on foster care allowances, and other costs and benefits to foster parents in 15 countries (the EU, Australia, Norway and the US). Purchasing power parities have been used as a common currency. A model average earning foster family has also been used to simulate how foster care allowances interacted with other state benefits and costs. A limitation of this methodology is that it measures what foster parents ought to receive rather than what they receive.

A comparative analysis of the allowances, benefits, costs and fostering wages to foster parents, indicated that the UK was ranked in the middle range of generosity to foster parents. The UK paid foster parents on average £60 a week compared to Norway which paid an equivalent £116 each week and Portugal £35 each week, in 1992. As a proportion of the disposable income from an average wage in each country, the UK was low down the scale of countries in 10th place. The foster care package in the UK was worth 28% of the average income defined, in France 56% and in Australia 17% of a similar average net income.

A severely disabled foster child, however, is generously supported in a UK foster placement compared to the other 14 countries. The supplement, paid in addition to the usual package of allowances in the UK, is estimated at £215 a week in 1992. In Denmark, US, Norway and Ireland the support of severely disabled foster children is still considerable, £197, £192, £148 and £98, respectively, whereas, in Luxembourg the supplement is just £8 each week (1992 prices).

It is concluded the level of foster care allowance paid in the UK is not adequate compared to levels of payment elsewhere.

Implications of this research for policy

The main implication to be drawn from this research is that the basic foster care allowance is not adequate to meet all the costs of foster child rearing. There are shortfalls for all ages of foster children but particularly those under the age of 11 years. To maintain these children in foster care, the allowance in one particular authority would have to be increased by £28 per week for a child under the age of 11 years and £14 each week for an older child, based on 1991 prices.

There are moral and legal reasons why the shortfalls should be made good. The law places a duty on each local authority to meet the costs of maintaining foster children at a socially acceptable and approved standard of living, and in many cases the state has legal custody of the child. The shortfalls arise because the local authority has been left to make decisions about the minimum amount paid. Government funding to local authorities is through a block grant system which forces local authorities to make decisions not only about payment levels but also in the light of priorities given to other services and the availability of top-up funds. One way of regulating local authorities is through a system of direct funding from central to local Government. This would encourage the authorities to be more accountable for the spending of public money on children, but at the expense of some loss of freedom for authorities to be innovative, and to take account of local needs and conditions. Another solution would be to determine a national standard allowance based on the real cost of child rearing which takes into account regional bias in costs of living. Ten of the 15 countries explored in the comparative analysis of foster care allowances used a system of nationally determined payment which left some scope for local autonomy.

This research has also provided information and an estimate of the indirect costs for foster parents of caring for a foster child. The authority is not obliged to reward carers for their services but as a policy initiative for foster mothers, the universal payment of a reward may ease the problems of the supply and retention of foster carers. It has long been accepted some mothers would have liked to foster but could not because of financial constraints. Six of the countries examined were found to pay a reward to all foster parents, in most situations this was equivalent to a low proportion of the average female labour market wages. None of the countries based their payments on an objective measure of hours spent, as suggested here. An appropriate level of the hourly rate of pay in this study emerged from an evaluation of the tasks of foster mothers. The rate was set at a Residential Child Care Workers middle service rate.

This research contributes in a number of ways to the general debate on living standards. The State implies, through the paying of foster care allowances, that the medium standard of living is the approved living standard for a foster child. Should this then be the minimum for all children? Arriving at a minimally accepted median standard for all children will produce a higher legal standard than presently imposed. A child supported on Income Support will need a weekly increase of between 45% to 57% to meet the costs of a modest but adequate lifestyle. If the same child were, however, allowed to claim the universal child benefit without counting this as income in the means test then the increase would be 17% less.

A contribution is also made in the current debate on equivalence scales. These scales are used to give direct comparisons between households of different sizes and with children of different ages, usually they are derived from expenditure data. Here, implied equivalence scales are derived from the FBU couple household and child budgets. The scales are similar to the ones used by the Government in policy formulation and the measurement of poverty. Equivalence scales for foster children are, however, much higher which has implications for other children on welfare benefits with extra costs such as children with disabilities or illnesses.

Further research

This research has demonstrated the potential of budget standard methodology for measuring the adequacy of non-means tested benefits. There are practical uses for this work and scope for further exploration of the methodology.

This research could be extended to other local authority areas or as a national survey of foster child costs. The present study has been based on a small sample of foster parents' perceptions which raises concern about regional differences and generalisations.

Disability has not been treated as a separate variable in this study. The degree of difficulty in caring for the average foster child is increasing and defining disability is complex. Authorities, however, are in the legal and moral position of having to meet the extra costs of 'special needs' which arise in a disabled or vulnerable child. Some costs are so great that they can only be reimbursed on an ad hoc basis. The UK has been found generous in the support of severely disabled foster children compared to other countries. To what extent foster parents actually claim benefits such as the Disability Living Allowance on behalf of their foster child, and how practical this is for children in temporary accommodation, is not known. The question about how many children receive this benefit and whether the benefit is adequate to pay for the extra costs should be of interest to policy makers.

The cost of living of young people past the age of 16 years is another example of where knowledge is lacking and yet in demand. Young people are encouraged by Government to join training and education schemes. There has been little research into the adequacy of the grant or benefit system to support such people, or the impact of student loans and the burden of their study on supporters such as parents, spouses, partners or the impact on their dependants. The present budgets for children aged 16 years can be adapted using budget standards methods for older children and children of different sexes.

Cultural differences in household consumption and the financial impact of an ethnic background have not been addressed in relation to children.

In respect of children in 'normal circumstances' there is scope and demand for knowledge on the cost of a baby. Roll's 1986 review of the cost of babies was based on estimates now some years old. The cost of a child aged 13 years would also be useful to give a fuller range of ages for policy makers, courts, insurance companies and others.

Further scope for exploration of the methodology arises from the methodological problems found in this research.

The budget standard methodology has some limitations. There are the problems of updating the budgets. The RPI is suitable for short term updating, after which there is scope for creating new budgets which account for changes in consumption patterns. Furthermore there are regional variations in some of the components, especially housing and in general the budgets do not reflect living costs in London or Northern Ireland.

This study also highlights the scope for further cross country comparisons of foster care allowances to be added to the existing 15 country frame.

Lastly, this study has been concerned with the costs of fostering to the foster family. It has not attempted to assess the broader costs (and benefits) of fostering to the local authority and the community. It has acknowledged that there are other costs in fostering including the administrative cost of recruitment of foster parents, matching child to placement family, social workers' time in support, inspection, monitoring and so on, and also the cost of services germane to health, criminal justice, community and educational services to foster children. Also outside the scope of this study has been any consideration of the quality of foster care.

References

Abrams, P. (1986) *Neighbours; The Work of Philip Abrams* (Biographer) Bulmer M., Cambridge University Press, London.

Adamson, G. (1968) 'Should Foster Mums be Paid', in *New Society*, 22nd August 1968.

Aldgate, J. (1990) 'Foster children at school: success or failure?' *Adoption and Fostering* Volume 14, 4.

Australian Institute of Family Studies (1983) 'Survey of Pocket Money', cited in *Lovering* (1984) op cit.

Baldwin, S. (1985) *The Costs of Caring, Families with Disabled Children*. Routledge Kegan Paul Plc, London.

Banks, J. Johnson, P. (1993) *Children and Household Living Standards*, Institute for Fiscal Studies.

Banks, J. Brundell, R. Preston, J. (1991) 'Adult Equivalence Scales: A Life-cycle Perspective', *Fiscal Studies Journal*.

Bardsley, P. and McRae, I. (1982) 'A Test of McClements' Method for the Estimation of Equivalence Scales'. *Journal of Public Economics* 17 pp 119-122.

Barnes, M. W.(1979) *'Curtis' to 'Seebohm'*, Coventry, Topshop.

Bartlett, J. (1980) *A Study of the Costs of Caring for Foster Children*. Foster care Westernport. (Unpublished)

Bebbington, A. Miles, J. (1989a) *The Supply of Foster Families for Children in Care*, PSSRU Discussion Paper 624/3, University of Kent, PSSRU.

Bebbington, A. Miles J. (1989b) 'The Background of Children who enter Local Authority Care' in *British Journal of Social Work*, 19, pp 349-368.

Bebbington, A. Miles, J. (1988a) *Children's GRE Research: Children Entering Care, A Need Indicator for In-care Services for Children*. DP 574/A PSSRU University of Kent.

Bebbington, A. Miles, J. (1988b) *Children's GRE Research: Report of the Survey of Foster Families: Predicting the Supply of Foster Families in Areas.* DP 572/2 PSSRU University of Kent.

Beckerman, W. (1966) *International Comparisons of Real Incomes,* Development Centre of the Organisation for Economic Co-operation and Development.

Berridge, D. Cleaver, H. (1987) *Foster Home Breakdown,* London, Basil Blackwell.

Birds Eye Wall's Ltd (1991, 1992) *Wall's Monitor 1991,* Bird's Eye Walls Ltd., Surrey.

Bittman, M. (1991) 'Juggling Time': *How Australian Families Use Time.* Report of the Secondary Analysis of the 1987 Pilot Survey of Time Use, Prepared for the Office of the Status of Women, Department of the Prime Minister and Cabinet, May 1991.

Blackburn, C. (1991) *Poverty and Health: Working With Families,* Open University Press.

Bolderson, H. (1988) 'Comparing Social Policies: Some Problems of Method and the Case of Social Security Benefits in Australia, Britain, and the USA' in *Journal of Social Policy,* 17, 3, pp 267-288.

Bowes, C. F. Church, H. N. (1970) *Food Values of Portions Commonly Used,* 11th Ed. revised by C. F. Church and H. N. Church, Philadelphia, Lippincott.

Bowlby, J. (1952) *Maternal Care and Mental Health: A Report prepared on behalf of the World Health Organizations,* 2nd Edition, Geneva, World Health Organization.

Bradshaw, J. (Ed) (1993) *Budget Standards for the United Kingdom,* Aldershot, Avebury.

Bradshaw, J. Morgan, J. (1987) *Budgeting on Benefit,* London, Family Policy Studies Centre.

Bradshaw, J. Holmes, H. (1989) *Living on the Edge: A Study of the Living Standards of Families on Benefit in Tyne and Wear,* London, Child Poverty Action Group.

Bradshaw, J. Ditch, J. Holmes, H. Whiteford, P. (1992) *Comparing Child Support* paper to the Conference Social Security: 50 years after Beveridge, University of York.

Bradshaw, J. Hicks, L. Parker, H. (1992) *Summary Budget Standards for Six Households,* Working Paper No. 12 (Revised), Family Budget Unit, University of York.

Bradshaw, J. Morgan, J. (1987) *Budgeting on Benefit: The Consumption of Families on Social Security,* Family Policy Studies Centre Occasional Paper 5, London, Family Policy Studies Centre.

Bradshaw, J. Piachaud, D. (1980) *Child Support in the European Community,* Occasional Papers on Social Administration 66. Great Britain, Bedford Square Press of the National Councils for Voluntary Organisations.

Bradshaw, J. Ditch, J. Holmes, H. Whiteford, P. (1993) *Support for Children, a Comparision of Arrangements in Fifteen Countries*, DSS Report 21, London, HMSO.

Bullock, R. (1990) 'The Implications of Recent Child Care Research Findings for Foster Care', in *Adoption and Fostering*, V 14, 3.

Cass, B. Keens, C. Wyndham, D. (1983) 'Child Rearing - Direct and Indirect Costs' in *Retreat from the Welfare State* by Adam Graycar.

Cliffe, D. (1990) *An End to Residential Child Care? The Warwickshire Direction*, A Paper at the National Children's Bureau and Warwickshire County Council Conference, 11th October 1990.

Cm 2144 (1993) *Children Act 1989*: A Report by the Secretaries of State for Health and for Wales on the Children Act 1989 in pursuance of their duties under Section 83(6) of the Act. London HMSO.

Cm 2184 (1988) *Children and Young Persons, The Boarding-Out of Children (Foster Placement) Regulations*, 1988, London, HMSO.

Cmd 6922 (Curtis Report) (1946) *Report of the Care of Children Committee*, London, HMSO.

Cohen, B. (1988) *Caring For Children. Services and Policies for Childcare and Equal Opportunities in the UK*. Family Policy Studies Centre.

Colton, M. Hellinckx, W. (1993) *Child Care in the EC: A country-specific guide to foster and residential care*. Arena, Aldershot.

Cooke, K. Baldwin, S. (1984) *How Much is Enough? a review of supplementary benefit scale rates*, London, Family Policy Studies Centre.

Cooke, K. (1988) *The Costs of Childrearing* in Walker R. (Ed) (1988) *Money Matters, Income, Wealth and Financial Welfare*, London, Sage.

Cousins, J. (September 1988) 'Foster Mothers: A Feminist View' in *Social Work Today*: 25.

Crowther, M. A. (1981) *The Workhouse System, 1834-1929: The History of an English Institution*. Georgia Press.

Culley, J. D. Settle, B. H. Van Name, J. B. (1975) *Understanding and Measuring the Cost of Foster Care*. University of Delaware.

Culyer, A. J. (1973) Quids without Quos - A Praxeological Approach, an essay in *The Economics of Charity*, The Institute of Economic Affairs.

Curry, L. (1993) 'Adopting a professional approach to foster care' in *The Independent*, Tuesday, 28th September 1993:15.

Curtis Report (1946) *Report of the Care of Children Committee*, Cmd 6922, London, HMSO.

Dean, M. (1992) *Breakdown Services* in Schorr A., Search 14, York, Joseph Rowntree Foundation.

Demb, J. M. (1991) 'Reported Hyperphagia in Foster Children' in *Child Abuse & Neglect*, Vol 15 pp. 77-88.

Department of Education and Science (1990) 'Pupils under Five Years in each LEA in England', *DES Bulletin*, April, London, HMSO.

Department of Employment (1989) *1988 Family Expenditure Survey*, London, HMSO.

Department of Health (1992,1993) *Health and Personal Social Services Statistics for England*, 1992,1993 Edition, 1991 Edition, HMSO.

Department of Health (1991) *Patterns and Outcomes in Child Placement: Messages from current research and their implications*. London HMSO.

Department of Health and Social Security (1979) 'Dietary Reference Values for Food Energy and Nutrients for the UK', *Report on Health and Social Subjects* No. 41, London, HMSO.

Department of Health and Social Security, Scottish Education Department (1976) *Guide to Fostering Practice*, London, HMSO.

Department of Health and Social Security (1985) *Reform of Social Security*, Vol 2 Cmnd 9518, London, HMSO.

Department of Health and Social Security, Supplementary Benefits Commission: *Memorandum 79 (1968) Memorandum 268 (1970) Memorandum 1042 (1978)* (Unpublished).

Department of Health and Social Security (1969) 'Recommended Intakes of Nutrients for the United Kingdom'. *Reports on Public Health and Medical Subjects* No. 120.

Department of Social Security (1988) Memorandum to Social Services Committee submitted by Department of Social Security *'Benefit Levels and a Minimum Income'*.

Ditch, J. (1993) 'The European Community: A developing social dimension?' *Benefit 5* Jan/Feb.

Edwards, C. S.(1981) *United States Department of Agriculture Estimates of the Cost of Raising a Child: A Guide to their Use and Interpretation*, Publication No. 1411, United States Department of Agriculture.

Espenshade, T. (1972) The Price of Children and Socio-economic Theories of Fertility. *Population Studies 25* pp. 207-222 quoted in, Robinson, Warren C., The Time Cost of Children and Other Household Production, *Population Studies* 41 (1987).

Espenshade, T. J. (1977) 'The Value and Cost of Children.' *Population Bulletin.* Vol. 32 No. 1 April.

Euromonitor (1987-90) Market Research in Great Britain, *Euromonitor.*

FES (1987) *Family Expenditure Survey 1986*, London, HMSO.

Fenyo, F. (1989) 'Economic Perspectives on Foster Care' in *Social Work and Social Welfare Yearbook.* 1989 pp 175-189 Milton Keynes: Open University Press.

Field, F. (1985) *What Price a Child? A historical review of the relative cost of dependants*, Policy Studies Institute.

Furnham, A. Thomas, P. (1984) *Pocket Money*, cited in Hill, M. (1990) *op cit.*

Furnham, A. Lewis, A. (1986) *Economic Mind: The Social Psychology of Economic Behaviour*, Brighton, Wheatsheaf Books.

George, V. (1970) *Foster Care Theory and Practice*, London, Routledge & Kegan Paul.

Gershuny, J. Thomas, G. S. (1979) *Changing Patterns of Time Use*, Data Preparation and some preliminary results UK 1961-75, SPRU Occasional Paper Series No. 13.

Gershuny, J. (1983) *Social Innovation and the Division of Labour*, Oxford University Press.

Gilligan, R. (1991) *Irish Child Care Services: Policy, Practice & Provision*, Institute of Public Administration.

Ginn, J. Arber, A. (1992) 'Adult Children and Women's Employment in Mid-life'. Paper to the *SPA Conference 1992* (Unpublished).

Ginsburg, N. (1991) 'The wonderful World(s) of Welfare Capitalism' in *Critical Social Policy*, Issue 31 Summer 1991.

Glickman, L. L. (1980) Foster Parenting: An Investigation of Role Ambiguity, Dissertation, Brandeis University, USA (Unpublished).

Goldstein, J. Freud, A. Solnit, A. J. (1973) *Beyond the Best Interest of the Child*, London, Macmillan.

Graham, S. (1987) *The Extra Costs Borne by Families who have a Child with a Disability*, SWRC Reports and Proceedings No. 68 University of New South Wales, Australia.

Gray, B. K. (1905) *A History of English Philanthropy*, P.S. King.

Guardian (1993), 'Education Supplement', January 5th.

Hantrais, L. Mangen, S. O'Brien, M. (eds) (1985) *Doing Cross National Research*, Aston University, Birmingham.

Hartnell, M. (1974) The Professional Foster Parent. in *Health and Social Service Journal*, Vol 84 II.

Henley Centre Leisure Futures - Time Use Survey (1991-1992) cited in Central Statistical Office *Social Trends 22* (1992).

Heywood, J. S. (1978) (3rd ed) *Children in Care: The development of the service for the deprived child*, London, Routledge & Kegan Paul.

Hicks, L. and Ernst, J (1992a) *Modest-but-adequate Budget Standards, Housing Budgets for Six Household Types*, Working Paper No. 5, Family Budget Unit, University of York.

Higgins, J. (1986) 'Comparative Social Policy' in *The Quarterly Journal of Social Affairs*, 1986, 2 (3) 221-242.

Hill, M. (1990, unpublished) *Children and Money: An Exploratory Study of Children's Knowledge and Understanding of Financial Arrangements Affecting the Families*, University of Glasgow, Department of Social Policy and Social Work.

Hill, M. (1991) 'Social Work and the European Community', *Research Highlights in Social Work* 23, London, Jessica Kingsley Publishers.

Hill, M. (1992) 'Children's roles in the domestic economy' *Journal of Consumer Studies and Home Economics* 16, pp. 33-50.

Holman, R. (1975) 'The Place of Fostering in Social Work' in *British Journal of Social Work 5,1.*

Home Office/Ministry of Health (1946) *Memorandum on Boarding Out of Children and Young Persons, Children and Young Persons (Boarding Out) Rules: 1946., Public Assistance (Boarding Out) Order 1946.* London, HMSO.

Home Office (1955) *Memorandum on the Boarding Out of Children Regulations 1955,* London, HMSO.

Horna, J. (1989) 'The Leisure Component of the Parental Role', *Journal of Leisure Research,* Vol 21, No. 2, pp 228-241.

Horsburgh, M. (1983) 'No Sufficient Security: The Reaction of the Poor Law Authorities to Boarding Out', in *Journal Social Policy,* 12,1:51-73.

Howard, D. R. Madrigal, R. (1990) 'Who Makes the Decisions: the Parent or the Child? The Perceived Influence of Parents and Children On the Purchase of Recreation Services'. in *Journal of Leisure Research.* Vol. 22, No. 3, pp. 244-258.

Humphries, J. Rubery, J. (1991) *Position of Women in the Labour Market in Britain.* Report to the European Commission.

Hutton, S. Wilkinson, B. (1992) *Modest-but-adequate Budget Standards, Fuel Budgets for Six Household Types,* Working Paper No. 8, Family Budget Unit, University of York.

Jervis, M. (1990) 'Payment where it's due' in *Social Work Today,* July 1990.

Jones, C. (1985) *Patterns of Social Policy: An Introduction to Comparative Analysis.* London, Tavistock Publications.

Joshi, H. (1992) *Child care and mother's lifetime earnings: some European Contrast.* Centre for Economic Policy Research Discussion paper 600.

Joshi, H. (1984) *Women's Participation in Paid Work,* Department of Employment Research Paper No 45.

Joshi, H. (1987) *The Cash Opportunity Costs of Childbearing: an Approach to Estimation Using British Data.* Centre for Economic Policy Research. Paper 208.

Kamerman, S. B. Kahn, A. J. (1983) *Income Transfer for Families with Children: An Eight Country Study,* Philadelphia, Temple University Press.

Kavanagh, S. (1988b) 'Foster carers have allowed themselves to be used to subsidise childcare'. in *Foster Care,* March 1988.

Kavanagh, S. (1988a) 'The true cost of caring' in *Foster Care Journal* 56 December 1988.

Knapp, M. (1980) 'A penny a minute', in *Community Care,* March 1980.

Knapp, M. (1982) *The Cost Implications of the Changing Pattern of Child Care* - evidence submitted to the House of Commons Social Service Committee. December 1982.

Knapp, M. Fenyo, A. (1988) *Economic Perspectives on Foster Care,* DP 586/5 PSSRU University of Kent.

Lakhani, B. Luba, J. Ravetz, A. Read, J. and Wood, P. (1988) *National Welfare Benefits Handbook*, London, Child Poverty Action Group.

Le Grand, J. (1991) 'Some Implications of 1992 and Beyond for Social Security in Europe.' *Planning a Strategy for Social Security Research in the 1990s*: a DSS/ESRC Consultation Seminar. 23-24 January 1991, School for Advanced Urban Studies.

Leat, D. (1988) 'Using Social Security To Encourage Non-Kin Caring' in Baldwin (Ed) *Social Security and Community Care*, Aldershot, Gower.

Leat, D. (1990) *For Love and Money: The role of payment in encouraging the provision of care*. England, JR Joseph Rowntree Foundation.

London & Regional Fostering and Adoption Group *(1990) Expenditure Survey* (Unpublished).

Lovering, K. (1984) *Cost of Children in Australia* Working Paper 8, Australian Institute of Family Studies.

Lowe, M. (1989) 'Black Children, Black Homes?' in *Community Care* 31.8.89.

Lynes, T. (1979) *New Society*, 15th November 1979.

Maclean, K. (1989) 'Towards a fee-paid fostering service' in *Adoption and Fostering* V13, 3, pp 25-29.

Martin, J. (1986) 'Returning to work after childbearing: evidence from the Women and Employment Survey', *Population Trends* No 43 Spring pp 23-30.

McCabe, M. Waddington, A. (1992) *Modest-but-adequate Budget Standards, Leisure Budgets for Six Household Types*, Working Paper No. 11, Family Budget Unit, University of York.

McClements, L. D. (1978) *The Economics of Social Security*, Heinemann: London.

Meyer, C. H. (1985) 'A Feminist Perspective on Foster Family Care: A Redefinition of the Categories' in *Child Welfare*, V LXIV, 3.

Mintel (1988) *Leisure Intelligence*, Mintel Intelligence.

Mintel (1987-1991) *Mintel Intelligence Journals*.

Mitchell, D. and Cooke, K. (1988) 'The Costs of Childrearing' in Walker, R. and Parker, G. (eds) *Money Matters, Income, Wealth and Financial Welfare* (1988), London, Sage.

Moss, P. (1988) 'The indirect costs of Parenthood: a neglected issue in social policy', in *Critical Social Policy* Issue 24.

Murphy-Lawless, J. (1992) *The Adequacy of Income and Family Expenditure*, Dublin, Combat Poverty Agency.

Napier, H. (1972) 'Success and Failure in Foster Care' in *British Journal of Social Work*, Vol 2, 2, pp 187-204.

National Food Survey (1985-1989) *Household Food Consumption and Expenditure, 1983-87*, Ministry of Agriculture Fisheries and Food London, HMSO.

National Foster Care Association (1987-93) *Foster Care Finance: Advice and Information on the Cost of Caring for a Child*, London NFCA.

191

National Foster Care Association (March 1993) *Foster Carers: Payment for Skills* pp 10-21.

Nelson, M. (1986) 'The distribution of nutrient intake within families', *British Journal of Nutrition*, 55, pp 267-277.

Nelson, M. Peploe, K. A. (1990) 'Construction of a Modest but Adequate Food Budget for Households', *Journal of Human Nutrition and Dietetics*, Vol 3. pp 121-140.

Newell, P. (1991) *The UN Convention and Children's Rights in the UK*, National Children's Bureau.

Nissel, M. Bonnerjea, L. (1982) *Family Care of the Handicapped Elderly: Who Pays?* London, Policy Studies Institute.

Office of Population Censuses and Surveys (1989) *General Household Survey*, Participation in Sport Supplement B 1987, London, HMSO.

Office of Population Censuses and Surveys (1988, 1989, 1992, 1993) *General Household Survey*, No. 19,20,22,23, London, HMSO.

Oldfield, G. F. (1990) *The Adequacy of Foster Care Allowances.* (unpublished dissertation) University of York.

Olson, L. (1982) *Costs of Children*, Massachusetts, Lexington Books Mass, USA.

Orlin, M. (1977) 'Conflict Resolution in Foster Family Care' in *Child Welfare* LVI, 1. pp 769-775.

Packman, J. (1975) *The Child's Generation: Child Care Policy from Curtis to Houghton*, London, Robinson.

Packman, J. (1968) *Child Care Needs and Numbers*, London, Allen.

Pashardes, P. (1991) 'Contemporaneous and Intertemporal Child Costs', in *Journal of Public Economics* 45, pp 191-213.

Pember Reeves, M. (1913) *Round about a Pound a Week*, London, Virago - reprint 1988.

Piachaud, D. (1979) *The Cost of a Child*, London, Child Poverty Action Group Ltd.

Piachaud, D. (1984) *Round about fifty hours a week, The Time Cost of Children*, London, Child Poverty Action Group.

Piachaud, D. (1987) 'Problems in the Definition and Measurement of Poverty', *Journal of Social Policy* 16,2, pp 147-164.

Piachaud, D. (1981) *Children and Poverty*, London, Child Poverty Action Group Ltd.

Rhodes, P. (1991) 'The Assessment of Black Foster Parents: The Relevance of Cultural Skills - Comparative Views of Social Workers and Applicants'. *Critical Social Policy*: Issue 32.

Rhodes, P. (1989) 'Fostering as employment: the mobility component', in Crieco M. Pickup L. Whipp R. (1989) *Gender, Transport and Employment*, Oxford Studies in Transport, Aldershot, Gower.

Rickford, F. (1992) 'Squaring Roots' in *Social Work Today*. March 19.

Robinson, J.(1991) 'Beyond the frontiers of fostering - the employment of a 'professional carer' in *Adoption and Fostering Journal* Vol. 15 No.1, pp 47-49.

Robinson. C. W. (1987) 'The Time Cost of Children and Other Household Production' in *Population Studies* 41, pp 313-323.

Rodgers, B. Doron, A. Jones, M. (1979) *The Study of Social Policy: A Comparative Approach*, London, George Allen & Unwin.

Roll, J. (1986) *Babies and Money: Birth trends and costs*. Family Policy Studies Centre.

Rowe, J. Lambert, L. (1973) *Children who wait: A study of children needing substitute families*, Association of British Adoption Agencies.

Rowe, J. Hundleby, M. Garnett, L. (1989) *Child Care Now: A Survey of Placement Patterns*. British Agency for Adoption and Fostering.

Rowe, J. (1987) 'Fostering Outcomes: Interpreting Breakdown Rates', in *Adoption and Fostering*, V.11,1 pp 32-34.

Rowntree, B. S. (1901) *Poverty: A Study of Town Life*, London, MacMillan.

Rowntree, B. S. (1941) *Poverty and Progress: A Second Social Survey of York*, London, Longmans.

Schorr, A. (1992) in 'Breakdown Services?' by Dean, M. *Search* 14, J.R. Foundation.

Shaw, M. Hipgrave, T. (1989) 'Young people and their carers in specialist fostering', in *Adoption and Fostering Journal* V13:4.

Shaw, M. Lebens, K. (1977), 'Foster parents talking', in *Adoption and Fostering*, Vol 88, 2, 1977.

Simon, L. J. (1975) 'The Effect of Foster-Care Payment Levels on the Number of Foster Children Given Homes', in *Social Service Review* No. 49 September.

Smith, B. (1988) 'Something you do for love: the question of money and foster care' *Adoption and Fostering Journal*, Vol 12, No. 4.

Smith, B. Smith, T. (1990) 'For Love and Money: Women as Foster Mothers'. *AFFILIA* Vol 5. No. 1, Spring pp 66-80.

Social Planning Council of Metropolitan Toronto (1984) *Guide for Family Budgeting*. Toronto, SPCMT.

Southon, V. (1986) *Children in Care: Paying Their New Families - A look at payments to foster and adoptive families in Denmark, Manitoba, New York State, Ontario and West Germany*. DSS: London HMSO.

Spicker, P. (1992) *Can European Social Policy be Universalist?* Paper presented to Social Policy Association Conference, July 1992.

Stroud, J. (1975) *In the Care of the Council: Social Workers and their World*, London, Victor Gollancz Ltd.

Swedish National Board for Consumer Policies (1989) *Calculations of Reasonable Costs*, SNCPCRC.

Szalai, A. (1972) *The Use of Time: Daily Activities of Urban and Suburban Populations in Twelve Countries*. The Hague, Paris, Mouton.

The Family Welfare Association, 78th Edition, *Guide to the Social Services 1990*, The Family Welfare Association.

Titmuss, R. M. (1970) *The Gift Relationship*, London, George Allen and Unwin Ltd.

Triseliotis, J. (1989) 'Foster Care Outcomes: a review of key research findings', in *Adoption and Fostering* Vol 13,3, pp 5-16.

Tunnard, J. Ryan, M. (1991) 'What does the Children Act mean for family members?' in *Children and Society* 5,1,67-75 Unwin.

Van Praag, B. M. S. Hagenaars, A. van Weeren, H. (1992), 'Poverty in Europe', in *Review of Income and Wealth*, 28, 345-59.

Veit-Wilson, J. (1994) *Adequacy for What and Whom? Poverty Lines, Minimum Income Standards and Social Security Benefits*, Paper for the International Research Meeting on Social Security: A Time for Definition, Vienna, Austria.

Verity, P. (1988) 'In response to Brenda Smith', in *Adoption and Fostering Journal*, Vol 12, 4, p40.

Walker, R. (1992) Poverty and Inequality in Childhood: A National Survey of Family Expenditures on Children. A research proposal (Unpublished).

Walker, R. (Ed) (1988) *Money Matters, Income, Wealth and Financial Welfare*, London, Sage.

Walker and Wood (1967) in Culley 1975.

Wandsworth Foster Care Association (1987) *Survey of higher costs*. (Unpublished)

Watts, H. (1980) *New American Budget Standards: Report of the Expert Committee on Family Budget Revision*, University of Wisconsin, Institute for Research On Poverty.

Webb, S. Webb, B.(1929) *English Poor Law History*, Part II, Vol III, London, Longmans Green.

Webb, S. Webb, B.(1910) *English Poor Law Policy*, London, Longmans, Green.

Which? (October 1990) 'Car Insurance, Insuring your car' *Which Journal* pp 553 -559.

Which? (September 1991) 'Car Safety', *Which Journal* pp 491-495.

Which? (March 1991) 'Ford Popular? Escort and Orion?' *Which Journal* pp 141-155.

Which? (June 1992) 'Guide to New and Used Cars', *Which Journal* pp 1-130.

Which? (November 1989) 'Big Estate Cars, the Family Estate', *Which Journal* pp 577-584.

Which? (May 1989) 'People-carriers, A Tall Order', *Which Journal* pp 248-253.

Which? (February 1991) 'Cars at Risk', *Which Journal* pp 107-109.

Which? (March 1991) 'Second-Hand Cars, How to find a bargain Second-hand Car', *Which Journal*, pp 150-155.

Which? (June 1991) 'Guide to New and Used Cars' *Which Journal* pp 1-68.

Whiteford, P. (1987) 'The Cost Children: Implications of Recent Research for Income Support Policies'. *Social Security Journal* Winter pp 3-19.

Whiteford, P. (1985) *A Family's Needs: Equivalence Scales, Poverty and Social Security.* Research Paper Number 27, Development Division of Department of Social Security.

Whiteford, P. (1992) *The Use of Purchasing Power Parities in the Comparative Study of Child Support* DSS 4.92 SPRU University or York. Memoranda.

Wilensky, H. L. Luebbert, G. M. Hahn, S. R. Jamieson (1985) *Comparative Social Policy: Theories, Methods, Findings* University of California, Institute of International Studies.

Wulczyn, F. (September 28, 1993) in correspondence from Kamerman S. B. Columbia University School of Social Work.

Wynn, M. (1972) *Family Policy: A study of the economic costs of rearing children and their social and political consequences*, London, Michael Joseph.

For Product Safety Concerns and Information please contact our EU
representative GPSR@taylorandfrancis.com Taylor & Francis Verlag GmbH,
Kaufingerstraße 24, 80331 München, Germany

Printed and bound by CPI Group (UK) Ltd, Croydon, CR0 4YY
08/05/2025
01864362-0004